i-DOCS

i-DOCS

The Evolving Practices of Interactive Documentary

EDITED BY
Judith Aston, Sandra Gaudenzi and Mandy Rose

WALLFLOWER PRESS
LONDON & NEW YORK

For Chloe, Wilf, Lara, Matthias, Hannah, Rowan and Shauna

A Wallflower Press book
Published by
Columbia University Press
Publishers Since 1893
New York · Chichester, West Sussex
cup.columbia.edu

A complete CIP record is available from the Library of Congress

ISBN 978-0-231-18122-8 (cloth : alk. paper)
ISBN 978-0-231-18123-5 (pbk. : alk. paper)
ISBN 978-0-231–85107-7 (e-book)

Columbia University Press books are printed on permanent
and durable acid-free paper.
Printed in the United States of America

Design by Tom Cabot

CONTENTS

ACKNOWLEDGEMENTS

Firstly, our gratitude goes to Yoram Allon, Commissioning Editor at Wallflower Press, and his colleagues there and at Columbia University Press for giving us the opportunity and support, which has led to this book.

Special thanks go to Jonathan Dovey for appreciating the importance of convening a dialogue around interactive documentary and making the first i-Docs symposium possible; to Jess Linington for passionately looking after the i-Docs website and activities for many years, even during her current sojourn in Australia; to Nick Triggs for his steadfast support for i-Docs in all its forms, and in particular for bringing his rigour, and his eye for quality and detail to the i-Docs Symposia. Among supportive colleagues at UWE Bristol we'd also like to thank Lynn Barlow and Yiota Demetriou.

Our students have been a constant source of inspiration, challenging our assumptions and keeping us on our toes. Without them i-Docs would never have happened. Additionally, we are blessed in our home at the Digital Cultures Research Centre within the creatively and intellectually stimulating Pervasive Media Studio, and we'd like to thank Verity Macintosh and Clare Reddington for their generosity in embracing i-docs as a studio theme. William Uricchio and Sarah Wolozin at MIT's Open Doc Lab, in a sense our North American counterparts, have also been collegiate and generous with their time and engagement.

We'd like to thank Andrew Dade, Rob Gordon and Marc Nahum, and all our families who have collectively shown endless patience in giving us the time, space and safety to concentrate on this book. Thank you for all those wider 'distractions' that have helped to keep us sane! We would like to express our deepest gratitude to all in the i-Docs community for feeding our curiosity and intellectual appetite since we started our first Symposium in 2011. Special thanks to those that actively contribute to our website and social media platforms, and to cherished critical friends - Sharon Daniels, Arnau Gifreu-Castells, and Brian Winston.

Finally, we must express our gratitude to Anna Wiehl, who has read the whole manuscript and advised on formatting and much more. Thankyou for your brilliant editorial input.

Judith, Mandy and Sandra – January 2017

NOTES ON CONTRIBUTORS

Christopher Cekay Allen is a producer and director of documentary media projects and a programmer of multi-disciplinary events. After graduating from Columbia University and studying at Trinity College Dublin, he co-founded UnionDocs and has been responsible for the organisation's growth from grassroots as the Executive Artistic Director. He has initiated many collaborative projects, uniting the creative efforts of hundreds of artists, documentary-makers and communities including *Yellow Arrow* (2004), *Documenting Mythologies* (2013), *Living Los Sures* (2014) and *Capitol of Punk* (2016). In 2014 and 2016, *Brooklyn Magazine* named him one of the most influential people in Brooklyn culture. He collaborates on live-media performance projects with his partner, artist A.S.M. Kobayashi.

Judith Aston is a Founding Director of i-Docs, a Senior Lecturer in Filmmaking and Creative Media at the University of the West of England and a core member of the University's Digital Cultures Research Centre. She began her career in the late 1980s developing a documentary-based videodisc project with Apple Computing, the BBC Interactive Television Unit and the University of Cambridge, and has been developing innovative interdisciplinary projects across academia and industry ever since. Her PhD in visual anthropology and interaction design, received from the Royal College of Art in 2003, reflects a long-standing interest in using nonlinearity and split screen to juxtapose multiple points of view. Taking an expansive view of interactive documentary, she also contributes to music, film and theatre projects, which bring screen-based media and interaction design into a live, performative context. She lectures and publishes widely on her work, acts as a curator, discussant and mentor, and was recently invited to be a judge for the One World Digital Media Award.

Jon Dovey is Professor of Screen Media at the Faculty of Arts, Creative Industries, and Education at the University of the West of England, Bristol. He has taught at Plymouth University, UWE and Bristol University teaching a wide range of film, media and digital courses in both practice and theory, including documentary studies. In 2008 he launched UWE's Digital Cultures Research Centre which he Directed until 2012. In 2012 he became the Director of REACT (Research and Enterprise for Arts and Creative Technologies), one of four Hubs for the Creative Economy funded by the AHRC. Led by UWE and Watershed, REACT is an Arts, Technology, and Business Collaboration aiming to produce fifty innovative media prototypes in four years. He was also Co-Investigator on the AHRC Connected Communities Creative Citizens Project where he led a strand on the impact of informal creative economies on communities. Recent publications include a contribution to *New Documentary Ecologies* (2014).

Nonny de la Peña is the founder of Emblematic Group, was selected by *Wired Magazine* as a #MakeTechHuman Agent of Change and has been called 'The Godmother of Virtual Reality' by *Engadget* and *The Guardian*. Additionally, Fast Company named her 'One of the People Who Made the World More Creative' for her pioneering work in immersive storytelling. A Yale Poynter Media Fellow and a former Annenberg fellow at the USC School of Journalism and communications, Nonny has more than twenty years of award-winning experience in print, film and TV including as a former correspondent for *Newsweek Magazine*. She is widely credited with helping create the genre of immersive journalism and her virtual reality work has been featured by the *New York Times*, BBC, *Mashable*, *Vice*, *Wired* and many others. Showcases around the globe include the Sundance and Tribeca Film Festivals, The World Economic Forum in Davos, The Victoria and Albert Museum, Moscow Museum of Modern Art, and Games For Change.

Paolo Favero is Associate Professor in Film Studies and Visual Culture at the Department of Communication Studies, University of Antwerp. With a PhD in Social Anthropology from Stockholm University focusing on questions of globalisation and cultural identity among young people in New Delhi (resulting in a book entitled *India Dreams*, 2005), Paolo has devoted the core of his career to the study of visual culture in India and Italy. He is also a specialist on the integration of new technologies within ethnographic methods. Presently he conducts research on image-making practices in contemporary India. Paolo has taught at the University Institute Lisbon (Portugal), University College London (UK), University of Foggia (Italy) and Stockholm University (Sweden). He has published, among others, in *Cultural Anthropology*, *Visual Studies*, the *Journal of Material Culture*, *Social Anthropology* and *Anthropological Quarterly*. His most recent publications focus on interactive documentary filmmaking and on the meaning images in a digital landscape. Paolo is also an active photographer and filmmaker. In 2004 he directed *Flyoverdelhi*, a film on youth in New Delhi that was screened by Swedish and Italian national broadcasters. He is presently an elected member of the Executive Committee of the European Association of Social Anthropologists (EASA) and the vice-chair of the ECREA Visual Culture network.

Samuel Gantier is Associate Professor at the University of Valenciennes, France, where he coordinates a Master's degree in Design Interaction and Interactive Documentaries. He conducts research in the design of multi-supported interactional audio-visual artefacts. Over the last fifteen years, Samuel has worked as a film director, film editor and UX designer on documentary films and i-docs for different broadcasters. His writings have appeared in many volumes, including *Empowering Users Through Design* (2014) and *Entrelacs, Les enjeux des nouvelles formes audiovisuelles documentaires* (2016).

Sandra Gaudenzi consults, researches, lectures, writes and blogs about interactive factual narratives. She is Senior Lecturer at the University of Westminster and Head of Studies of !F Lab – a Creative Europe training scheme for interactive documentary-makers. She is also a Visiting Fellow at the Digital Cultures Research Centre (University of the West of England, UK) where she co-directs the i-Docs conference and website. In Belgium, she co-convenes *WebDox*, an annual conference on interactive storytelling, while in London she co-hosts a regular storytelling event, The Flying Monkeys, with fellow digital creatives. In 2015, she created *Digital Me* with Helios Design Labs, a digital experiment in storytelling and personalisation for the BBC Taster platform.

Arnau Gifreu-Castells is a lecturer, researcher and director in the audiovisual and multimedia field. He is a doctor in communications and has a master's degree in digital arts from the Pompeu Fabra University (Barcelona). He is a research affiliate at the Open Documentary Lab (Massachusetts Institute of Technology) and part of the i-Docs group (University of the West of England). He has published various books and articles in his research area, interactive and transmedia non-fiction, and specifically on interactive documentaries. Arnau has been a research lecturer at Harvard University (Harvard Metalab), York University (Future Cinema Lab,

Canada) and Universidad de los Andes (CEPER, Colombia). He is a lecturer at ESCAC (University of Barcelona) and at ERAM (University of Girona) and acted as producer on a wide range of projects.

Craig Hight is Associate Professor in Creative Industries at the University of Newcastle, New South Wales. His current research focuses on the relationships between digital media technologies and documentary practice, especially the variety of factors shaping online documentary cultures. His most recent book is *New Documentary Ecologies* (2014), co-edited with Kate Nash and Catherine Summerhayes.

Anandana Kapur is an award-winning filmmaker and co-founder of Cinemad, India. Previously an executive producer for non-fiction programming on TV, she has worked on information and video campaigns for the Government of India and UNICEF. Her films *Blood on My Hands* (2006), *Chamba Nede Aa ki Door* (*Is Chamba Near or Far* (2010)), *Much Ado About Knotting* (2012) and *The Great Indian Jugaad* (2015) have received critical acclaim globally. Anandana also teaches courses on Documentary Practice and Researching Media and Culture. Her published work is on gender and film studies. A Shastri India Canadian Institute Fellow, she is currently pursuing practice-based research on the interactive documentary genre.

Michel Labour is Senior Associate Professor at the University of Valenciennes, France. He is a specialist in the design of interactive decision processes and decision-aiding information systems. His recent writings have appeard in *Theories of Information, Communication and Knowledge: A Multidisciplinary Approach* (2014) and *Sens décisionnels et facteurs humains* (2016).

Ben Moskowitz is an advocate for open standards, content and technology. Ben teaches interactive design and storytelling at the Interactive Telecommunications Program at the New York University's Tisch School of the Arts and is Visiting Associate Arts Professor at NYU Shanghai. As former Director of Development Strategy at the Mozilla Foundation, he has held senior roles leading the design, implementation and management of public interest media productions and video technologies. He is the founder of the Open Video Conference, a forum to coordinate free and open technologies, policies and practices in online video.

Kate Nash is Lecturer in Media and Communication at the University of Leeds, UK. Her research focuses on the relationship between the cultures and practices of documentary and those of digital media. Her work has appeared in a number of leading journals including *Media Culture and Society*, *Continuum* and *Studies in Documentary Film*. Kate is co-editor (with Craig Hight and Catherine Summerhayes) of *New Documentary Ecologies: Emerging Platforms, Practices and Discourses* (2014) and she is currently working on a monograph on interactive documentary for Routledge

Mandy Rose is Co-Director of i-Docs, Associate Professor and Director of the University of the West of England's Digital Cultures Research Centre. A pioneer of UK interactive and participatory media, she was co-producer of BBC 2's ground breaking *Video Nation* project (1994–2000); devised *Voices* (2005), a major pan-BBC investigation of language, accent and dialect in the UK; and was Executive Producer of the *Capture Wales/Cipolwg ar Gymru* digital storytelling project (2001–8). Mandy's research looks at the intersection between documentary, digital media and networked culture. Her recent writing appears in *The Journal of Documentary Studies*, *The Documentary Film Book* (2013) and *DIY Citizenship; Critical Making and Social Media* (2014).

William Uricchio is Professor of Comparative Media Studies at MIT in the US as well as Professor of Comparative Media History at Utrecht University in the Netherlands. He is principal investigator of the MIT Open Documentary Lab, which works at the frontiers of interactive, immersive and participatory reality-based storytelling. He has written extensively about the emergence of new media forms and practices, at times using a historical lens and at others by working with interactive and algorithmically-generated media forms. William has received numerous awards for his work including Guggenheim, Humboldt and Fulbright research fellowships and most recently, the Berlin Prize.

FOREWORD

The late Peter Wintonick banished the word 'documentary' insisting instead on 'docmedia' to convey a vision of 'cyber-docs, digidocs, transmedia docs, cross-docs, cross-media, 360-degree docs, netcast docs, interactive docs, 3D-docs, made-for-mobile docs'; to which others add: 'soft-', 'interactive-', 'data-', 'dynamic-' or 'multi-linear-docs'. Clearly, we face a landscape in considerable need of maps.

Nowhere has this necessary cartographic work been attempted more thoroughly and clear-sightedly than within the i-Docs research group at the Digital Cultures Research Centre at the University of the West of England. Through their website and in a series of symposia in 2011, 2012, 2014 and 2016, the DCRC has created fora wherein docmedia's terrain can be delineated and its flora and fauna (as it were) catalogued. This collection well represents the progress to date of the community these symposia have brought together.

Understanding the consequences of digitizing the documentary project is no easy matter. For one thing, 'documentary', a term used in connection with film from 1915, if not before, has itself defied definition in the century since. It is no wonder that its 'other', docmedia, is equally resistant to easy categorization. The problems of doing so, however, are compounded because debate about the digital is suffused with obfuscating technicist enthusiasm. (The terminological 'tsumani' above – Wintonick again – in play to name what we think we are talking about is evidence enough of that). This volume's editors' useful contribution defines an i-doc as 'any project that starts with the intention to engage with the "real" and does so by using digital technology'. Unlike the traditional linear 'closed', Barthesian 'readerly' documentaries, with i-docs, at the intersection between the linear and the digital, 'the audience become active agents within a "writerly", more open, documentary text'.

This radically rewrites the tripartite division between the filmed, the filmer and the spectator. Hybridic figures emerge, not only dissolving the boundary between filmmaker and audience, but also between filmmakers and their subjects. Whatever else they might be, most obviously i-docs are the work of filmed/filmer or filmer/audience or filmed/filmer/audience hybrids.

There have been illuminating explorations of this junction over recent years and the hybridity digital technology allows has been not only examined but also enthusiastically celebrated. The practical challenges of the act of documenting in the new environment has also been described. But, given the seductions of the new, this literature has not much absorbed the debate about what has gone before or penetrated that deeply into what is at hand. Docmedia's context is largely uninformed by the history, dilemmas and challenges of the traditional linear documentary, although the pertinence of the old can be easily justified. Moreover digital wonders have beglamoured many observers. This anthology moves to correct these lacuna.

This collection affirms, with much argument and the evidence of case studies, i-docs to be transformative development. It presents both overviews and detailed studies to outline not only the dimensions i-docs add to social issue storytelling or the challenge they can be to Eurocentrism, but also how they impact on a variety of other documenting practices. *i-Docs: The Evolving Practices of Interactive Documentary* importantly adds details to our map of i-docs in the still largely *terra incognita* that is docmedia. It is very welcome.

Prof. Brian Winston

INTRODUCTION

Judith Aston, Sandra Gaudenzi and Mandy Rose

This volume represents the latest iteration of an ongoing research project into the creative practices and social meanings of interactive documentary (i-docs) that has been underway within the framework of i-Docs since 2011. That year, Judith Aston, Jon Dovey and Sandra Gaudenzi convened the first i-Docs Symposium at the Digital Cultures Research Centre (DCRC) at the University of the West of England (UWE) in Bristol. Since then, joined by Mandy Rose, we have continued to convene the dialogue began there through the i-Docs research project – which includes the website, Facebook group, a special edition of *Studies in Documentary Film* (2012) and three subsequent symposia in 2012, 2014 and 2016.

This collection draws on what we have learned through all of the endeavours undertaken within the i-Docs project to date. It seeks to amplify aspects of the discussions that we have fostered with a growing community of i-docs makers and researchers, it being fitting that these discussions take a variety of forms and have a life on a variety of platforms. They have taken a live, physical form in the symposium; an interactive form on the website; they are reflected in a lively daily conversation on social media in the Facebook community; and, after their articulation within the *Journal of Documentary Studies*, they are now emerging in print form again as this book.

Our definition of i-docs is deliberately open ended. We embrace any project that starts with the intention to engage with the real, and that uses digital interactive technology to realise this intention. For us the notion of the 'real' embraces the breadth of lived experience; as Clifford Geertz would have it, 'rocks and dreams are both of this world'. We therefore use the term 'real' in full acknowledgement that our understanding of reality is a shifting concept, which lends so many twists and possibilities to Grierson's 'creative treatment of actuality'.

In a fast-moving field, we want i-docs to be an expansive concept that can provide a platform for interrogating diverse forms and embracing a variety of emerging trends. We continue to use the term 'i-docs' to include projects that may be found elsewhere described as web-docs, transmedia documentaries, serious games, locative docs, interactive community media, docu-games and now, also, forms including virtual reality non-fiction, ambient literature and live performance documentary. We do not focus only on visual screen practices as i-docs can include work where audio leads, or where immersive and mixed reality projects use actuality and reportage, aural history and poetry, all opening up new terrains for documenting away from the lineage of documentary film.

As we consider the repercussions of i-docs, we find these interactive and experiential works prompting us to ask not what documentary means but *what documentary does*. What has changed in the last five years is that we have moved from a preoccupation with questions about what i-docs are, to interrogate how we make them, what forms they take in different cultural contexts, and where they might be going. We see interactive documentary-making as being as much about process as about product, and also believe very strongly that it is first and foremost about people as opposed to machines.

At its heart, therefore, the i-Docs project is an arena for a series of conversations, which bring together a broad spectrum of makers and theorists from across the globe to consider how documentarians and other producers of non-fiction are taking advantage of the developing affordances of computerisation. If, as Bill Nichols has suggested, documentary is engaged with telling stories about our shared world, our interest is in what happens as the former audience become agents in that process. At the very least the work unfolds through their interaction with it, with the potential also existing in some projects for them to be involved in the co-creation of content. This is a proposition which highlights a humanistic approach to agency. We are, however, fully aware that agency takes on another twist now that artificial intelligence is being applied to storytelling, this being an issue of developing importance that is also addressed in the book.

The field is, if anything, expanding, and this collection tackles recent trends and highlights longer-term themes. Over time, the hybrid forms emerging in the context of digital media – most notably between games and documentary and between digital journalism and interactive documentary – become more apparent. i-Docs provides a space where we can look across disciplines at what interactivity brings to these engagements. Meanwhile, the collection picks up certain longer-term themes, which have received little attention. At the same time, we have also honed in on the craft of interactive documentary-making, by looking at hack and co-design practices, as well the role of user testing.

This volume reflects our belief that the multi-disciplinary nature of i-docs calls for a multi-disciplinary debate, and a dialogue between thinking and making. This is not to set up a binary between academia and creative industry, or between theory and practice, as some of the foremost i-docs practitioners are academics and some of the most astute critical thinking comes from outside the academy. To express this dialogue across disciplines and between making and thinking, this collection explicitly brings together theoretical papers, case studies and interviews with influencers.

The i-Docs Symposium has been dedicated to making a space where those currents can mingle. In our welcome address to i-Docs 2016, we talked of the event as providing an opportunity to zoom in to grapple with the detail of particular projects and also to zoom out and see those projects in context – cultural, geographical, historical, political. In this collection, case studies, interviews and papers zoom in to consider processes of design and making, and the dynamics at work between producers, subjects and users, while other papers zoom out to consider the wider implications of i-docs, their contribution to today's media ecology and consequences for the creative industries.

We have designed the volume with the objective that it might be of use to academic researchers, digital makers, media decision-makers and students, and we invite all interested to continue the discussion by contributing to the i-Docs website and Facebook group. As such, we hope that the collection reflects something of the spirit that Patty Zimmermann generously describes having felt at i-Docs 2016: 'i-Docs was a marvel of assembling different communities and constituencies to probe and unpack new developments in interactive documentary. The swift dialectical shifts between theory and practice, local and global, ideas and tech, established and emerging, left me unsettled and engaging new unexpected ideas. I left intellectually nourished and fortified for the rapids needing navigation.'

This book is structured around three themes and each section is introduced by its editor: 'Co-Creation', by Mandy; 'Methods', by Sandra; and 'Horizons', by Judith. Some of the contributions were originally papers at i-Docs 2014 and 2016.

1 CO-CREATION

PREFACE

Mandy Rose

Digital media and networked connectivity have the potential to reconfigure the relationship between media producer, subject and audience at the heart of documentary, bringing them into a dialogic relationship and into play with interactive systems. In this section we take 'co-creation' as a broad term for the collaborations that emerge within that space. The contributions are interested in the production processes that allow co-creation – in engagement strategies and design approaches. They are also concerned with the contribution of users, and with the ethics, social meaning and values that arise within co-creative encounters. They address co-creation between media makers and documentary subjects, with academic researchers and communities, and through algorithms (having been programmed by humans) and online users.

Kate Nash explores two projects to consider how interactive media develops documentary's citizenship role. She examines evidence of user engagement with *Fort McMoney* (Dufresne 2013) and *Hollow* (McMillion Sheldon 2013) and makes a case that the civic value of these projects is linked to their capacity to bridge between private and public media.

Anandana Kapur offers a case study of her own work-in-progress – a cross-class collaboration between domestic workers and their employers in Delhi. She describes the process through which she is harnessing everyday technology – the mobile phone – to surface hidden dimensions of female life, agency and friendship in India's 'rape capital'.

In an extensive interview, the award-winning interactive documentary maker Kat Cizek discusses what it means for her practice to make work 'with partners instead of just about them'. From her first experiments in interactive as National

Film Board of Canada filmmaker-in-residence to the final piece within the *High-rise* project 'The Universe Within' (2015), she shows how a collaborative ethos has shaped her work.

Mandy Rose explores co-creation as a strategy for activism. Through a consideration of *Question Bridge: Black Males* (Johnson *et al* 2012) and *The Quipu Project* (Court *et al* 2015), she considers interactive documentary as a platform for convening dialogue between documentary subjects and audiences, and suggests how forms of shared editorial control can enable media making for change.

Christopher Allen turns the reader's attention towards the practice of exhibition. His case study of the *Living Los Sures* (Allen *et al* 2014) project explores the multiple collaborations and encounters involved in this multi-year process through which a 'hipster' Brooklyn micro-cinema and a local community re-examine a lost 1980s documentary classic and the meaning of neighbourhood.

Craig Hight draws on Software Studies to highlight the ubiquitous but generally overlooked collaboration between machine and user on which interactivity depends. Considering the interfaces and affordance of two interactive documentary platforms – Klynt and Korsakow – his chapter makes an urgent case for the opening up of discussions around agency and ethics within these encounters.

I-DOCS AND THE DOCUMENTARY TRADITION
EXPLORING QUESTIONS OF CITIZENSHIP

Kate Nash

Documentary media's relationship to the social world is distinctive. This is particularly the case in relation to questions of citizenship, with documentary long claiming a particular, albeit historically variable, role in its mediation. Central to the civic role of documentary is the claim that documentary serves as a source of public knowledge that serves to inform political participation. While i-docs are formally and technically distinct from linear documentary media, there is some evidence for continuity at the level of their social functions, with citizenship a continuing touchstone for documentary practice. I-docs frequently aspire to expand documentary's political role, particularly by providing new ways of engaging with social issues and opportunities for forms of self-representation. In these aspirations is a continuation of documentary's political ambition, but also a response, shaped by the cultures and possibilities of digital media, to the contemporary challenges of representing and attempting to impact on the real. Documentary's social functions, its connection to social participation and citizenship, journalistic investigation and the exploration of alternative perspectives (Corner 2002), inform the use of digital technologies just as these technologies, their representational possibilities and cultures, are shaping the political uses of documentary.

This chapter engages with ways in which i-docs connect to citizenship. In particular, it considers how we might capture i-docs' multiple modes of address and forms of participation and their implications for public engagement. Focusing on two examples, *Fort McMoney* (Dufresne 2013) and *Hollow* (McMillion Sheldon 2013), I consider both what documentary makers seek to achieve civically and politically and what we know about how audiences have responded to these projects. While these two projects cannot be considered representative of the many ways in which i-docs intersect with politics, they highlight different ways of thinking about citizenship and interactive documentary and reveal some of the implications of i-docs for current debates in digital media citizenship. The analysis presented here suggests that i-docs' particular significance may lie in their potential to foster connections between the private realm of media engagement and of public participation.

I-DOCS AND DIGITAL MEDIA CITIZENSHIP

Citizenship has been a central, if variable, concept in documentary history and scholarship. It is invoked in John Grierson's vision of documentary as a promotional vehicle in the service of government (Aitkin 2013: 131), television documentary's informational and watchdog role (Corner 1996, Ellis 2000: 44–7), and independent documentary's ability to 'give voice' to alternative perspectives (Chanan 2007). Across this difference there has been a central focus on the ability of documentary – as with other factual 'mass' media – to enhance (or not) 'public knowledge' (Corner 1998), providing citizens with the informational resources required for informed decision-making. This focus on the informational role of documentary has, in recent years, included recognition of the significance of emotion, entertainment and culture for citizenship (Hartley 2012, Smaill 2010). However, because documentary scholarship has predominantly assumed film and television as media platforms, it has also assumed that audience engagement with documentary is necessarily separate from political action. This is captured in Jane Gaines' question about the connection between political film and action: 'What is it that moves viewers to want to act … to do something instead of nothing in relation to the political situation represented on screen?' (1999: 89). Whatever the 'something' is that moves audiences, any action they take happens after their engagement with documentary. The role of documentary is essentially one of providing information of different kinds that might motivate political action.

In the case of i-docs, this question is potentially altered, as audiences are not only positioned as interpreters of political representations – although this is part of the experience of engaging with i-docs that can be too easily overlooked; they are also invited (at times perhaps compelled) to act in politically significant ways. Of course these actions vary considerably in their significance for the individual and for society, connecting in different ways to formal and informal political spaces. Nevertheless, what they point to is the potential expansion of documentary's civic role beyond the provision of 'public knowledge' as a preparation for political participation. There is a need to rethink the relationship between documentary and society, considering the connections between representation and dialogue, participation and co-creation (to highlight some of the relevant practices).

Audience practices and their political implications have been the focus of much recent i-doc scholarship. In exploring documentary through ideas of 'open space', Helen de Michiel and Patricia Zimmermann, for example, argue that interactive documentary is less about 'changing lives or establishing deductive rhetorical arguments' but more about 'opening up complex dialogues that reject binaries through polyphonies and which creates mosaics of multiple lenses on issues' (2013: 356). Similarly, Dale Hudson and Zimmermann (2015) draw attention to the ways in which interaction, participation and relationships can be structured around social issues. Jon Dovey and Mandy Rose highlight documentary's participatory heritage while suggesting that digital platforms reinvigorate co-creative documentary authorship, understood as storytelling shaped not by a singular voice (be that an individual author or a specific collective) but emerging 'within a network of relationships' (2013: 371).

These ways of thinking about the politics of interactive documentary draw strongly on the ideal of polyvocality and the theoretical framework of the public sphere as a normative model for mediated citizenship. Drawing on the work of Jürgen Habermas, the public sphere has been influential as a way of thinking about the democratic role of the media, highlighting its significance as a source of information but also as a platform for the exchange of ideas and the formation of collective public opinion. While film and television documentary was most significant in terms of its provision of information (Chanan 2000), i-docs are potentially also platforms for action, and it is their ability to link documentary representation and forms of participation in the public sphere that has been a key focus of scholarly attention. However, the political potential of digital media is both claimed and contested. In order to understand how i-docs might link documentary representation to forms of politically significant action there is need to critically explore the ways in which participation is fostered and different voices positioned or potentially silenced within specific projects.

In relation to participatory i-docs, Mandy Rose (2014) has argued that their significance lies in their ability to address gaps in participation by creating interactive architectures and discursive structures that support different voices to speak with authority and purpose. She draws attention to the potential for participatory projects to eschew overall synthesis allowing for the creation of issue frames grounded in recognition of different perspectives. While there has been a tendency to see i-doc participation as something quite distinct from documentary's traditional representative function, Rose draws attention to the importance of documentary discourse as framing the offer of participation. While she focuses particularly on the potential for documentary discourse to promote polyvocality, this need not exhaust the relationship between discourse and participation. This is something that will be taken up further in the analysis below.

Rose also points to a broader range of questions, asking whether there are differences in the extent to which audiences feel informed and confident to participate. In doing so, she connects analysis of i-doc participation in the public sphere to a critical question in digital media research: 'What does it take for people to participate in public?' (Livingstone 2005: 29). This is an important question for any critical engagement with i-doc participation in that it moves from a consideration of what is technically possible for people to do with an i-doc to analysis of the ways in which these technical possibilities intersect with documentary discourse and individual subjectivities.

Peter Dahlgren's civic cultures framework (2009: 104–5) seeks to provide a way of examining the political potential of digital media that acknowledges the complex relationships between technology, communication and subjectivity. He identifies six interdependent dimensions of the socio-cultural world, including those facilitated by the media, that he argues that are important for public sphere participation. Citizens need: information and increasingly strategies for acquiring knowledge; democratic values such as tolerance, equality, responsibility and respect, among others, which underpin participation; a degree of trust in each other in order to engage in democratic exchange; communicative spaces in which to encounter others; practices, which may vary but whose significance lies in helping them to acquire the skills and competencies required to engage democratically; and finally, they need identity in order to see themselves as members of a democratic collective (2009: 108–22).

Central to Dahlgren's analysis is a recognition of the value of the private sphere for political action (2009: 74). While the public sphere is where mediation and political action intersect, participation in this political sphere depends on identities, skills and relationships that are formed in the private realm. The media can play a role at this level that has the potential to support participation in the public sphere. To ask, as Rose does, about when people might feel confident to participate in the public sphere through i-docs is to consider the relationship between civic cultures, documentary discourse and the private and public spaces that i-docs create. Looking at i-docs from this perspective highlights the potential for an expansion of documentary's civic role, beyond the provision of information i-docs may offer spaces in which collective identities, civic values and communicative skills can be developed. Dahlgren notes, however, that the move from the private spaces of media engagement to participation in the public sphere is always possible but not always realised. It is a move that, he argues, depends on the emergence of a collective orientation and commitment to action. In the following analysis, I consider how i-docs might contribute to the formation of civic cultures. At the same time, I look for evidence that they work to connect private engagement to public participation and the realm of formal politics.

FORT McMONEY: FROM CIVIC CULTURES TO PUBLIC SPHERE?

'The Fort McMoney experience will be a kind of web-era platform for direct democracy. The winner, if there is one, will be the battle of ideas.'

David Dufresne (2013)

The documentary game *Fort McMoney* is grounded in a specific vision of digitally mediated citizenship that owes much to the ideal of the public sphere. Addressing the social, economic and environmental impacts of Canada's oil sands industry as they impact on the town of Fort McMurray and the surrounding region, its storytelling, interaction and participation foster a playful performance of deliberative citizenship that involves gathering information and engaging in collective debate and decision-making. In analysing *Fort McMoney*, I will consider the connections made by the production team between play and players' experience of agency and community. The game is built on the idea that play has the potential to scaffold political participation. This scaffolding links play not only to the documentary itself but also to social media and the mainstream media providing some opportunities for players' voices to enter into public debate.

Fort McMoney is a hybrid media object, combining audiovisual representation, game-play and simulation with real-time chat. It addresses players as active decision-makers. In an unpublished project proposal David Dufresne details that players were originally conceptualised as members of a virtual 'Fort McMoney council' who engage with documentary content as a basis for debate and collective decision-making. Game-play explicitly references the norm of informed decision-making with 'influence points', rewarding the player for – among other things – their engagement with documentary content. The game integrates the traditional 'informational' role of documentary with a deliberative platform that seeks to foster informed debate (weekly forums), the formation of public opinion (reflected in various 'polls') and, ultimately, collective decision-making (weekly referenda). The structure of game-play reflects in key ways the ideal of the public sphere as a democratic space that is public, inclusive, informed, persuasive (players are invited to make their world view 'triumph') and participatory.

However, in seeking to create this kind of public discursive space, the creators of *Fort McMoney* were conscious of the importance of players' private experience of game-play. In proposing the project, Dufresne makes the point that while the investigative content of the documentary (interviews and video sequences) aims to represent issues objectively, game-play and simulation present opportunities to foster a different mode of engagement. Play in particular is seen as a way of promoting a more personal relationship to the issues: 'The spectators really become actors, forging their opinion, evaluating their thoughts and expressing their emotions and subjectivity at the heart of the programme. *Fort McMoney* does not want to moralise, it's the players themselves who, through their actions, develop their critical sense.'

To play is to engage imaginatively with possible futures for Fort McMurray, but it is also to engage reflexively with one's own political identity. In forging a personal opinion players are encouraged to draw connections between the issues represented and their own values. They have the opportunity to see themselves as political agents and to become conscious of their responsibilities as actors and as citizens. Game-play is also grounded in democratic values; to play is to acknowledge the existence of political difference, the value of expressing alternative perspectives and respect for collective decision-making. The game design emphasises community, by organising play into 'cycles' so that players 'quickly learn that they aren't alone'. The game proposals emphasise the value of collective engagement both in terms of shared experience but also understanding, allowing players to understand different perspectives on the issue, a form of 'collective conscience'.

At the level of the game's design, there is evidence both of the significance of the public sphere as a democratic model, but also recognition of the value of play as a foundation for the emergence of civic identity and collective orientation. However, looking for evidence of player experience, there is some evidence of a tension between the structure of game-play and the desire to foster a sense of civic agency. Blogger Melissa Aronczyk (2014), for example, highlights agency as an issue in her participation in weekly fora: 'While the game's players debate whether taxes should be higher, workers better treated, and environmental concerns alleviated, there is no space to say "Stop. This shouldn't be happening at all" ... nor does it offer alternatives, asking what political possibilities might exist, what other arrangements of people money and energy might be assembled.' She describes the experience of feeling alienated from a conversation that does not have space for her contribution. Several other players cited technical constraints to dialogue – not being able to search for specific issues, for example – that meant that genuine dialogue was difficult (see player responses cited in Mal 2014: 6).

Measures of audience participation in round one, while impressive, also point to something of a participation gap with more than 300,000 players but only

1869 contributing to the debates (Mal 2014). While this is not atypical for digital projects (versions of the 1 per cent rule attempt to capture this in relation to internet culture generally, emphasising the relatively small numbers engaged in actively producing media content), it is a gap that cannot be easily explained in terms of a lack of digital skills or knowledge (see for example Henry Jenkins on the participation gap; 2006: 23).

In contrast, civic cultures as a conceptual framework may offer some explanation. As a game, *Fort McMoney* depends on players trusting its democratic model. However, the algorithms underpinning the game are not transparent – a fact that resulted in at least some players experiencing a lack of trust. One player, commenting on the 'Bienvenue à Fort McMoney/Groupe de Joueurs page', for example (Uthagey 2014), expresses this view (see figure 1). In response, another player stated that they didn't feel that their votes in the polls were taken into account. In addition to the challenge of inspiring trust in the underlying algorithm, the mechanism of polling can also have implications for civic identity and agency. Reflecting on the increasing role of opinion in contemporary politics Susan Herbst (1993) has argued that polls can have the effect of contributing to feelings of political alienation. She highlights the reactive nature of opinion polling suggesting that they offer little scope for thoughtful analysis and limit choice to binary oppositions in ways that can contribute to feelings of powerlessness. Joke Hermes (2006) has similarly critiqued the increasing reliance of opinion polls in the news media, arguing that if they play any role at all in informing citizens then they do so only in the most cursory way, fuelling scepticism and working against the emergence of publics.

Fig. 1: Questioning the virtual democracy of *Fort McMoney* on the Facebook, 'Group de jouers' page

While the game structure – particularly the for and against structure of the debates – suggests a space that is welcoming of divergent opinion, the documentary elements – the interviews and visual sequences – and the principles underpinning the simulation (which like the voting were opaque to players) may have alienated those with a pro-industry perspective and some of those from Fort McMurray itself. The pro-environmental perspective 'won' the first round of play and players with pro-environmental perspectives were conspicuously more active in the debates. Dufresne (cited in Wohlberg 2014) speculated that those arguing for the status quo were simply less interested in debate. Alternatively, it might be that those with pro-industry views felt alienated by the documentary's discourse. This is, of course, highly speculative, although it is interesting to note the relative visibility of pro-industry sentiment expressed on Canadian news site *The Globe and Mail* (2013a, 2013b), which ran ongoing coverage of *Fort McMoney*.

In evaluating *Fort McMoney*'s significance for citizenship, however, it is also important to take into account the value of its pro-environmental frame, in terms of its ability to amplify this perspective in broader public debate. Lincoln Dahlberg has argued that while public sphere perspectives have led us to value diversity of opinion, we should also consider the importance of online spaces in which citizens encounter like-minded others; he highlights the importance of such spaces for nurturing counter-discourses (2007: 837). From this perspective, *Fort McMoney* can be seen as a space for those wanting to explore environmentalist perspectives to gather evidence and test arguments while feeling part of a discursive majority. Such an opportunity is significant given the political, economic and communicative imbalance that may foster feelings of powerlessness in relation to the issue.

In evaluating the impact on the broader mediated public sphere, the media partnerships surrounding the *Fort McMoney* game should also be considered. One partner, the Canadian newspaper *The Globe and Mail,* regularly reported on the game, focusing on the results of the weekly referenda and adding to this further analysis and discussion spaces. The effect was to translate players' in-game action – voting – into a news story that drew attention to players' collective perspectives, connecting them to the mainstream media public sphere.

Similarly social media, particularly Twitter, provided a connection between the public sphere and the space of game-play. Here again, the project team and media partners were active in fostering a discussion of the project and the issues raised. Interestingly, however, analysis of the 222 posts made using the #fortmcmoney hashtag during the second half of game-play in December 2013 reveals that the project (rather than the issues) was the focus of 70 per cent of posts.[1] This is in spite of the fact that 'issue focused' hashtags such as '#oilsands', '#tarsands' were present in 30 per cent of posts (as opposed to game-focused tags such as '#webdoc' or '#idoc' which were included in only 10 per cent of posts). Again the project's media partners were instrumental in fostering discussion as they were responsible for 18 per cent of issue-focused posts. On social media, while *Fort McMoney* succeeded in fostering a very active conversation through its novel use of digital media, it was predominantly the novelty of the game itself that, rather than the oil sands, that was the focus of conversation.

HOLLOW: COMMUNITY DOCUMENTARY AND SOCIAL NETWORKS

Hollow is an interactive documentary and participatory project addressing the social and economic problems facing residents of McDowell County, West Virginia. It is a multiplatform project, with web content surrounded by forms of social media content. It can be considered socially layered cinema, a social media discourse centred on a 'cinematic' text (Atkinson 2013). But importantly, in Alex Juhasz's (2014) terms, it also 'cedes' the digital, foregrounding community and relationships and moving beyond the domain of representation in order to achieve its political goals. While documentary makers have a long history of working with communities, *Hollow* highlights the potential for social media to support such activity.

In proposing *Hollow*, the production team highlighted two key objectives: to facilitate community self-representation as a response to the unequal power relationships in media production that typically result in communities like McDowell being portrayed as victims in the mainstream media; secondly, to create the conditions for the community to collaborate in order to address social, economic and environmental problems. The project therefore established a series of relationships oriented toward co-creation, but also relationships that might link the symbolic realm of documentary storytelling and the political realm of coordinated action. Director Elaine McMillion Sheldon describes the connection: 'Storytelling online and offline increases social capital, spreads local knowledge and encourages efficacy among residents as they become empowered to form a new community identity' (2013a: 25).

Here storytelling becomes a catalyst for strengthening collective identity, community knowledge and social capital. Further, she describes the project as 'about getting people talking; not to me necessarily, but to each other, because it's not something that happens very often without some facilitation on the ground' (personal communication, 6 August 2015). Relationship formation is a key goal with the project conceptualised as creating a space where residents will 'interact with fellow community members, thereby increasing their associations'

(McMillion Sheldon 2013a: 24). The project is grounded in storytelling as both self-representation and as a path to fostering civic cultures, creating communicative spaces, collective identity, trust and relationships. While there is arguably nothing novel in this connection between documentary's representative and civic projects (see for example Abrash and Whiteman 1999), social media was integral to how these goals were achieved.

COLLABORATIVE (SELF-)REPRESENTATION

Hollow sought to support community members to become citizen journalists providing access to cameras, storytelling workshops and events designed to build media literacy. A community advisory board provided editorial input and helped to connect residents to the projects and community screenings provided an opportunity to show community work. In spite of encouraging community engagement in the summer of 2012, however, the project team has reported a subsequent drop off in participation that they attribute to a range of structural and cultural issues, such as a lack of infrastructure and a degree of political apathy (McMillion and Adams n.d.). In addition, McMillion thinks that community members' sense of their relationship to the media was also a factor: 'When I wanted them to participate and tell their own story, many of them just wanted to be interviewed. [...] I had some people where I thought they would be great contributors, to contribute their own story from their voice, rather than me editing a version of their voice, but they just really felt more comfortable and just wanted to be part of the traditional side of me documenting' (personal communication, 6 August 2015).

Social media, in contrast, provided a range of options for residents to contribute to storytelling, which, while very small scale, are important in connecting representation to people's everyday engagement with media. In particular the project's Facebook page became a space where the production team was able to support a range of activities oriented to challenging dominant media representations of McDowell and producing alternatives.[2]

During the production of *Hollow* the production team made regular posts (79 in total) in which they shared images of McDowell – archival images, community events and images of natural environments. These images serve a number of different functions (including promotional functions) but a key one is to position the project politically, creating a frame for participation. The album 'out and about', for example, contains 165 images of people, events and places in the region that constitutes a substantial visual archive; importantly, one that challenges dominant media representations of the McDowell region. In addition, the project team shared short stories about their interviewees and included images of community members engaged in storytelling. These posts serve to foreground questions of representation and help to foster a community identity tied to the practice of collective of storytelling.

There were several ways in which people contributed content to Facebook during the production phase of *Hollow*. While comments on content posted by the team were modest (47 per cent of posts attracting no comments and only seven attracting ten or more comments), the posts did serve as invitations for people to contribute memories and personal connections to McDowell (see figure 2). While often not considered to be storytelling, the personal stories contained in the comments can also be seen as a contribution to the overall project of collaborative storytelling. Posting to the page also provided opportunities for participation; 53 posts were made to the page during production, and while much of this activity (22 posts) related to the project itself (funding and promotion), there were eight posts suggesting content (interviewees, locations) and another eight posts in which people shared alternative media representations of McDowell. People also used posts to connect with the production team and other community members, linking people to the project (through tags) and sharing their experience of being interviewed. While there are a few photos submitted to the page, there is surprising little video or photography by community members (although they are often depicted filming in the content posted by the project team).

Following the launch of *Hollow* in June 2013, the Facebook page continued to play a role as a space for collaborative representation. Taking the period between March and July 2015 as indicative, the team continued to post regularly making

11 August 2012 ·

Northfork is now a ghost town, but, once was a thriving little community that hosted the families of coal miners and railroad workers. My grandfather was the Station Master there and he built their home in Crumpler ('up the hollar'). My mother and her siblings were born there and all moved away as soon as they were of age, became professionals and/or homemakers. As a child, my Mother played the piano for the silent movies in Northfork. She talked about the dances held 'in town' when they were older teens and dating. Now, there is little left, except abandoned buildings, remnants of old house foundations, and blackened roadsides of coal dust from the past. Drove up there recently... Sad sight. Extraordinarily beautiful countryside. Financial potential for WV if investors could develop varied recreational resorts that would interest a broader population. Good luck with your project. I hope it will draw more attention to the area and, perhaps, some big investors with creative ideas.

Like   Comment   Share

Fig. 2: *Hollow*: an example of a story contributed as a comment to Facebook

Fig. 3: Sharing media
representations of
McDowell on the *Hollow*
Facebook page

Fig. 3: Sharing media representations of McDowell on the *Hollow* Facebook page

48 posts. These posts served several functions, including sharing updates on the project and its impact (17 posts). Importantly, the team also shared various items of content (including art, music, photographs and videos) produced by locals (11 posts) and media coverage about McDowell, including stories that address issues of representation (16 posts). The effect of this activity is to create an active and supportive social space that foregrounds collaborative representation. It is also to create an opportunity for the emergence of a form of 'monitorial citizenship' (Schudson 1998) with residents sharing and challenging dominant media representations of McDowell County (see figure 3). There is also a level of (admittedly modest) content creation. Of the 94 posts to the site from launch to 29 May 2015, there were several posts sharing pictures and video (six), personal stories (two) and drawings (three). The page therefore functions, to some extent, as a space for collective representation grounded in acts of vernacular creativity (Burgess 2007) and communication that adds up to an alternative representation of the region.

A PLATFORM FOR POLITICAL ENGAGEMENT

As previously noted, *Hollow* was also intended to be a tool for community development. '*Hollow* will offer a platform for decision-making, collaboration and encourage change in the region. [...] We want this site to live and evolve well beyond launch and act as a useful tool for the community – this will happen through social media tools, organizing community workshops and developing online tools that entice users to contribute ideas and support' (McMillion 2013a). Although the project included a community page – *Holler Home* – this was relatively unsuccessful, attracting fewer than 70 posts over two years. In contrast, the Facebook group 'McDowell Community Initiatives', set up by the documentary team in 2012, has developed over time into a fairly active community group with over five hundred members. This is particularly significant since most of those who are active in the group did not know each other prior to *Hollow* (personal communication 6 August 2015).

In contrast to the *Hollow* project site where the voice of the team dominates, on the 'McDowell Community Initiatives' group page it is the voice of the community that is most evident, with a handful of community members accounting for the bulk of the posts. The focus of the page is much more explicitly on the issues facing the community and on facilitating action. Posts made between January and August 2015 (239) are indicative, serving several functions including promoting and coordinating events, networking and discussing issues. General discussion is frequently prompted by one community member posting 'discussion starters' such as: 'lots of the time when we turn on the news we [sic] exposed to negative news stories of the county and community.... What do ya'll [sic] think is one key positive thing McDowell County does or offer? (post date 22 May 2015). More specific discussions emerge around issues and events such as the demolition of a school gym (21 April 2015) and water quality (2 March 2015). These discussions include debate, knowledge sharing, relationship building (including tagging people to put them in touch with each other) and linking group members to decision-makers and relevant information.

Connections between the public sphere and civic cultures are evident on the page. In addition to the semi-public debates described above, the community is also very active in seeking and promoting news media coverage. There are several examples of stories posted on the site being picked up by the local media (15 Febuary, local exercise initiative; 23 May young footballers' achievement), and when two local journalists join the group (23 April 2015), several members make contact to press the importance of the local media in achieving the groups' aims. At the same time, there are a number of posts focused on the formation and maintenance of relationships (there is also evidence of interpersonal tension and conflict resolution). The importance of identity is reflected in individuals posting 'inspirational quotes', pictures and their own creative content. Even when addressing pressing issues such as a gym demolition, memory, personal stories and relationships are significant.

The 'McDowell Community Initiatives' Facebook Group is indicative of the way in which i-docs, dispersed across and beyond digital platforms, can create civic cultures and foster dialogic spaces and relationships from which forms of public and political engagement can emerge. The discursive frame established by the documentary-makers, while open, is not infinitely so. As with *Fort McMoney,* there is a value here in creating a space of relatively like-minded people that is supportive of shared alternative perspectives. Also important are the connections that social networks facilitate between everyday lives and documentary content.

CONCLUSIONS

In this chapter I have considered how i-docs might expand documentary media's civic role beyond the provision of 'public knowledge'. In my analysis of *Fort McMoney* and *Hollow* I have drawn attention to documentary-makers' desire to use digital media to support a range of practices that connect documentary to the public sphere of political action but also support the emergence of civic cultures, private spaces that foster skills, relationships and identities that are fundamental to citizenship. Both projects address their audience as citizens, promote civic values and provide opportunities for relationship building and communication. In both cases, the documentary makers aspired to create communicative/collaborative communities around their projects and in so doing to create a space where civic and political engagement might be fostered.

A key idea that I have explored here is the potential for i-docs to create productive connections between the private spaces of media consumption and the public sphere. If i-docs support civic cultures, when and how might they also facilitate the emergence of publics? Although preliminary, the research presented here suggests this as a fruitful avenue for further investigation. *Fort McMoney* and *Hollow* both seek to engage their audiences as members of a political collective, building on the civic cultures they foster to promote forms of action in the public sphere. This raises further questions about the relationship between these forms of participation and the sphere of formal politics. Differences between the projects also highlight the need to better understand the intersections between documentary production and interactivity but also the impact of discourse on interaction and participation. It is not a question of replacing questions about the politics of representation with questions about participation, but of understanding the complex relationships between them.

However, it is important to note that the creation of mediated civic cultures and political engagement are not inevitable outcomes of audiences' consumption of i-doc content. They are significant potentials and more research is needed to understand how documentary media might best support civic cultures and social/political participation.

NOTES

1. The analysis presented covers the period from 9 to 22 December 2013.
2. This analysis of community self-representation is based on the *Hollow* Facebook page, covering two key periods: production (March to September 2012) and the second anniversary of the project (March to July 2015).

REFERENCES

Abrash, Barbara and David Whiteman (1999) 'The Uprising of '34: Filmmaking as Community Engagement', *Wide Angle*, 21/22, 87–99; http://muse.jhu.edu/login?auth=0&type=summary&url=/journals/wide_angle/v021/21.2whiteman.html. Accessed 31 October 2016.

Aitken, Ian (2013) 'John Grierson and the Documentary Film Movement' in Brian Winston (ed.) *The Documentary Film Book*. London: British Film Institute/Palgrave McMillian, 129–37.

Atkinson, Sarah (2014) *Beyond the Screen: Emerging Cinema and Engaging Audience*. London: Bloomsbury.

Aronczyk, Melissa (2014) 'Fort McMoney: Media for the Age of Oil', Antenna blog. blog. commarts.wisc/2014/02/03/fort-mcmoney-media-for-the-age-of-oil. Accessed 31 October 2016.

Burgess, Jean (2007) *Vernacular Creativity and New Media*. PhD Thesis. Queensland University of Technology; http://eprints.qut.edu.au/16378/1/Jean_Burgess_Thesis.pdf. Accessed 31 October 2016.

Chanan, Michael (2000) 'Documentary and the Public Sphere', in John Izod and Richard Kilborn (eds) *From Grierson to the Docu-Soap: Breaking the Boundaries*. Luton: University of Luton Press, 221–30.

____ (2007) *The Politics of Documentary*. London: British Film Institute.

Corner, John (1996) *The Art of Record: A Critical Introduction to Documentary*. Manchester: Manchester University Press.

____ (1998) *Studying Media: Problems of Theory and Method*. Edinburgh: University of Edinburgh Press.

____ (2002) 'Performing the real: Documentary diversions', *Television and New Media*, 3, 3, 255–69.

Dahlberg, Lincoln (2007) 'Rethinking the fragmentation of the cyberpublic: from consensus to contestation', *New Media and Society*, 9, 5, 827–47.

Dahlgren, Peter (2009) *Media and Political Engagement: Citizens, Communication and Democracy*. Cambridge: Cambridge University Press.

De Michiel, Helen and Patricia Zimmerman (2013) 'Documentary as Open Space', in Brian Winston (ed.) *The Documentary Film Book*. London: British Film Institute, 355–64.

Dovey, John and Mandy Rose (2013) 'This Great Mapping of Ourselves: New Documentary Forms Online', in Brian Winston (ed.) *The Documentary Film Book*. London: British Film Institute, 366–75.

23

Dufresne, David (n.d.) '*Fort McMoney*: Une Connexion, Une Voix, un desastre, Un web-documentaire ludique écrit et proposé par David Dufresne, produit par TOXA'. Unpublished project proposal provided by the Director.

___ (2013a) *Fort McMoney*. Web Documentary. Co-produced by NFB, ARTE and TOXA; http://fortmcmoney.com/#/fortmcmoney. Accessed 31 October 2016.

___ (2013b) 'Fort McMoney: Make your world view triumph', *Huffington Post Canada*; http://www.huffingtonpost.ca/david-dufresne/fort-mcmoney-webdocumen-tary_b_4319259.html. Accessed 31 October 2016.

Ellis, John (2000) *Seeing Things: Television in the Age of Uncertainty*. London: I.B. Tauris.

Gaines, Jane M. (1999) 'Political Mimesis', in Jane M. Gaines and Michael Renov (eds) *Collecting Visible Evidence*. Minneapolis: University of Minnesota Press, 84–102.

Globe and Mail, The (2013a) 'Should we stop exploiting the oil sands? Fort McMurray players say "yes"', 16 December 2013; http://www.theglobeandmail.com/report-on-business/industry-news/energy-and-resources/should-we-stop-exploiting-the-oil-sands/article15969027/comments/#dashboard/follows/?2389. Accessed 31 October 2016.

___ (2013b) 'Should oil be nationalised? Fort McMoney players say "yes"', 20 December 2013; http://www.theglobeandmail.com/report-on-business/industry-news/energy-and-resources/should-oil-be-nationalized/article15809881/. Accessed 31 October 2016.

Hartley, John (2012) *Digital Futures for Cultural and Media Studies*. Oxford: Wiley-Blackwell.

Herbst, Susan (1993) *Numbered Voices: How Opinion Polling has Shaped American Politics*. Chicago: University of Chicago Press.

Hermes, Joke (2006) 'Citizenship in the age of the Internet', *European Journal of Communication,* 29, 3, 295–309.

Hollow (n.d) *Hollow the Project*. Facebook page. https://www.facebook.com/hollowtheproject?fref=ts. Accessed 31 October 2016.

Hudson, Dale and Patricia Zimmerman (2015) *Thinking Through Digital Media: Transnational Environments and Locative Places*. New York: Palgrave Macmillan.

Jenkins, Henry (2006) *Convergence Culture: Where Old and New Media Collide*. New York: New York University Press.

Juhasz, Alex (2014) 'Ceding the Activist Digital Documentary', in Kate Nash, Craig Hight and Catherine Summerhayes (eds) *New Documentary Ecologies: Emerging Platforms, Practices and Discourses*. New York: Palgrave Macmillan, 33–49.

Livingstone, Sonia (2005) 'On the relationship between audiences and publics', in Sonia Livingstone (ed.) *Audiences and Publics: When Cultural Engagement Matters for the Public Sphere*. Bristol: Intellect, 17–41.

Mal, Cedric (2014) 'Webdoc: Retour d'expériences sur *Fort McMoney*', Le Blog Documentaire; http://leblogdocumentaire.fr/2014/01/22/webdoc-retour-dexperiences-sur-fort-mcmoney-le-jeu-documentaire-de-david-dufresne. Accessed 31 October 2016.

McDowell Community Initiatives (n.d.) Facebook Group Page. https://www.facebook.com/groups/hollerhome/. Accessed 31 October 2016.

McMillion Sheldon, Elaine (2013a) *Hollow: A Masters Thesis*, unpublished. Emerson College, Boston, MA.

___ (2013b) *Hollow*. Web documentary; http://www.hollowdocumentary.com. Accessed 31 October 2016.

McMillion Sheldon, Elaine and Megan Adams (n.d.) 'Moving from Perceptions to Realities: Lessons Learned from *Hollow*'. MIT Civic Media Project; http://civicmediaproject.org/works/civic-media-project/hollow. Accessed 31 October 2016.

Rose, Mandy (2014) 'Making Publics: Documentary as do-it-with-others citizenship', in Magan Boler and Mat Ratto (eds) *DIY Citizenship: Critical Making and Social Media*. Boston: MIT Press, 221–12.

Schudson, Michael (1998) *The Good Citizen: A History of American Civil Life*. New York: Free Press.

Smaill, Belinda (2010) *The Documentary: Politics, Emotion, Culture*. New York: Palgrave Macmillan.

Uthagey, Euquinimod (2014) 'Bienvenue à Fort McMoney/Groupe de Joueurs'. Facebook Group Page, posted 11 Feburary 2014; https://www.facebook.com/groups/2080157160 50856/?fref=ts. Accessed 31 October 2016.

Wohlberg, Meagan (2014) 'Environment wins in first round of *Fort McMoney*', *Northern Journal*; http://norj.ca/2014/01/environment-wins-in-first-round-of-fort-mcmoney/. Accessed 31 October 2016.

CO-CREATION AS TALKBACK
USING THE COLLABORATIVE AND INTERACTIVE DOCU-FORMS TO (RE)IMAGINE THE 'RAPE CITY'

Anandana Kapur

After 16 December 2012, when 23-year-old Jyoti Singh was brutally gang raped and fatally beaten, the city of Delhi and the rest of India saw an outpouring of grief, protest and rage (see figure 1).[1] As a filmmaker who lives in the city herself, I too was re-examining my relationship with the city by participating in and/or observing the various forms of protests and efforts to reclaim the city space. During that time, I was struck by a hitherto unseen image – of women enjoying homosocial intimacy across class and caste boundaries. Of the many women who took to the streets were Delhi's domestic workers who are often excluded from feminist imaginations of the city. Commonly referred to as 'invisible workers', domestic workers are a sizeable but under-appreciated demographic in urban India.[2] The existence of class- and caste-based specificities alongside 'hegemonic notions of women's experiences' (Ali 2012: 586) deny them spaces to express their concerns and subjectivities. Their life-worlds also tend to be excluded from documentation of urban life and culture. This despite 'the real employment growth story for Delhi's women [being] paid domestic work' (Shrinivasan 2013).

However, the dismissal of Delhi as a 'rape capital' in mainstream media denies the reality of the domestic workers – their mobility, experiences and successful negotiation of the city. And not just domestic workers, this also affects their employers and other women who inhabit the city. The homosocial intimacy sparked by the protests begged exploration on the lines that these moments of co-existence had the potential to be extended to creative co-creation. The necessity of producing a collaborative narrative space had already been established by a need to transcend definitions that cast women as 'lacking and passive' (Peake and Reiker 2013: 1).

Fig. 1: Women take to the streets after 16 December 2012, demanding gender equity.

Despite official narratives suggesting uniformity, the narrative on the ground is predicated on choice and openness. As a response, an auto-ethnographic documentary project was conceptualised, wherein pre-existing sites of bodily coherence such as interiors/domestic spaces, public transport and social events were invoked as authentic homosocial categories. In order to explore the experience of domestic workers in conjunction with the experience of women of my class, I adopted an interactive approach that was as open-ended as possible. The women would be co-creators and have ownership over deciding the frequency, nature and themes of their documentations. This reduction of 'directorial necessity' (Delaney 2011) was further underscored by the existing technology landscape. The affordances of digital technology are increasingly suited to allow open-ended exploration. The capacity to produce images and narratives can easily be located in the domain of the 'amateur' user. Further, when one is interested in the idea of empowerment and participation, the provocation is to use participants' existing media practices because they have the potential to be a more authentic source of archives of the city that 'talk back' to hegemonic narratives. Here, the proliferation of mobile phones[3] and resulting DIY content[4] in the form of selfies, everyday photography, testimonies or mobile-video diaries provided a rationale for moving away from traditional video cameras. According to media and urban studies scholar Ravi Sundaram (2015), there is at the disposal of a documentary filmmaker a robust 'sensory infrastructure … a neurophysiological zone amplified by the mix of mobile computing objects, moods, and sensations … a remarkable infrastructure of agility and possibility'.

The documentary project under discussion is a work-in-progress wherein domestic workers and their employers document their experience of and conversations about the city using mobile phones. Formalised as part of a practice-based PhD programme in India, the origins of this project lie in a social change project titled Baat-Cheet (i.e. 'conversations'), conceptualised by me in early 2011. Its central aim was to facilitate cross-class conversations by women on issues of common concern such as the city, self-image, nutrition, etc. Despite positive reactions from lay and activist audiences, I was unable to identify collaborators for rolling out the idea. Eventually, the events of December 2012 led me to reflect on the potential of my own professional practice as a filmmaker and I ended up choosing the current focus and form to incubate the idea.

The cross-class and cross-caste interactions between participants are conceived as cues to an alternate discourse of the city that may be exemplary in terms of commonality and coherence. Interactivity is both a methodological process as well as the desired language of the film. This exegesis is a reflection on the different facets of collaboration involved in the documentation process and their implications for creating an i-doc that positions the city of Delhi as a site for mobility and the 'seeking of pleasure' (Phadke *et al* 2014: xiii).[5]

The intimacy of domestic spaces is often charged with differences of context, access and power. Consequently, using them as incubators for non-transactional dialogues on the city necessitated that both domestic workers and their employers were agreeable to the nature and intent of the project. It was also imperative that they had access to mobile phones and were capable of sharing and recording audio and video materials. In instances where domestic workers did not have 'smart' mobile phones, these were provided along with usage guides in regional Indian languages and hands-on training of key functions. The project envisages that women will use platforms like Whatsapp and Telegram for sharing insights as well as commenting on challenges that arise in documenting the city using the mobile phone.

My co-creators were identified using the snowball technique, i.e. leveraging of my personal networks. Both domestic workers and homemakers recommended households and/or volunteered to be a part of the study after detailed discussions on the motivations and possible outcomes of the project. A gender-rights facilitator was also invited to observe these interactions and ascertain that my own class location should not lead to any participant, especially domestic workers, being coerced in to participation. Personal mobile video documentations of the city along with images of my participation in gender-rights initiatives also helped create consensus on the politics of co-creation in the project. Since the project is self-funded, participants were able to openly discuss, debate and self-select aspects that they would prefer documenting or reflecting upon.

With this context, explicit conventions of authority (on the part of the employer) were first challenged with the request to convey the informed consent of both parties through a digital self-portrait, i.e. a selfie (see figure 2). It is a testament to the engagement of the co-creators to contribute to a re-imagination of the city-space that the domestic workers were willing to take on, and their employers were disposed to share, the authority of self-representation. The aesthetic qualifier for the image was that the duo would choose to pose in a space of the domestic workers' liking. Several domestic workers chose the kitchen, some the living room and one the baby's nursery. For many employers and domestic workers this was not just a new dimension of physical intimacy but also their first experience of clicking selfies.[6] This was captured in a message that I received from a participant's daughter – 'Mum's asking how to click a "good" selfie. ROFLOL!' (Anon. 2015a). The momentary collapse of conventions of conduct seemed to accord them agency in self-representation and also allowed them to reflect on their levels of technological literacy. The shift in gaze brought about by the shared self-portraiture proved a powerful and productive moment, disrupting the usual hierarchy in the relationship and signifying the taking of control over the narrative being created. The documentary practice seeks to adopt several such strategies of lateral collaboration 'to facilitate properties necessary in an ideal conversation' (Torres 1995: 3). Few of these strategies include encouraging the more mobile savvy of a domestic worker/employer duo to help the other resolve challenges in mobile use; nudging employers to use their influence to ensure domestic workers' ownership of their handsets is not compromised under the influence of male family members or children; encouraging domestic workers

Fig. 2: Inscribing the self in a world of media monopolies.

to reflect on the effectiveness of footage created by their employers and other participants from the upper class. I foresee more strategies being evolved as the filming proceeds over time and as class dynamics are observed to be changing or unchanging. The desire to curate such experiences emerges from recognising that homosociality is a locative gesture that can help us explore ontological metaphors of collaboration as well as recognise subjectivities in participatory frameworks.[7]

The use of mobile phones also makes the process of media creation accessible and identifiable for the participants.[8] In a recording sent to me by a collaborator, her eight-year-old takes over the mobile phone because she thinks she can compose a better frame than the adults i.e. her mother and the domestic worker. The resulting low-angle tilt-up as well as the accidental shake, when she sneezes or prompts questions, are invaluable collaborative events. In addition, its capacity for the creation of immediate and intimate portraits makes mobile cinema an 'embodied experience' (Hansen 2004: 11). The mapping of people, objects and places also lends itself to a distinctive, 'playfulness ... a dizzying array of possibilities for temporal ecstacy' (Lange 2010: 201). In her Nokia N95 mobile film *Tehran Without Permission* (2009), Sepideh Farsi lingers on quivering lips, helping our eyes travel beyond crevices we may have overlooked. Being privy to conversations that are forbidden, censored or denied successfully subverts all that surveillance prevents outsiders from seeing – including Tehran as experienced by Iranian women. Similarly, Mumbai-based artist collective CAMP's experimental documentary *From Gulf to Gulf* (2013) stitches together videos and images from mobile phones of sailors from Kutch in India to present experiences of seafarers and their co-travellers. Taking the form of 'video-letters' addressed to 'loved ones', the video film is a result of 'four years of dialog, friendship and exchange' (CAMP 2013). Filmed using mobile phones the narrative is 'embellished with cheerful music deliberately chosen by these improvised directors' (ibid.), i.e. the sailors. Relinquishing authorial control and enabling self-representation, directors Shaina Anand and Ashok Sundaram ably portray, 'full time intimate spheres' (Matsuda 2005: 133).

In my current work in progress, joint reflection on the assumptions that are made about women – the work they do, their choices and behaviours, psychological motivations that affect decisions and perceptions of mobility – reveal a more expansive vocabulary about the city than is currently accessible. The 'rape city' is considered a food capital, a melting pot, a green oasis and so much more. The conversations show that middle- and lower-class women in the city of Delhi have distinct experiences of creation, engagement and negotiation in the city. They reveal it as a 'site of social movement, including feminist politics, class struggle, economic independence and an array of freedoms' (Peake and Reiker 2013: 6).

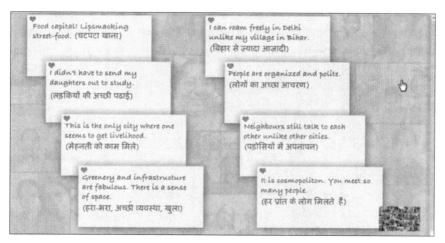

Fig. 3: Transcribed excerpts of women's descriptions of Delhi in Hindi and English.

The narrative is further nuanced when discussions on risk and violence are always accompanied by strategies to counter/address these problems. While safety is a concern, women do not surrender agency or accept paternalism. In a discussion on the aftermath of the rape and protests, a domestic worker tells her employer: 'One felt unsafe. The city suddenly seemed dangerous. So, we decided that we would go out in twos and swore that if any man harassed us we'd simply round him up and thrash him with our slippers. We were prepared' (Taiyab 2015).[9] The articulation is clear and emphatic: 'Their right to be in that space should remain unquestioned. Choosing to take risks, even of possible sexual violence in public spaces, undermines a sexist structure where women's virtue is prized over their desires or agency' (Phadke *et al* 2014: 60).

The audio-visual materials (photographs, audio and video clips, text messages, emails) generated as a result of these interactions inherently allow for establishing links and meta-tagging. Frequently used terms or referenced locations, as well as reflections on individual memories and events, together constitute a counter-discourse that can help reclaim the city space. The social and psychological mobility that the project accorded to the collaborators was given an added dimension via the mobility of the very media being created. The exchanges and observations forwarded to me through messaging applications like Whatsapp and Telegram further contributed to the creation of an ensemble via existing sensoria. Neither my mobile phone nor I are 'causes' i.e. 'singular, stable, and masterful initiators of effects' but instead they are 'sources' i.e. complex, mobile and heteronomous enjoiners of forces (Bennett 2005: 459). The formation of an 'assemblage ... not governed by a central power' (2005: 445) intuitively foreshadows the intended outcomes of the project, i.e. 'an assumption of … power to intervene in/with what is' (Gaudenzi 2013: 53). In this regard, a multi-perspectival and expansive i-doc can extend the lateral collaborations between the domestic workers and their employers into the distribution and consumption phases. Here, my co-creators will be able to alter the narrative arc, outcomes and therefore pleasures of viewing the documentary.

Central to all the contextual, technical and structural choices in collaborative projects, however, is the question of whom I am eventually accountable to 'self, film subject or audience, and which audience?' (Elder 1995: 96). The answer lies in acknowledging the limits and challenges to the co-creation framework developed for the documentary project. At the very outset, access to and ownership of mobile devices excludes those domestic workers who are on the wrong side of the digital divide. I would ill afford a subscription to the notion of 'digital utopianism or the idea that the digital era has democratised culture and that greater access means increased choices and content, as well as greater potential for community and participation' (Monaghan 2015). Half of my co-creators are from a demographic that is traditionally excluded from screening spaces on the basis of caste/class, literacy and technology ownership. Explicating strategies like subtitling only in English, fixed duration and distribution along established social and technological networks further alienate them even though they may be central protagonists or sources of narratives. Further, co-creation also demonstrates anxieties that reveal how social perceptions of relationships, including those between a domestic worker and her employer, impact the quality and nature of the interactions being sought. In this particular case, resistance to the relevance and outcomes of the practice has manifested itself several times (see figure 4) as a direct challenge to the affordances of interaction.

In addition, the intimate nature of mobile phone content not only causes anxiety about social hierarchies but also invokes tropes of voyeurism. Mobile phone media is unwittingly evocative of secretly taped, sexy or sexed moments. One collaborator found filming using a mobile phone 'downright creepy-like' and comfort could only be found in 'sticking to my big, fat camera'. In another thread, the askewed digital and social power structures at work were revealed when the collaborator wrote: 'I knew she was not very comfortable by the end of it. And then she mentioned that the "bhaiyya" at the last household she worked at had also taken her pictures once. Am trying not to think too much about it' (Anon. 2015b).[10] This points to the realisation that vulnerabilities faced by domestic workers in the city space are not always operational or enacted in public view. Acknowledging this increases the importance of challenging the predominant perceptions or gaze within homosocial transactions as well. Also, 'ficto-graphic atrocity stories (im-

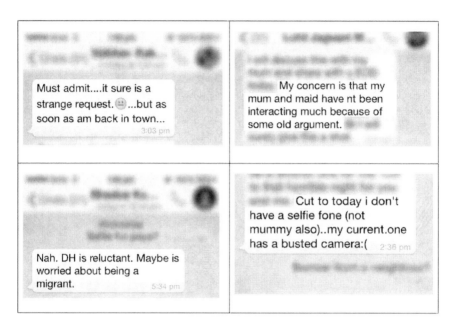

Fig. 4: Embodying unspoken anxieties of a creative homosociality.

ages, sounds, videos) circulate and attach themselves to sites of violence; in India, for instance, "fake" videos have been held out as reasons for disturbances in various cities and for the intimidation and killing of minority populations' (Sundaram 2015). By implication, the ease and convenience of using mobile phones as devices for self-expression are not only privileged instances but the resulting media content may also be suspect in its ontological claims. The ease of handling a mobile phone also does not translate to engaging filmmaking. It is therefore imperative that self-reflexivity is an important ethical parameter and strategy to re-examine the techno-centric nature of interactive modes of documentary.

Unlike documentaries that are created by non-human aggregators online or whose viewing necessitates access to the internet or data services, an 'inclusive' interactive documentary would have to take more varied forms. Gestural activation in simulation environments, android-based applications that function on older generation phones or the use of localized distribution devices including Bluetooth and memory cards may prove to be the modes in which the documentary is eventually realised.[11] The absence of advanced literacy and technological skills among the co-creators also necessitates conceptualisation of an alternate to the web-based i-doc. Eventually, one hopes that, through the experience of approaching and allowing oneself to be confronted by diverse points of view, the ongoing i-doc project can help alter the stories we tell ourselves and those around us.

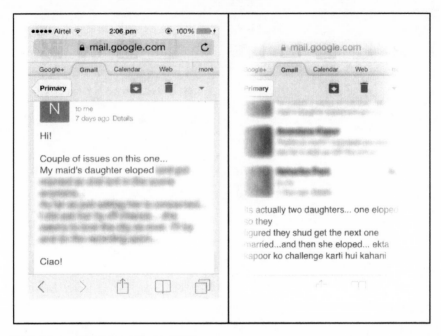

Fig. 5: When resilience is manifest in flight!

The project currently has ten co-creators on board and videos are being created as per the schedule and convenience of the participants over a period of five months. The duration, image orientation and portrayals vary based on individual choice and interpretation of everyday experiences. Some are more prolific than others and some speculate on constraints of time and technical ability. Yet, despite these anxieties, each video reveals an under-represented or under-explored dimension of what women observe and experience in the city. An excerpt from a collaborator's email a few weeks into the project, requesting that she suspend filming because her domestic workers' daughters have eloped one after the other says it all (see figure 5). Delhi's vast population allows lovers to melt into anonymity in defiance of class and caste conventions. Surely, the 'rape capital' nomenclature does injustice to the story of the two young women from a village in central India and their love stories.

At the end of the current phase of filming, I hope to take a step back from the process and critically examine the kinds of symmetries of experience between women across class that have been surfaced by the project. Based on these, I plan to facilitate another phase of filming with a new set of co-creators. Previous co-creators will be invited to share their experiences including co-facilitating mobile literacy sessions wherever necessary. The new group of co-creators will be accessed via domestic workers' networks. My role as a curator of this project will enable me to transcend the limits of my own class-based networks. In the interim I will continue to examine the various modes of i-docs being created and identify a technological framework that will enable me to create an inclusive i-doc.

NOTES

1. As per the Indian penal code names of rape victims cannot be made public. In this instance, Jyoti Singh was dubbed 'Nirbhaya' ('the fearless one') by popular media. However, on 16 December 2015 at a memorial meeting, her mother urged everyone to acknowledge her name in recognition of the need to challenge social stigma around rape that shames women and denies them ownership of their identities and bodies.
2. According to the National Sample Survey Organisation (NSSO) there was an increase of 68 per cent in the number of domestic workers in urban areas in India in the decade from 1999 to 2009.
3. The Internet and Mobile Association of India has estimated that the existing mobile phone user base in India will grow from 159 million users in 2014 to over 300 million users by 2017. The resulting ecosystem has great potential for collaborative content creation, interactions driven by data services and mediatised aesthetics.
4. The documentary *District Zero: What is Hidden Inside the Smartphone of a Refugee?* (2015) produced by EUROLIVES captures the interactions of the owner of a mobile phone repair workshop with Syrian refugees when they try to access/retrieve photographs of loved ones stored in their mobile phones. The chief protagonist helps his customers to recover, print and frame those memories. The film acknowledges the mobile sensoria operational in represented reality.
5. Pleasure-seeking may be interpreted as a spontaneous exploration of the city-space such that spatial limits imposed on women are rendered redundant (Phadke *et al* 2014).
6. While selfies i.e. self-representation through the digital medium have been sharply criticised as symbolizing a proclivity for narcissism, they have also been used by several artists, communities and individuals to claim ownership of identities, bodies and representations. See works of Rupi Kaur, Petra Collins, Vivian Fu, Mayan Toledana.
7. The term 'locative media' refers to media that help correlate and connect events and experiences over geospatial and temporal coordinates. Locative media are an integral part of urban culture and include mobile technology, interactive and immersive applications, GPS-enabled devices, etc (Frissen *et al* 2015).
8. The screen shots and photographs presented here (figures 1–5) were generated using Apple, Micromax, Nokia and Samsung phones.
9. Nirmala and Shahina Taiyab have known each other for four years. Shahina is Nirmala's employer. They live approximately four kilometres away from each other's house and less than three kilometres away from Munirka, New Delhi i.e. the site where Jyoti Singh and her male friend were abducted by her rapists and killers.
10. 'Bhaiyya' is a term in Hindi which translates to 'brother'. It is used colloquially by women to address men who are not family members, including strangers. It echoes the protectionism that operates in Indian culture because there are several rituals and festivals where

brothers take oaths to protect their blood sisters. There is also an evocation of a 'sexless' interaction between men and women. The sub-texts of honour, vulnerability and submission are inherent in its use.

11. Several older-generation phones are still in operation in India and are likely to be owned by domestic workers and economically disadvantaged sections despite being phased out globally. While these handsets are integral to the digital India story, they may not be ideal for recording or storing media.

REFERENCES

Ali, Kamran Asdar (2012) 'Women, Work and Public Spaces: Conflict and Co-existence in Karachi's poor neighbourhoods', *International Journal of Urban and Regional Research*, 36, 3, 585–605.

Anon. (2015a) 'Text message during co-creation/self-selection'. Sent 10 August 2015.

_____ (2015b) 'Text message during co-creation/self-selection'. Sent 16 August 2015.

Bennett, Jane (2005) 'The Agency of Assemblages and the North American Blackout', *Public Culture*, 17, 3, 445–65.

CAMP (2013) 'From Gulf to Gulf to Gulf'; http://studio.camp/event.php?id=173. Accessed 31 October 2016.

Delaney, Edward J. (2011) 'Documentary vs. Video Art: Catching up with RISD's Dennis Hlynsky'; http://www.pbs.org/pov/blog/news/2011/11/documentary-video-art-risd-dennis-hlynsky/. Accessed 31 October 2016.

Elder, Sarah (1995) 'Collaborative Filmmaking: An open space for making meaning, a moral ground for ethnographic film', *Visual Anthropology Review*, 11, 2, 95–101.

Farsi, Sepideh (2009) *Tehran Without Permission*. Film. Produced by Rêves d'Eau Productions.

Frissen, Valerie, Sybille Lammes, Michiel de Lange, Jos de Mul and Joost Raessons (2015) *Playful Identities: The Ludification of Digital Media Cultures*. Netherlands: Amsterdam University Press.

Gaudenzi, Sandra (2013) *The Living Documentary: From Representing Reality to Co-creating Reality in Digital Interactive Documentary*. PhD Thesis. Goldsmiths, University of London; http://research.gold.ac.uk/7997/. Accessed 31 October 2016.

Hansen, Mark (2004) *New Philosophy for New Media*. Cambridge, MA: MIT Press.

Lange, Michiel de (2010) *Moving Circles: Mobile Media and Playful Identities*. Unpublished PhD Thesis. Rotterdam: Erasmus University.

Matsuda, Misa (2005) 'Mobile Communications and Selective Sociality', in Mizuko Ito, Okabe Daisuke and Matsuda Misa (eds) *Personal, Portable, Pedestrian: Mobile Phones in Japanese Life*. Cambridge: MIT Press, 123–42.

Mayoral, Jorge Fernandez, Pablo Tosco and Pablo Iraburu (2015) *District Zero: What is Hidden Inside the Smartphone of a Refugee?* Film. (2015) Co-produced by Eurolives, Arena Communication Audiovisual and TXALAPART.

Monaghan, Whitney (2015) 'From iPhone to iFilm: The queer experience of Tangerine'; http://theconversation.com/from-iphone-to-ifilm-the-queer-experience-of-tangerine-45302. Accessed 31 October 2016.

Peake, Linda and Martina Reiker (2013) *Rethinking Feminist Interventions into the Urban*. New York: Routledge.

Phadke, Shipla, Shilpa Ranade and Sameera Khan (2014 [2011]) *Why Loiter? Women & Risk on Mumbai Streets*. New Delhi: Penguin.

Shrinivasan, Rukmini (2013) 'Only 8% of Delhi's Women Work', *Times of India*, 16 March 2013; http://timesofindia.indiatimes.com/city/delhi/Only-8-of-Delhis-women-work/articleshow/18999280.cms. Accessed 31 October 2016.

Sundaram, Ravi (2015) 'Post-colonial sensory infrastructure'; http://www.e-flux.com/journal/post-postcolonial-sensory-infrastructure/#_ftn17. Accessed 31 October 2016.

Taiyab, Shahina (2015) 'Interview with Nirmala'. Interview with Nirmala Taiyab, New Delhi, 16 August 2015.

Torres, Fernando Arturo (1995) *Towards a Universal Theory of Media Interactivity: Developing a Proper Context*. Fullerton: California State University.

DOCUMENTARY AS CO-CREATIVE PRACTICE
FROM *CHALLENGE FOR CHANGE* TO *HIGHRISE*: KAT CIZEK IN CONVERSATION WITH MANDY ROSE

Edited by Anna Wiehl

Kat Cizek was recruited by the National Film Board of Canada in 2004 as Filmmaker-in-Residence, with a brief to reinvent the influential NFB project *Challenge for Change* which, from 1967 to 1980, sought to put media to work for social change by turning documentary subjects into collaborators.[1]

Since then Cizek has been experimenting with forms of interactive media practice that are grounded in co-creation, collaborating with partners including media-makers, academics, city planners, architects and – most importantly for her – 'the people formerly known as the subjects'.

Fig. 1: Katerina Cizek – Portrait of the Artist (2011) – photo by Jamie Hogge, courtesy of the National Film Board of Canada.

From her first experiments at the NFB as Filmmaker-in-Residence to her multi-year, multi-faceted Interactive Emmy award-winning documentary project, *Highrise* (Cizek *et al* 2009–15), forms of collaboration have been at the heart of her practice.

In a conversation with Mandy Rose, Kat Cizek explains the ethos which underpins her work, and explores the potential and challenges of a co-creative approach.

Mandy Rose: One of the key concepts of your creative work is co-creation. What does this idea mean to you?

Kat Cizek: Co-creation for me is a method or an intention to make media with people that aren't media-makers. As I go into different disciplines and worlds I see that there are very specific definitions of co-creation as being a type of, for example, social entrepreneurial approach. So the term is causing as many problems as it's solving. But for me co-creation is a very broad term that implies a thoughtful process, which involves a collaboration with the intent to make quality media *with* partners instead of just *about* them, to make media as a media-maker together with people that aren't media-makers: citizens, academics, professionals, technologists, organisations.

MR: You're talking about making media together, but in your projects your collaborators don't necessarily record media themselves?

KC: I would make a distinction between participatory and co-creative media-making. Many times I work with people who are highly specialised in their fields, and want to be involved in the creation of media, but have absolutely no interest in picking up a camera, recording or editing – medical doctors and architects, for example. Co-creation is about having a broader sense of the co-design and the spirit behind making something. Participation is only one specific methodology that is appropriate for certain contexts and not others.

MR: Do you think of co-creation as an approach specific to digital and to interactive media?

KC: I think it's a social and political response to the new capacity that technology affords us. Technology allows us to be collaborative in new ways. However, for me it's important not just to fall back on technological collaboration; but to think very specifically, politically and socially about how and why we are doing things. So co-creation comes about in dialogue with the technology as the tools for collaboration change and evolve.

Approaches to collaboration have really evolved in the last ten years. When I was in the middle of Filmmaker-in-Residence ten years ago, I wasn't seeing much of this kind of collaborative practice. It existed and it has existed for decades; but in the last five years I've seen much more collaborative media happening, and the breakdown of silos and disciplines in journalism, in the academy, in media-making, going along with the idea of coalitions and partnership building.

MR: Let's take that apart in terms of how that has played out in *Highrise*. Who would you say were your co-creators in this project?

KC: There are many individuals and organisations. My closest collaborator throughout the process was veteran NFB producer Gerry Flahive. The first inspirations for even creating *Highrise* were some of the world-class urban thinkers and practitioners here in Toronto; Graeme Stewart, architect, the thinker behind the Tower Renewal project; Deborah Cowen, a critical geographer at the University of Toronto who has spent a lot of time talking and thinking about urban issues, about how Toronto has become extremely segregated and how that maps out into the city socially and geographically; Emily Paradis who is a collaborator on this recent project, 'The Universe Within' (Cizek *et al* 2015), and was there already in the early days of Filmmaker-in-Residence when she was doing her PhD with homeless women; she was an early advisor. Another urban thinker at York University who has been key is Roger Keil, who was just beginning a large research project into global suburbanisms, with the hypothesis that suburban cultures and infrastructures often have more to do with each other globally than they do with the centres of the cities that they are attached to. The starting thesis for *Highrise* was that something was happening at the edges of our cities that wasn't related to our conventional notions of urbanism, and that we needed to approach it in new ways.

MR: How do you initiate these co-creative processes? What kind of conversations do you have?

KC: When I'm beginning a collaboration with a potential co-creator, I try to move the conversation away from 'I'm making a film about you and your ideas' to 'We are making something together and we don't know yet what it's going to be. It involves your expertise, it involves my expertise, but I'm not pointing the camera at you.' This is certainly a shift of focus away from a conventional documentary approach.

MR: So how did you get started with *Highrise,* and how did it evolve?

KC: One of the first and really important partners was the City of Toronto who had just opened a Tower Renewal office and were looking for pilot sites in the city. I started exploring those sites which brought me to the west side of the city – to Kipling Avenue.

It was one of the pilot sites for the Tower Renewal project, but I was also closely connected to Microskills, a community organisation that had been working in Etobicoke for 25 years. It was a wonderful example of suburban community organising. The organisation had taken over a strip mall by the airport. It was run by a Jamaican-Canadian community organiser who had some support from Microsoft. She had hundreds of computers and was running large-scale professional training for people in the neighbourhood.

Everything about that community organisation was nothing like what we think of when we imagine organising in the city centre. It was responding to the needs and the demands of the local community. It really was humbling for me to see what organising might look like in the suburbs. There is so little of it, so it was impressive what they had achieved, and they were slowly taking over the strip mall with these courses and classes in professional development. They had just gotten a grant to bring a civic engagement office in the pilot site of the highrise that the City of Toronto had chosen.

The day I walked into one of the offices, they had just hired a community organiser who had worked in eastern London – Russ Mitchell. He was very experienced, and I loved his modest, practical, from-the-ground-up approach. We really hit it off.

Out of eleven new neighbourhood offices around town, he was the only one in Toronto who actually put one of these offices inside a highrise. A lot of them ended up in shopping malls or other community organisations. He said: 'I've got to be where the people live. That's where I've got to be.' He had no media experience, but he got the principle of what we were doing right away, as a frontline worker he really understood it.

So with him we started doing participatory media projects at Kipling, very early in the process of *Highrise*. The six residents who joined our group were further key co-creators, giving us insight into what it's like living in a highrise in contemporary Toronto.

So – residents, architects, community organisers, community organisations, the City of Toronto and academics – those were the early players. Then later we were approached by the *New York Times*.

MR: Would you describe your relationship with the *New York Times* as a co-creative one?

KC: Sure, and it was unprecedented and unusual for both the *New York Times* and the NFB at that time. Here were two institutions trying to figure out how to work with one another across multiple departments in order to create something that neither of them would have considered even five years earlier.

It was, for example, unusual for the *New York Times* to be in video let alone interactive audio-visual media. They'd done a lot of interactive data journalism, but creating an interactive documentary was new for them.

MR: Was 'A Short History of the Highrise' (Cizek *et al* 2013) one of their first short-form documentaries?

KC: Video-based, absolutely. They had a burgeoning video department at that point, really cutting edge, and they also had amazing multimedia. We ended up working with the designer/developer from *Snow Fall* (Branch 2012), which had been their biggest multimedia project, but that was text-based. It was essentially a very well done piece of conventional journalism that had these multimedia design applications on top of it. Whereas our project was video-based, with interactive elements that the *New York Times* had never done, and it was built as a multimedia piece.

MR: So this called for some deep collaboration.

KC: It was a really deep collaboration, and we worked mainly with the interactive team. We collaborated also very closely with the archives and the photography department, with the rights department as well as with the social media desk, because Part IV of 'A Short History of the Highrise' was user-generated. We put a call out to *New York Times* readers to submit photographs. So I consider that a really interesting example of co-creation.

'Universe Within' (Cizek *et al* 2015), the most recent project, was also a really unique form of collaboration. The work was built on this fantastic grant that Deborah Cowen and Emily Paradis were able to get from the SSHRC.[2] They received a substantial partnership development grant, and with that we were able to fund the research and the development of what became 'Universe Within', and they'll also be publishing a book based on that research.

MR: So that was a separate research collaboration to the global suburbanisms work.

KC: Yes, first Deb and Emily were advisors on *Highrise* as a whole, and then we collaborated on a specific project. I'd been talking about digital citizenship with both Deb and Emily and they didn't know each other though they are both at the University of Toronto. At the time neither saw digital as their area of expertise (Emily's expertise is participatory methodology). So we had long conversations and then finally they said, 'Okay, maybe digital citizenship is something we should be concerned with'.[3]

MR: What was your initial research question for the project?

KC: While Heather Frise, my colleague at *Highrise*, and I were working at the Kipling site, we kept wondering, what are the digital lives of the people in this building? This was tricky, as we only knew six people well, we knew about twenty fairly well, and as to the rest in these two highrises, two thousand people, we had no idea who they were, where they came from, what kind of digital connections they had. We assumed that if people have recently arrived in Canada, digital media must be an important part of their lives. So we decided to put together a survey of the buildings. With Deb and Emily we co-designed a research survey and we hired fourteen people from the buildings to interview their neighbours door-to-door. We did this in fourteen languages, as the idea was to represent as many languages in the building as possible.

Over the course of six weeks, we interviewed over a hundred households. We had this amazing team, with the academic researchers and peer researchers in the buildings, who brought so many ideas to the project too.

One aspect that sets our process apart from other research is that often surveys are done and the people involved have no idea what the results are, so the research is useless for the people who actually live there. Our goal was to analyse the data and put it into a newsletter as quickly as possible. Within two weeks of having finished, we came back with a thousand copies and put them under the door of every household. Thanks in part to that research, they were able to get a grant to build a playground, because the data showed how many people under twenty were in the building – 50 per cent of the population, which is incredibly high and an unusual statistic for a Canadian neighbour-hood. That's more like a figure you'd see in a First Nations community here in Canada, or in the Global South.

MR: It sounds like the collaborative relationships and research enabled you to surface information that wasn't otherwise accessible.

KC: That's right, and that information then helped define what the media project would be. That's the difference: it is not going in and saying, 'I'm going to make a film about your ideas.' It's more like, 'We're interested in seeing how media might work to advance some of the ideas and knowledge that exist in this community.' It's a completely different starting point in terms of the relationship. We are really rolling up our sleeves and trying to figure out what is going on here and what we can learn from each other.

So even just the act of doing a neighbour-led survey, where it was neighbours interviewing each other as opposed to some researchers coming down and knocking on the doors; that had an impact. Once the tenant/researcher had gone into those apartments, the next day they would see those people and talk again. Then it's, 'There's a tenant's association meeting next week, why don't you come?' So the product of the work wasn't just the data that we collected. The process itself helped develop community spirit and provided networking opportunities for people. Beyond that, some of the work got a lot of media attention, and that brought some funding, and interest in the community, or helped develop that interest.

MR: To what extent have you delved into histories of community media in this process of thinking about your own co-creative practice? Have you looked back at *Challenge for Change*?

KC: Well I've definitely come out of a tradition of alternative media, and when I started Filmmaker-in-Residence in 2004, the direct mandate for me was to reinvent *Challenge for Change* in the digital age.

So I wouldn't say that I went back and watched every *Challenge for Change* project, but I certainly did some reading about it, watched some stuff, and talked to people within the NFB about what *Challenge for Change* was. In particular, *The Fogo Island Process* (Low 1967) was something I was really interested in, and one of the projects of Filmmaker-in-Residence out of the seven that I did at the hospital was specifically an adaptation. The question was, 'Can I take *The Fogo Island Process* and adapt it to the contemporary academic hospital? How would that look?'

What happened in *Fogo* was a process in which Colin Low, the filmmaker, worked with Memorial University to use film as a way to document the lives of members of a community who were destined to be relocated.

The provincial government had decided that they would remove them from the island. The people on the island didn't want to go. Colin Low went in and documented their lives, in what were really film fragments. He brought that material to the provincial politicians and civil servants and had them watch it and respond to it on camera, and then he brought that back to the community, and then through that process, the community began to organise and articulate their goals and hopes and dreams for how they could stay. Through that process they came up with the idea of a community co-op cannery that is still in existence today. It's a pretty amazing example of how the process of filming can make a difference. So, yes, I was absolutely inspired by that example.

Then, beyond community media, we are just standing on the shoulders of giants of critical community organising, strong traditions in many places around the world, I was inspired by that as well as; for example, in Filmmaker-in-Residence, I was really inspired by interventionist research – doctor and nurses who weren't satisfied with the conventional model – that you do research and then you publish it and then somehow expect that miraculously your work becomes of service to the community ten years after the fact. There is a sense of urgency and responsibility, and I really felt that that was the tradition of *Challenge for Change*.

MR: What other experiences have informed your co-creative approach?

KC: The most formative experience I had was collaborating with homeless young parents with no fixed address in the context of a hospital. We were asking: How can we make these parents get into contact with the service providers of the hospital that provides them with services? How can they be invited to speak more honestly? What might really make a difference in the way the hospitals and healthcare providers work with young parents?

Healthcare, as troubled as some of it can be, has some really interesting innovations happening within it. For example, technology is being applied, which is helping to break down silos and create a more collaborative, patient-centred approach. This affects both the delivery of healthcare, and even co-creation itself, when appropriate. So there is innovative thinking, institutional change and social innovation that we have a lot to learn from as media-makers.

MR: Did you know that when you chose St Michael's hospital as the location for Filmmaker-in-Residence?

KC: Well I didn't choose St Michael's, that's what was so humbling about the experience. I left the academy, I'd gotten a degree in anthropology and I was so sick of postmodernism [*laughter*]. I really felt disgruntled and disenchanted by it. So it was a hugely humbling experience to be given this assignment to go into this hospital and I learned so much at every level.

For very practical reasons, we decided to align ourselves with the frontline workers at the hospital, and we were in principle being accepted by the hospital, but the corporate arm and particularly the public relations arm of the hospital was very, suspicious of us. They'd had a previously bad experience with a reality TV show in there. So they were like, 'What, Filmmaker-in-Residence, you're just going to wander around with a camera?'

So, the frontline workers that we immediately hit it off with and had this co-creative relationship with, they said: 'Well why don't we frame this as academic research. We'll go through the research and ethics board of the hospital and in that way it protects what we do as knowledge gathering and academic research. It's not for PR, and they have to respect the academic freedom in the project.'

So we were asking all these questions; what is informed consent? What is ethical practice? How do you really work in a research context with people in a way that provides them with rights and responsibilities?

We often just pay lip service to these issues in documentary and don't think through them carefully enough. This project, in contrast, was an opportunity to gather benefits and learning from a co-creative process in terms of understanding risk, mitigating and figuring out ethical ways to have people to be able to make their own choices when possible, but also protect them when they can't.

MR: How did these experiences inspire your concepts of co-creation and collaboration in *Highrise*? What were the terms of the relationships with people you worked with? And how do you conceive of authorship or your own role in the co-creative process?

KC: I don't see authorship and co-creation as a dualism, but I do see shifts with regard to new evolving and transitioning forms of relationship. Mostly I think it's about finding a pragmatic moment – the moment in which you think 'Yes, we can collaborate on *this* specific thing at *this* moment.' Then, however, there is also the point where you realise that it's your turn, and you want to continue making a documentary where you have people participating but not having them in your editing room eight hours a day.

So, I consider myself definitely a director, but the relationship that I have with the people that I work with is quite different, I hope, than a conventional documentary project and it's a scale, it's a spectrum.

MR: What do you think are the biggest challenges of working in this way?

KC: The messiness [*laughter*]. There is no obvious way to do it, no formula. No co-creation process is like the one you have done before, and just managing expectations or even figuring out what those expectations might be is starting anew.

MR So how do you steer a path in terms of your co-creative practice to make sure that you are on firm ethical ground?

KC: Part of it is respecting people's investment and skills and energy. So paying the people when they do work is just one key ethical principle of ours. We've negotiated that differently with participants. So for example, in the end parts of *No Fixed Address* (Cizek *et al* 2009) we provided food, public transportation tokens as well as honoraria in the work.

When we started doing the *Street Health Stories* (Cizek *et al* 2007), which involved young parents being trained on photography and interview skills so they could create a portrait of the health and wellbeing of the homeless through their own voices, we actually hired the young women and paid them per hour. In *Highrise*, one of the community organisers was very adamant about not offering honoraria upfront because he felt that this could compromise some of the other work that they were trying to do that could not offer honoraria. So ethics of co-creation here included respecting that partner's limited resources as well, and above all, respecting the principle of civic engagement. The whole idea was that they weren't just hiring people to do work for them, but they were trying to develop a responsibility and a commitment on a part of those citizens *without* being paid for it.

So again, it was about how to create projects and space for these bigger dialogues across sectors, across disciplines, across ways of life that have a larger frame than the frames we have in the way that we create media. That is certainly a big goal, a kind of a metagoal of co-creation.

MR: Are you referring to political critique and systemic change?

KC: Yes, systems change, and larger, I am thinking about how we address things that are much bigger than we are, and what we normally do in our disciplines? How do we pull together coalitions? How can we work together and look at the bigger picture? I think that is the broader political goal.

MR: So it is a question of how you take things from the individual to the societal level.

KC: And it is also about how you keep it in an artful place where the readers or the audience or the users or whatever you want to call the people that you are pulling in are also allowed to co-create some of the answers. This differs from the preachy, didactic perspective of putting it like: 'Here are our solutions.'

MR: So it's about maintaining your critical relationship to what you're observing? Do you ever find that tension between a critical and a co-creative model?

KC: Having a background in journalism, I really like to defend editorial control, even if this model is changing. In all our projects we maintain editorial control: ultimately the decisions are ours to make – not just me as a director, but NFB as an institution and certainly the producers play an important role.

The same goes for other co-creators: the doctors in the *Challenge for Change* project at St. Michael's Hospital remained doctors in our process, I did not tell them how to administer medication. Still, that doesn't mean that we weren't learning and informing each other about our practices – respecting each other's expertise was part of the co-creation model. So the fact that I brought in my expertise in journalism and documentary and understanding in which ways a critical position can enhance a conversation – that became part of the game, too, though that was not something that I thought of when we entered the co-creative relationship, if that makes sense for you.

MR: It more than makes sense, and though it is certainly not the end point of the discussion on documentary co-creation, it's a brilliant point to end on.

NOTES

1 MicroSkills is a non-profit, charitable organization in the Greater Toronto Area supporting youth, women, unemployed, racial minorities, immigrants and newcomers to Toronto, as well as other community members of Toronto who address them. MicroSkills aims to develop programmes and workshops that allow their clients to participate in Canadian society most fully, to achieve self-determination and to attain economic, social and political equality. For more information see http://www.microskills.ca/. Accessed 31 October 2016.

2 The Social Sciences and Humanities Research Council is the national granting agency for social sciences and humanities.

3 Kat Cizek here refers to *Young Parents No Fixed Address* where she was working together with young women who were pregnant or parenting and had experience with homelessness. For more information see http://filmmakerinresidence.nfb.ca/. Accessed 31 October 2016.

REFERENCES

Branch, John (2012) *Snow Fall: The Avalanche at Tunnel Creek*. Web Documentary. Produced by New York Times; http://www.nytimes.com/projects/2012/snow-fall/#/?part=tunnel-creek. Accessed 31 October 2016.

Cizek, Kat *et al* (2007) *Street Health Stories*. Film. Produced by Gerry Flahive, co-produced by NFB.

_____ (2009) *Young Parents No Fixed Address*. Cross-platform. Produced by Gerry Flahive, co-produced by NFB; http://filmmakerinresidence.nfb.ca/. Accessed 31 October 2016.

_____ (2013) 'A Short History of the Highrise'. Web Documentary. Part of *Highrise* series. Produced by Gerry Flahive, co-produced by NFB and New York Times; http://www.nytimes.com/projects/2013/high-rise/. Accessed 31 October 2016.

_____ (2015) 'Universe Within – Digital Lives in the Highrise'. Web Documentary. Part of *Highrise* series produced by David Oppenheim and Gerry Flahive, co-produced by NFB; http://universewithin.nfb.ca/desktop.html#index. Accessed 31 October 2016.

Low, Colin (1967) *The Fogo Island Process*. Film. Produced by John Kemeny, co-produced by NFB.

NOT MEDIA ABOUT, BUT MEDIA WITH
CO-CREATION FOR ACTIVISM

Mandy Rose

AUTO-ETHNOGRAPHY

My interest in co-creation as a strategy for documentary production derives from an experience as a producer in the early days of digital media. I use that experience to frame this chapter in which I discuss two remarkable interactive documentaries whose power and significance derives from their co-creative approaches, and who employ these for their potential to contribute to processes of social change.

Between 1993 and 2000, I was co-producer of BBC 2's *Video Nation* project. Through an intensive research process, we identified fifty people to reflect the diversity of life in the UK, trained them to use camcorders, and invited them to record and reflect on aspects of everyday life during the course of a year. I have written elsewhere (Rose 2000: 173) about how we were inspired by the early *Mass Observation* project and, following their approach, we described the project as a 'self anthropology' of the UK.[1] We edited the recordings into a variety of programme outputs, with participants' contractual right of veto. The finished programmes became well known – particularly the two-minute Shorts that each featured one person and ran on weeknights just before the nightly news magazine programme. For broadcast we minimised editing, and often left the Shorts open-ended. After a brief generic title sequence, the viewer was in the presence of one member of the *Video Nation* for two minutes, largely uncut. We chose not to weigh the brief format down with production team credits. Not intending to obscure our role in the process, we wanted, rather, to foreground the participants' contributions.

When other media-makers asked how the Shorts came about, I would enthusiastically describe selecting, training, briefing participants, getting to know them; the fascination and privilege of watching their tapes, the pleasure of editing their footage. As I talked, I would sense their interest drain away. They'd imagined that these recordings turned up in the post fully formed – that we simply put them on air. Explaining the process seemed to burst a bubble. They didn't want to know about the relationship between the filmers and the production team – if we were so involved then it seemed that they felt the project was devalued, even fake.

I was troubled by this response. I knew that the contribution of both sides was what made the project work, that the collaborative dimension was not a necessary evil but a key value in the project. Reviews and feedback suggested that *Video Nation* was significant in challenging the prevailing account of UK life in a variety of ways – by countering stereotypes and prejudices of all kinds, offering a nuanced view of a multicultural UK intersected in unexpected ways by class, gender, age, education, political leaning. I also knew that these recordings felt different from what results when a filmmaker turns the camera on a subject. These diverse participants were each the subject of their own recordings, in control of their editorial agenda. Whatever their circumstances, no-one was constructed as an object or a victim.

We produced *Video Nation* within the Community Programmes Unit of the BBC – the BBC's Access TV space. But that framework didn't help me to articulate what was at play in the project. Access discourse foregrounds the handing over of the cameras, as if the technology itself makes things happen, whereas I knew that *Video Nation*'s success was about the dynamic between the production team and the subjects. When I first came across the term 'co-creation' around 2000, it felt like an epiphany – offering a positive designation for this type of media production arrangement. Rather than an anthropology of the self, I began to see *Video Nation* in Jean Rouch's terms as 'shared anthropology' (Rouch cited in Eaton 1979: 26).

CO-CREATION AS CONVENING

In an interview in this collection, Kat Cizek, perhaps the foremost proponent of co-creation within interactive documentary, defines that concept as 'a very broad term that implies a thoughtful process ... a collaboration with the intent to make quality media with partners instead of just about them, to make media ... with people that aren't media-makers: citizens, academics, professionals, technologists, organisations'. Cizek draws a distinction between co-creation which might take many forms, and participation, which she sees as one sub-set of co-creation, involving the subjects in making media by picking up a camera, or some other production device: 'Participation is only one specific methodology that is appropriate for certain contexts and not others. [...] Co-creation is about having a broader sense of the co-design and the spirit behind making something.'

The experience of *Video Nation* left me with the view that collaboration between media-makers and the public is a necessary method in particular for reflecting marginalised and disenfranchised viewpoints and experiences. A rhetoric of universal participation continues to cloak what Henry Jenkins has called the 'participation gap' (2008: 258). While production equipment might be relatively low cost and accessible and some platforms for media distribution no longer controlled by media gatekeepers, many are still excluded from media-making as much by their lack of editorial expertise and confidence as by a lack of access to media tools. Manuel Castells has argued that 'communications networks constitute by and large the public space in the network society. [...] Politics is media politics' (2009: 300). If this is so, how do those on the wrong side of the participation gap have agency within the public space of the media?

In this context, co-creation is a significant strategy for interactive documentary. However, if public involvement is mediated by experienced media-makers, how can disenfranchised and marginalised people take part in interactive media practices on their own terms? How can producers structure projects so that even though they may initiate the work, those taking part have ways of setting the agenda? What does such a co-creative production process look like? What kind of form might such a project take?

In this chapter, I consider two remarkable interactive documentary projects that offer some answers to these questions. I discuss the co-creative dimension of the projects, asking what cultural precursors and contexts inspired their divergent co-creative approaches. I also consider how the producers perform as facilitators, asking how co-creation is invited and structured? How is the project agenda set, and what is the participants' agency? Both projects stage processes of dialogue among communities, between participants and with audiences. My interest is in *how* the communicative structures of the projects are produced.

The first example – *Question Bridge: Black Males* (Johnson *et al* 2012) – engages those who take part in processes of dialogue and self-reflection in order to disrupt a problem of image and self-image with deep historical roots and dire contemporary consequences. The second – *The Quipu Project* (Court *et al* 2014) – provides a media platform through which witness testimony can be recorded, gathered and heard in order to support an activist movement in a struggle for legal redress that has been going on for twenty years. In both projects, the participants are the subjects of the respective struggles and the producers devise strategies which cede significant editorial control to them. Crucially, in order to bridge the participation gap, both projects stage face-to-face as well as digital engagement. Both projects are also interactive in the sense that online users are invited to get involved, though for reasons of space this is not the focus of this chapter.

In recent years, a number of scholars have turned their attention to the co-creative tendency within interactive documentary. A number of us have noted the precursors of these practices in community and alternative media (de Michiel and Zimmermann 2013, Gaudenzi 2013, Rose 2014) and asked how and if today's interactive projects bring novel dimensions to those counter-currents within documentary (Dovey 2015, Frankham 2015, Winston *et al* forthcoming). This chapter is a contribution to that continuing discussion. It starts where my previous writing in this area leaves off. In 'Making Publics; Documentary as Do-it-With-Others-Citizenship' (Rose 2014), I considered how documentary participation (meaning, in Cizek's terms 'making content') might contribute to a reworking of documentary's historic role in the public sphere. I discussed participation as a citizenship practice, in which participants come together in a collective address to common concerns. Here, I am concerned with the production strategies that can engage counterpublics – groups contesting hegemonic discourse or power structures – as co-creators.

Helen De Michiel and Patricia Zimmermann have developed the persuasive concept of 'Open Space Documentary' to reflect this generation of collabora-tive, iterative, often open-ended work. This body of work, they argue, replaces documentary rhetoric with, 'a politics of convenings' (2013: 365). Following Manuel Castells' argument (2009) that communications networks constitute contemporary public space, such convenings can make a significant contribution to contemporary politics. Whereas documentary rhetoric might intervene within the public sphere, interactive documentary can be a platform for a convening through which an audience becomes a public – a group conscious of itself and its shared sense of purpose. The projects I discuss here are fundamentally works of convening in which documentary as representation gives way to documentary as a process of staging multiple interactions and engagements – between partici-pants and with viewers/users. These projects suggest how co-creative interactive documentary can play a role in change making in our increasingly unequal and precarious economic and ecological times.

My interest in co-creation takes inspiration from Jean Rouch, the French an-thropological filmmaker, who rejected the dominant extractive ethos of knowl-edge generation within his discipline and came up with innovative strategies for collaboration with documentary subjects in West Africa in the 1950s. His wish was 'to transform anthropology, the eldest daughter of colonialism, a discipline reserved to those with power interrogating people without it' (Eaton 1979: 26). It has been possible to accuse some documentary practices of operating the same power dynamic. Co-creation can offer an alternative framework.

'AN ENSEMBLE OF EFFECTS' – *QUESTION BRIDGE: BLACK MALES*

In June 2012, I saw an installation called *Question Bridge: Black Males* at Sheffield DocFest. In a small gallery space, I stood among a semicircle of monitors arranged so that five life-sized talking heads were at my head height. On screen, men posed and answered each other's questions by talking directly to camera. As a viewer, I was positioned and addressed as if I was part of that group, as if those questions and answers were also mine to wrestle with. The filming strategy brought me into a complex affective space, called on as if part of the on-screen community to hear and imagine from many varied perspectives how the world and each other look through diverse African-American men's eyes – the sense of intimacy created by the to-camera address disarming the objectification that is intrinsic to a racist construction of the other.

The accompanying description explained that the installation was part of a transmedia art project, created by Chris Johnson, Hank Willis Thomas, Bayete Ross Smith and Kamal Sinclair, with a purpose, as described on the *Question Bridge: Black Males* website: 'to represent and redefine Black male identity in America through video mediated question and answer exchange, diverse members of this "demographic" bridge economic, political, geographic, and generational divisions'. Participants had been invited to offer a question that they would like to address to another black American man. Those questions – about class, values, politics, individual and collective responsibility – were filmed and played to other men who then answered them. The dialogue between participants produced through editing then made up the work. Standing in the Sheffield gallery space, I was moved, impressed by the project's ambition to have an impact on a deeply entrenched, urgent theme, and by the deceptive simplicity of the project's design.

Launched in 2012 as a gallery installation with the same video material reflected on the website, since then the *Question Bridge: Black Males* project has been a catalyst for numerous conversations across the USA. In museums, galleries, YMCAs, schools, prisons and online, men have asked, listened and replied on screen with audiences responding with their own thoughts, questions and answers. There have been 34 *Question Bridge* exhibitions. A 75-minute version of the videos is available for community screenings. A high school curriculum based on the project themes has been downloaded 1,200 times. In 2013, the *Question*

Bridge: Black Males team ran a Kickstarter campaign and raised $75,000 for an interactive version of the project which launched in 2014 with a mobile phone app allowing online users to contribute. In 2015, a book edited by Deborah Willis and Natasha Logan with essays by the artists and transcripts of the videos completed the multi-faceted project.

Described variously by the artists as a 'transmedia art project', a 'documentary-styled video art installation', a 'video-mediated megalogue', 'experimental non-fiction' – what is the project's cultural lineage? *Question Bridge* was first of all a methodology created in 1996 by Chris Johnson – a fine-art photographer who had become involved with socially engaged performance art, and also taught at California College of Arts. Johnson had collaborated with the artist Suzanne Lacy on her ten-year Oakland Projects which involved installations, performances and activism with youth in the Bay area. With Lacy and Annice Jacoby, Johnson had created *The Roof is on Fire* (1994) – a participatory art project which sought to make the voices of Oakland youth heard by the adult world. In a lecture to the Project for the Advancement of our Common Humanity, Johnson describes himself as deeply influenced by Lacy's socially engaged feminist art practice – her creation of 'innovative spaces to surface dialogue about difference' (Johnson 2014).

A couple of years later – invited to make an art project in San Diego, Johnson asked ten black Americans separated by class and geography to pose questions of each other, and facilitated their video dialogue. He called his project *Question Bridge*. Johnson showed his *Question Bridge* videos to his class on experimental non-fiction. Hank Willis Thomas – then a student at California College of the Arts – was taken aback by the raw, frank exchange and struck by the power of the question. Willis Thomas is a conceptual artist who works largely with photography on themes of identity, history and popular culture. When given a New Media Fellowship by the Tribeca Foundation in 2006, he thought of *Question Bridge* and got back in touch with Chris Johnson about developing a new version of the project (Willis Thomas 2014).

Chris Johnson has said that '*Question Bridge: Black Males* started with an audacious idea – that it was possible to change the way we think about black male consciousness' (2014), and the project seeks to do this by engaging both with black American men and with a wider public. A key reference point for the work is the idea of 'double consciousness' which was articulated by the black American sociologist W.E.B. Du Bois in his pioneering, formally radical 1903 study of black experience and culture – *The Souls of Black Folks*. As described by Du Bois, 'it is a peculiar sensation, this double-consciousness, this sense of always looking at one's self through the eyes of others, of measuring one's soul by the tape of a world that looks on in amused contempt and pity. [...] The history of the American Negro is the history of this strife' (1903: 3) This reference back, beyond the Civil Right era, to the ideas of one of the figures who influenced that movement, highlights the deep historical roots of the problems addressed by *Question Bridge* and their reach right back to slavery. The project can be seen as a collective interrogation of the lived experience of the category – 'Black Males'. It attempts to deconstruct this limiting monolithic construct, more than a century after Du Bois' book, with a black man in the White House reflecting the economic and social security that has been achieved by middle-class black Americans, while at the same time, in what Michelle Alexander has called 'the New Jim Crow' (2010: 5), the post-Civil Rights era has seen a radical erosion of liberty and experience in poor black urban communities – characterised by economic deprivation, civic marginalisation and mass incarceration.

In 2008, Hank Willis Thomas and Chris Johnson went on the road and invited black American men to speak to this context by asking each other questions. They gathered over a thousand question-and-answers on video. At that time, Bayete Ross Smith and Kamal Sinclair became involved, and the web project was developed, drawing on Sinclair's engagement with interactive documentary practices. Development was given added momentum when the team came across the Harvard Implicit Association project which had produced evidence of negative racial assumptions (which included impacts on black self-image) but which also showed that these could be subject to change through exposure to alternative ideas and images (Rose 2014b).

In the videos, those taking part come together as a virtual community to interrogate their situations, but face-to-face interaction is also key to *Question Bridge*. Inspired by a question in one of the videos from a younger man to the older generation – 'Why didn't you leave us a blueprint?' – the *Question Bridge* team developed an inter-generational format for a kind of Town Hall meeting – a format they called the 'Blueprint Roundtable'. By summer 2015, over 3,200 people had taken part in these community gatherings.

While *Question Bridge* takes advantage of digital media, its direct precursors are in relational art or what Grant Kester terms 'dialogical art' – with its interest in 'inter-subjective ethics and identity formation' (2008: 108). In these pieces, 'the meaning of a given dialogical work is not centered in the physical condition of a single object or in the imaginative capacity of a single viewer. Instead, the work is constituted as an ensemble of effects, operating at numerous points of discursive interaction' (2008: 120). The project's interest in transformation within the consciousness of those taking part has strong ties to ideas of self-actualisation and community capacity building that were developed within Community Media.

The content – first-person video testimony and the montage of multiple points of view – link it to documentary.

Question Bridge provides a response to the participation gap by engaging with participants face-to-face. Through the initial filming, and then through the Blue-print Roundtables, the project reaches out to men including marginalised people – prisoners, gang members for instance – who would have been very unlikely to respond to an online call. Yet, while face-to-face engagement can encourage di-verse participants to get involved in a media project, the challenge for co-creation is how to allow them to contribute on their own terms. *Question Bridge: Black Males* offers an elegant response to that problem.

By inviting the initial participants not to answer questions but to pose them, the artists delegate agenda-setting. That invitation to ask a question works at a number of levels. It's not an intimidating thing to do, so it's inclusive, and ques-tions are offered by lots of diverse men. At the same time, through their fram-ing of the invitation, specifying that questions should bridge 'economic, political, geographic, and generational divisions', the questions offered function as a criti-cal device to prise open the category, 'Black Males' – a category constructed as monolithic by a history of racial oppression. Posed across difference, the question in itself exposes the apparently innocuous idea of 'Black Males' as what Donna Haraway has called a 'non-innocent category' (1989: 341).

Question Bridge: Black Males was created in 2009, prior to the killings of Trayvon Martin, Michael Brown, Eric Garner, the protests that followed, and the emergence of Black Lives Matter. These events and the tentative emergence of a new Civil Rights Movement have repositioned *Question Bridge*. The durational aspect of the project and its multimodal nature have allowed it a flexibility to respond to these unfolding events. Blueprint Roundtables were held in St Louis and Ferguson in the aftermath of the protests, with the inter-generational format bringing diverse men into dialogue about police violence, activism, and the chal-lenges of building a political movement. Meanwhile, the website provides an on-going resource and offers the potential for anyone to get involved by uploading mobile content on these themes.

When the first *Question Bridge: Black Males* exhibition was staged at the Brooklyn Museum, the experience was structured around an expectation that visitors would watch the videos for around five minutes. In fact, the exhibit had to be reorganised as people stayed much longer, some compelled to watch the entire three-hour installation (Willis and Logan 2015: 243). Through its elegant co-creative design, the project has convened diverse men who, through speaking and listening attentively to each other, lift the lid on a corrosive problem at the heart of American life. Watched and debated by visitors in numerous locations and contexts across the USA, and engaging wider networks through associated events and convenings, the project produces an 'ensemble of effects' around its powerful collective demand for a future beyond 'double consciousness' (ibid). Although many of those encounters will leave no record, in 2017 the web project will be handed over to the Smithsonian Museum, which will provide a permanent home for this unique archive of black American male experience.

NETWORK BUILDING – *THE QUIPU PROJECT*

On the screen are video images of indigenous life in rural Peru – of children walking up a village street, people working on mountain fields, a woman talking on a phone. Overlaid are threads dotted with graphics that represent coloured beads. Selecting a bead, you listen to testimony recorded on a phone line by women and men who describe being tricked, coerced and forced into sterilization within a government programme nearly twenty years ago. First launched in 2014, *The Quipu Project* is a web documentary which seeks to support those indigenous Peruvian women and men in their continuing search for justice. The international exposure that the project has brought to this issue can be suggested by coverage in outlets including the *Guardian, New York Times, BBC World Service, La Republica* (Peru) and *Wired*.

A number of writers have already discussed the genesis of this powerful project (Mitchell 2015, Arnau Gifreu-Castell's contribution to this volume). My particular interest is in the unusual co-creative approach taken by the producers, Chaka Films. My discussion of that aspect of the project draws on an unpublished interview with project directors Maria Court and Ros Lerner from 2016. In 2012, Lerner, a Peruvian filmmaker, started to explore the possibility of making a documentary about the forced sterilisations that had taken place in Peru in the 1990s. Over four years, under President Alberto Fujimori's Reproductive Health and Family Planning Programme, around thirty thousand women and men were denied the capacity to bear children. A number of attempts to get legal redress had been attempted and failed. What Lerner found in her initial research was that there had been much media interest in the case, and that those affected had been filmed for various media projects, but they hadn't seen the finished results or known what impact these might have had, so were sceptical about the point and value of getting involved. Lerner determined to find a way to use documentary to engage with this disenfranchised community in a way that would offer them control in the process and would prove of value to them in their struggle for justice.

Over the next two years Lerner developed *The Quipu Project* with UK-based Chilean filmmaker Maria Ignacia Court, joined by Sebastian Melo as executive producer and by creative technologist Ewan Cass-Kavanagh. They decided to approach the case as an interactive documentary. It is worth quoting Lerner at length as she reflected at the 2016 i-Docs Symposium on the three interrelated objectives behind the approach that the team that became Chaka Films took: 'We didn't just want to tell a story from the past, we were more interested in what is happening now. For sure it is very important to get to know what happened in Peru in the 1990s because we are speaking about a massive and systematic human rights violation, but the ongoing story of those who have been fighting for twenty years for justice with no success seemed much more interesting to us (Lerner and Melo 2016).

For Chaka Films, the appeal of an interactive documentary rested in particular on its co-creative potential: 'We didn't want to tell a story *about* those affected, we wanted to tell a story *with* them, we wanted to create something that was truly participatory, where people could share their own stories in their own voices, but they could also experience the interactive documentary and become its first audience (ibid.; emphasis added). As Lerner explained, they wanted the media-making to be an agent in the fight for justice.

Both Court and Lerner had experience in South American participatory documentary. Lerner had worked within the 'Caravana Documental', an annual project that takes documentary out of Lima into regions of Peru where non-professionals are facilitated to make their own short films. Court had been an intern in community radio on Robinson Crusoe, an island West of Chile in the South Pacific Ocean. In the UK, she interned with me on the CollabDocs research project and worked as assistant director on my collaborative documentary *Searching for Happiness* (Rose *et al* 2013).

In developing the project, the team looked at what they might draw from a number of participatory media projects which engaged with disenfranchised groups. A first point of reference was *The Fogo Island Process* (Low 1967) – generally considered the originary community media project, which was an initiative within the National Film Board of Canada (NFB) in what became the *Challenge for Change* project. In the late 1960s, various papers circulated at the NFB which drew on Marshall McLuhan's ideas about how media might work beyond representing society to support social change. In 1967, inspired by academic Donald Snowden's critique of the metropolitan bias and disinterest in grassroots knowledge within Canadian public policy, NFB filmmaker Colin Low went to Fogo, a community of around five thousand people spread across small islands off the Newfoundland coast who were threatened with relocation. Through a process that involved the production of 27 films, Low engaged groups of islanders in reflecting on their situation and considering options for the future. Those films were not treated as mass media, but as tools in a process of reflection and dialogue among the islanders, and for communication with stakeholders in government (Waugh *et al* 2010).

Wondering how they might take advantage of digital media even though many of their subject-collaborators had no internet access, Chaka Films came across *We Farm*, a peer-to-peer service allowing small farmers to share information. Here, a system that routed questions sent via SMS to and from a website allowed farmers without the internet to post questions and receive answers from around the world. *We Farm* offered Chaka two important ingredients – a platform that could enable dialogue between subjects and audience, and one which the subjects might use independently. Another key reference point was *New Day New Standard* (Jahn *et al* 2012), a hotline set up to inform nannies, housekeepers and caregivers in New York State about the 2010 Domestic Workers Bill of Rights. *New Day New Standard* involved an approach which included narrative and an example where sound was the principle medium, which picked up on Court's experience in radio.

To create a tool that would be useable by indigenous people scattered across remote areas of Peru, with no interconnection and no online access, Chaka needed investment in development. It was timely that 2013 saw a call for participation in a suitable R&D scheme – the REACT Sandbox – on the theme Future Documentary.[2] Through REACT, Chaka Films developed a collaboration with University of Bristol researchers Matthew Brown, a Professor of Latin American history, and Karen Tucker, whose work concerns indigenous communities, both of whom had spent time in Peru and were aware of the enforced sterilisation programme. Between September 2013 and January 2014, the Sandbox provided a context for Chaka to work with Brown and Tucker and with a group of women in Peru in a process of participatory design. Together, they set out to devise a media system that could work across the digital divide and support those affected in their fight for justice.

Indigenous communities in Peru are socially marginalised in a number of ways. As well as living in remote rural communities, they are often illiterate and speakers of Quechua, a native Peruvian language. Development required thoughtfulness about the predominantly oral culture of those involved, and face-to-face dialogue was crucial. Lerner and Court made two trips to Peru during the Sandbox to consult with women there over the design of the media system and to test the first prototype. During that time, Court and Lerner came to understand that the project had an unexpected added dimension for their Peruvian co-creators, who saw the chance to record testimony as an opportunity to rehearse and refine their statements as potential future witnesses in court.

REACT provided a unique context in which Chaka and their academic collaborators were free to focus on the context and needs of their subjects, designing a system which put control of contribution into their hands. Of the academic researchers, Lerner says: 'Both of them had spent time in Peru. [...] They understood the context of what had happened. So the idea of consent ... of giving something back were things that were always in the middle of our brief. Matthew and Karen helped us to remember [that] and always think on the ethical side' (Rose 2016).

The system they came up with utilised a simple and highly appropriate mix of analogue and digital technology. Calling a VoIP (voice-over internet protocol) phone line, participants were invited to offer testimony that would be gathered on a website. Crucially, they could also listen back to their own recording, hear the recordings made by others, and be informed when others had listened to theirs. To put that system to use, partnership with three NGOs in Peru – Convenio IA-MAMC-AMHBA (Huancabamba, Piura), AMAEF-C-GTL (Cusco) and Independencia (Ayacucho) – provided a grounded relationship to local communities and a context through which workshops were organised. In partnership with these groups, Chaka Films taught people how to engage with the phone line, and then left phones with some women who they called 'story hunters' so that they could gather testimony among their friendship groups. Then Chaka Films partnered with radio stations to promote the project in places they hadn't been able to visit.

In 'Where voice and listening meet: participation in and through interactive documentary in Peru', Mary Mitchell offers a detailed examination of the pilot phase of *The Quipu Project*, considered from a vantage point of ICT for Development; she notes *The Quipu Project*'s unusual cycle of communication which is 'attentive to speaking, listening and responding' (2015: 6) and argues that the project provides an alternative to the emphasis on voice-over listening which has characterised much participatory media. Picking up on the project's reference point in the *The Fogo Island Process*, Mitchell cites Snowden's articulation of the dynamics of that process as one of horizontal learning and vertical communication. Horizontal communication is what goes on 'within a village or between villages, through sharing videotapes. Vertical communication takes place when those videotapes are brought to those in authority, facilitating communication between previously separated groups of stakeholders' (2015: 5). Within *The Quipu Project*, horizontal learning is of primary importance – with the phone line allowing participants to overcome isolation and stigmatisation by articulating their own experience, sharing testimony, developing their ability to bear witness, and hearing about the experience of others. Vertical communication is not, however, one of the project's objectives. *The Quipu Project* does not aspire to take those testimonies directly to those in power (although their recordings might be seen as rehearsals for future court appearances, so may function in that way indirectly). However, in place of vertical communication another significant dimension is an objective for *The Quipu Project* – one with particular synergy with digital media – network building.

Lerner recounted how, when they started the project, they noted that even though forcibly sterilised people had been speaking out for twenty years, they were disconnected, and therefore lacked strength as a movement. 'One of the main purposes of the project was not only to make this visible, but ... to start connecting them or helping them create this community and this network around this common experience, regardless of their physical location ... this idea of creating community became more and more important, I think, for the project.' Indeed, when Chaka were asked at GoodPitchArgentina to define the project's goals, prioritising between 'changing structures', 'building community', 'changing minds', they put 'building community' top of their list, with 'changing minds' second.

Network building has played out in a number of ways within *The Quipu Project*. Going from one remote community to another to engage people with the project, Chaka Films would invite a workshop participant to join them for the next event, as a community advocate for the project. Leaders of the movement had been in touch before, but here the network was being strengthened as grassroots activists were meeting up, gaining experience in public speaking and representing their cause. *The Quipu Project* also fosters networks of another kind – building virtual networks between those offering testimonies and those hearing them via the website. The sense of co-presence created by the knowledge that website users have heard their testimonies, and especially by those users who leave messages, has been an important dimension for those speaking out – affirming that their experience is no longer hidden, and that they are supported.

The Quipu Project demonstrates how interactive documentary co-creation can be harnessed to support activism. The media-making process is designed to develop capacity within an ongoing movement – by building self-confidence among individuals and connecting them to others, both in person and virtually, and by supporting movement building – through gathering voices together, connecting disparate activists, and building international awareness and support.

During the course of *The Quipu Project*, Esperanza Huayama Aguirre, one of the project's initial collaborators, who was not previously an activist, has become increasingly engaged with campaigning. She is now the president of her local women's organisation – the first illiterate appointee in that role – and one of the best-known advocates for justice around forced sterilisation in Peru, appearing in national and international media. In May 2016, Alberto Fujimori stood for re-election as President. Forced sterilisation was an issue his opponents foregrounded in their campaign. Just before the election, Huayama Aguirre became the signatory to a pledge by the opposition candidate to right the wrongs of the sterilisation programme, if elected to power. In the event Fujimori was defeated, by a small margin. While it is impossible to be sure, it is quite feasible that Huayama Aguirre's role played a part in the outcome by encouraging indigenous voters to turn out.

CONCLUSION

Question Bridge: Black Males and *The Quipu Project* demonstrate significant advances within the trajectory of co-creation which has been developing within interactive documentary for some time. As I have shown, the projects adopt novel approaches to shared authority and decision-making with documentary subjects. In one project, the careful framing of the call to action provides both an open space and a critical framework. In the other, a participatory design process informs the development of a media system that works on behalf of the subjects rather than representing them. Moving beyond forms of participation that focus solely on incorporating the voices of documentary subjects, both projects facilitate multi-faceted processes of dialogue among their subject communities and with audiences, and enable that dialogue through a combination of digital and material platforms and methods. These projects – which are not in thrall to digital affordances and don't assume that connectivity is ubiquitous – offer a powerful reminder that purpose, and an agnostic view of technology, should drive project design.

Thinking back twenty years to Video Nation when, in an otherwise top-down broadcast system, the only co-creative strategy available was to train people in the use of camcorders, serves to underline the palette of co-creative potentials now at the disposal of documentary. At a time when there is growing awareness of the dark side of networked culture, *Question Bridge: Black Males* and *The Quipu Project* affirm how online networks can be put to use for activism by media makers with a deep commitment to the communities they are working with.

When I talked with Lerner and Court in July 2016, they were downcast. Another attempt to bring the case of the forced sterilisations to court had been thrown out, and the two were questioning their project. While they didn't promise a successful outcome to those taking part in *The Quipu Project*, justice was their shared agenda. Had they in some way let their co-creators down? It's an important question – about the responsibility and answerability of media professionals in co-creative projects – and one which deserves its own chapter. It's also a question about the relationship between documentary and social transformation. In *Hope in the Dark* (2016), Rebecca Solnit reminds the reader of the slow advances and surprising turns that can be involved in processes of social transformation, and how changing ideas provide a bedrock for radical shifts. Citing 'Founding Father' John Adams, who said of the American Revolution that all the work in the minds of the people was 'accomplished before hostilities commenced', she argues that 'this means that the most foundational change of all … is hardest to track. [...] The revolution that counts is the one that takes place in the imagination; many kinds of change issue forth thereafter, some gradual and subtle, some dramatic and conflict-ridden – which is to say that revolution doesn't necessarily look like revolution' (2016: 26).

At a critical historical moment, *Question Bridge: Black Males* and *The Quipu Project* demonstrate how, within a context of interactive documentary, co-creation can be a route to convening dialogues that can provide significant resources in those ongoing processes of change.

NOTES

1   In the *Mass Observation* project, which was initiated in 1937 by anthropologist Tom Harrisson, journalist Charles Madge, and painter, poet and filmmaker Humphrey Jennings, fused Surrealism and social science, with members of the public writing diaries on the practices of everyday life.

2   As i-Docs and the REACT Hub shared a home at the Pervasive Media Studio in Bristol, and Jon Dovey was REACT director, documentary was an obvious choice for a Sandbox theme. Mandy Rose and Sandra Gaudenzi were Advisers on the Future Documentary Sandbox, and Sandra working closely with Chaka Films, while Judith Aston was academic lead on one of the other projects – *Orion: Behind the Mask*.

REFERENCES

Alexander, Michelle (2010) *The New Jim Crow – Mass Incarceration in the Age of Colorblindess*. New York: New Press.

Castells, Manuel (2009) *Communication Power*. Oxford: Oxford University Press.

Court, Maria, Ros Lerner and Sebastian Melo (2014) *The Quipu Project*. Web documentary. Co-produced by Chaka Studio and Helios Design Labs. First presented at i-Docs 2014. https://interactive.quipu-project.com/#/en/quipu/intro. Accessed 31 October 2016.

De Michiel, Helen and Patricia Zimmermann (2013) 'Documentary as an Open Space', in Brian Winston (ed.) *The Documentary Film Book*. London: BFI Press, 355–365.

Dovey, Jon (2014) 'Documentary Ecosystems: Collaboration and Exploitation' in Kate Nash,

Craig Hight and Catherine Summerhayes (eds) *New Documentary Ecologies: Emerging Platforms, Practices and Discourses*. New York: Palgrave Macmillan, 11–32.

Du Bois, W.E.B. (1903) *The Souls of Black Folks*. Chicago: A.C. McClurg.

Dovey, Jon and Mandy Rose (2013) '"This great mapping of ourselves" – New documentary forms online', in Brian Winston (ed.) *The Documentary Film Book*. London: British Film Institute, 366–75.

Eaton, Michael (ed.) (1979) *Anthropology, Reality – Cinema: The Films of Jean Rouch*. London: British Film Institute.

Frankham, Bettina (2015) 'Moving Beyond Evidence: Participatory online documentary practice within the poetic framework of Cowbird', *Media International Australia, Incorporating Culture and Policy*, 154, 123–31.

Gaudenzi, Sandra (2013): *The Living Documentary: from representing reality to co-creating reality in digital interactive documentary*. PhD Thesis. Goldsmiths, University of London. https://research.gold.ac.uk/7997/1/Cultural_thesis_Gaudenzi.pdf. Accessed 31 October 2016.

Haraway, Donna (1989) *Primate Visions: Gender, Race and Nature in the World of Modern Science*. New York: Routledge.

Jahn, Marisa *et al* (2012) *New Day New Standard*. Multi-platform project including participatory website, mobile app, and public art project. Produced by Murmur, MIT Media Lab and TF1 New Media Fund'; http://www.studiorev.org/p_ndns.html. Accessed 31 October 2016.

Jenkins, Henry (2008) *Convergence Culture: Where Old and New Media Collide*. New York: New York University Press.

Johnson, Chris (2014) 'Creative Expression and Transformational Change, Project for the Advancement of our Common Humanity.' Lecture, 7 February 2014, New York University, PATCH lecture series. https://www.youtube.com/watch?v=7blgKa3plXc. Accessed 31 October 2016.

Johnson, Chris, Thomas Willis, Ross Hank, Bayete Smith and Karmal Sinclair (2012) *Question Bridge: Black Males*. Web documentary; http://questionbridge.com/. Accessed 31 October 2016.

Kester, Grant H. (2004) *Conversation Pieces – Community and Communication in Modern Art*. Los Angles: University of California Press.

Lacy, Suzanne, Annice Jacoby and Chris Johnson (1994) *The Roof is on Fire*. Performance with 220 teenagers. Oakland, California.

Lerner, Ros and Sebastian Melo (2016) Presentation at i-Docs Symposium, 4 March, Bristol, UK. Unpublished video.

Low, Colin (1967) *The Fogo Island Process*. Film. Produced by John Kemeny, co-produced by NFB.

Madge, Charles and Tom Harrisson (eds) (1970) *Mass Observation – The First Year's Work 1937-1938*. Faber: London.

Mitchell, Mary (2015) 'Where voice and listening meet: participation in and through interactive documentary', *Peru Global Times* online, 22/23; http://ojs.ub.gu.se/ojs/index.php/gt/article/viewFile/3268/2728. Accessed 31 October 2016.

Rose, Mandy (2000) 'Through the Eyes of the Video Nation', in John Izod, Richard Kilborn and Matthew Hibberd (eds) *From Grierson to the Docu-Soap: Breaking the Boundaries*. Luton:

University of Luton Press, 173–84.

____ (2014a) 'Making Publics: Documentary as do-it-with-others citizenship', in Megan Boler and Matt Ratto (eds) *DIY Citizenship: Critical Making and Social Media*. Boston: MIT Press, 201–12.

____ (2014b) Interview with Kamal Sinclair on *Question Bridge*. May 2014; http://docubase. mit.edu/lab/interviews/interview-with-kamal-sinclair/. Accessed 26 October 2016

Rose, Mandy *et al* (2013) *Searching for Happiness*. Web documentary. See credits on website for details of collaborators; http://theareyouhappyproject.org. Accessed 31 October 2016.

Solnit, Rebecca (2016) *Hope in the Dark: Untold Histories, Wild Possibilities*. Chicago: Haymarket Books.

Waugh, Thomas, Ezra Wiston and Michael Baker (2010) *Challenge for Change*. Activist Documentary at the National Film Board of Canada. Montreal/Kingston: McGill-Queens University Press.

We Farm (n.d.). Online platform; http://wefarm.org/. Accessed 26 October 2016.

Willis Thomas, Hank (2014) 'Question Bridge Keynote', i-Docs 2014. https://vimeo. com/130855264. Accessed 31 October 2016.

Willis, Deborah and Natasha Logan (eds) (2015) *Question Bridge: Black Males in America*. New York: Aperture.

Winston, Brian, Gail Vanstone and Wang Chi (forthcoming) *The Act of Documenting: Documentary Film in the 21st Century*. London: Bloomsbury Academic.

LIVING COLLABORATIONS IN LOS SURES, BROOKLYN
1984 AND TODAY

Christopher Cekay Allen

SHOT 212

A powerful stream rushes from an open fire hydrant. A young man redirects the spray with a tin can that has been opened on both ends, vaulting it vertical and out of the frame. The camera pans through a line-up of smiling, soaked spectators, clothing clinging to wet bodies, all watching this waterfall on the street. Far in the background, a man making his way through the crowd motivates a zoom. Wearing a white deep-v-neck t-shirt and with obvious swagger, Cuso Soto weaves through tight clusters on the sidewalk until he is in close-up. The camera rotates over Cuso's shoulder at the very instant he is confronted by a shirtless man. Is

Fig 1: The starting frame of the 212th shot of Diego Echeverría's *Los Sures*.

this man's energetic stance a threat? No, a sly grin emerges to crack the tension. The camera re-focuses and orbits around the man, slowly revealing dozens of on-looking faces in the background, including a 'Beat Cop' with walkie-talkie raised in mid-conversation, before landing confidently back on Cuso. Shifts in the light show droplets of water on the lens, a camera truly in the middle of the action. The shirtless man re-enters the frame, locking together with Cuso in playful roughhousing that evolves quickly into an embrace. The shot cuts on the pair, arms intertwined.

In 23 seconds, this single shot provides an example of both masterful documentary cinematography and storytelling craft. It opens the fourth chapter of Diego Echeverría's *Los Sures* (1984), providing a delicate transition from an extended montage sequence of vibrant street scenes from the Puerto Rican barrio to the introduction of the protagonist for the chapter, Cuso Soto, in a moment that reflects his joyful character. But let's remove the shot from its function in the film. I'm watching it on a loop: hydrant, crowd, swagger, confrontation, crowd, Cop, embrace, hydrant, crowd, swagger... Now, other aspects attract attention, so many details of place and time captured in the background and margins of this frame: the surprising number of people (perhaps forty?), graffiti on the walls that seems to read 'Charli F.D.W.', a young woman in a black tank top staring back at the lens, a vehicle parked well into the sidewalk, boarded-up buildings across the street. Those two hands grasping window bars must belong to an invisible person looking out from a dark apartment. So much action, so many lives and stories beyond the director's narrative intersect in the strip of celluloid that holds this shot.

The encounter between a 16mm camera and a Brooklyn neighbourhood in the early 1980s – producing so many mysteries in the margins and background of the frame – inspired the expansive documentary project *Living Los Sures*. Beginning in 2010 and produced by UnionDocs, a centre for documentary art founded a few blocks from where much of the film takes place, the project grew to include the work of over sixty artists, filmmakers, technologists, librarians and designers and the cooperation of hundreds from the local community. *Living Los Sures* encompasses five main elements: i) the 16mm and digital restoration of the film *Los Sures* from 1984; ii) the creation of forty new short documentary projects about the neighbourhood today; iii) an ongoing interactive people's history that splices the stories of long-term residents into the narrative of *Los Sures*; iv) a web-doc with a game-like structure that catches up with Marta Avilés, one of the five main protagonists of *Los Sures*, as she considers leaving her apartment after forty years; and v) a public mural on the face of UnionDocs, telling a life history of Cuso, who continues to call the neighbourhood home.

TAKING IT SHOT BY SHOT

Whenever *Los Sures* is shown, a flood of memories is triggered. They gush like the hydrant in shot 212. In the recent theatrical re-release, we were surprised to find that folks from this special neighbourhood's diaspora showed up to screenings across the country, no matter how far flung. Inevitably they saw a friend, a shop, a fashion item, a building, a hairstyle, a dance move, or something else very familiar but long lost that brings a story so vividly to mind that they want – no, need – to share. We hoped to harness this latent energy in designing an interactive, participatory project that would utilise the film to access and sort stories from the long-standing community. We imagined collecting a large database of annotations that brought new meaning to particular images or moments from the documentary. We wanted stories and opinions that added breadth to the narrative or even directly challenged its assumptions. So, how best to gather these stories, and how best to make them available?

We didn't have the budget to create a fully functional user-generated content platform. We also were extremely sceptical that interesting stories would result from an open submission system. Having observed other participatory projects, and through my own successes and failures in designing a mobile storytelling project called 'Yellow Arrow', I knew we couldn't count on people to take the time and effort required to contribute details that would actually be worthy of sharing. We would have to do the groundwork ourselves to provide early exciting examples of the kind of content we were seeking, and we would have to add significant incentives. Rather than build an expensive interface, we used the resources we had available: a physical space in the community, basic equipment, and the time of both our staff and the fellows in our collaborative studio. Not a 'scalable approach', but something that seemed likely to produce quality.

Starting out, we showed the film in small groups of long-standing community members and simply recorded the conversation that followed, but we found this approach resulted in few completed stories and many unproductive tangents.

Fig 2: Index of *Living Los Sures*: Shot by Shot.

Then we showed the film to one individual at a time followed by an interview. This tended to produce only a couple of key stories as it relied solely on the participant's recall of the film. It was difficult to consistently connect these stories to specific moments or images in the film, which we needed to produce annotations. Aris Dilone, a filmmaker from a Dominican background who was formerly involved in local politics, conducted the majority of these interviews. Together, we brainstormed many alternate ways of designing the interaction. For instance, we also tried to watch the film alongside the interview subject, starting and stopping it to ask questions or discuss specific points. This approach took too much time, however, and it was simply awkward to stop in the middle of the narrative's flow. Throughout, we would always ask the participants for any photographs or ephemera they might have to illustrate a specific story.

Eventually, we learned that the best way to get the most relevant interesting material in the least amount of time involved chopping up the film into isolated single shots, literally deconstructing the edit. *Los Sures* is composed of 326 different shots. We'd play a shot once with sound and then let it loop silently in front of the interview subject. While the shot repeated, we simply asked 'what do you see?' Using this Rorschach-like method, people would notice so much more, offering comments and memories that were detailed and individualised and much less generic. We could present around ten shots in an hour-long interview and record dozens of interesting memories and ideas that were all very neatly connected to distinct points in the film. The isolated shot gave us a unit with which to work.

Discovering how to display this material alongside the film followed a similar trajectory. Initially, I imagined a database that one could navigate freely by author, topic, time and place. I thought of it as a B-side to the documentary, with the notion that you could pause the film at any moment and flip into this alternate interface. I had happy memories of reading *Ulysses* with Don Gifford's annotations in parallel and imagined something similar might be possible given the hundreds of perspectives that the project might engage. Text, images, video and audio contributed by the community would offer commentary and expand your understanding. In 2012, at the first hackathon offered by POV, our team of Andre Valentim Almeida, Danny Bowman, Kyle Warren, Lucas Carlisle and myself created a prototype that attempted to model this potential. Pausing the film, the frame shrunk to the corner of the screen and related content burst outward with guiding lines that traced back to the specific part of the image being referenced.

As our investment in the interview process grew, and as we started to get better and better stories – stories that fit together in clusters, that built on or contradicted each other – the database interface began to feel increasingly inappropriate. The material was good, so why create an experience that put it in a

Fig 3: Shot by Shot prototype developed at POV's first hackathon.

secondary position that demanded stopping the flow of the film? We had doubts that the audience would actually do that very often. Yet much of what made these annotations interesting was that they really did refer to the immediate context of the film. We also noticed that some annotations were stronger when delivered in a particular order and that it mattered how ideas were introduced and developed. Commentary on certain shots circled specific themes, forming a multi-voiced story around a focus idea. One shot might provoke memories about the relationship between the police and the residents, while another was all about the practice of watching people out of your apartment window. By creating their own random path through this material, the user seemed unlikely to understand these connections, missing much of the quality in what we had gathered.

I decided to tear up the earlier versions and see what could result if the stories were organised under the shot. Instead of allowing access to the entire film online, we'd have the 326 shots broken into discrete pages to allow the users to move through the shots one at a time. They could still jump around in the narrative, but they'd always have a single shot to watch. Just like the interview method, they could watch it first with sound and then it would loop in the background silently. The stories and media collected would appear in the foreground, in a linear interface that you could scroll through at your own pace. Everyone thought this new approach to be a much better match to the material. There was just one big problem. The change increased the editorial labour required to publish the project by an enormous amount. The planned premiere at the New York Film Festival was looming uncomfortably close as our tiny team went to work rearranging the database of annotations into an order that had logic, progression and sometimes even drama.

WHERE ARE WE?

Echeverría's film is set in the Southside of Williamsburg, Brooklyn at a time when the mostly Puerto Rican area, known locally as Los Sures, was one of the poorest neighbourhoods in America. It uses testimony gathered through the interview and observation of five otherwise unaffiliated individuals to represent the challenges residents faced across the Southside: poverty, drugs, gang violence, crime, negligent landlords, racial tension, single-parent homes and inadequate local services. Yet the portrait isn't motivated by pity. It celebrates the vitality of this largely Puerto Rican community, showing the strength of their culture, their creativity, and their determination to overcome a desperate situation.

The Brooklyn shown in the film is hard to reconcile with the borough's current popular imaginary. Today, Brooklyn has stepped well out of Manhattan's shadow to become its own global brand, signifying a pop intellectual and hipster lifestyle where hip-hop legacies, bespoke experience design and multi-cultural influence are framed by post-industrial urban grit. The influence of this idealised Brooklyn can be seen in cities all over the world. Introducing a screening of *Living Los Sures* in a public park in the summer of 2015, Borough President Eric Adams joked: 'The sun is not the centre of the universe. It's Brooklyn, baby.'

Having served for 22 years as a police officer for the NYPD, however, Adams knows that Brooklyn becoming a simple shorthand for gentrification leaves way

Fig 4: Tito is one of the principal subjects of the documentary *Los Sures*. He is pictured here (third from left) with his brother Danny and friends in 1983. Image courtesy of Ellen Tolmie.

Fig 5: An outdoor screening of short films from *Living Los Sures* turns a handball court into a cinema in the Southside of Williamsburg.

too much out of the picture. Brooklyn is enormous. If separated from the rest of New York City, it would be the fourth-largest city in America. It holds a vast mix of people, with extreme and increasing gaps between the rich and the poor. It is a place where homelessness is as high as it was in the Great Depression. Though apparently erased from popular imagination and most current media, it has always been home to very strong communities of immigrants. The neighbourhood of Los Sures, so clearly illustrates the tensions between these two ideas of Brooklyn, as the site of a battle between local identity and luxury lifestyle.

DIVISIONS

In the 1980s, Williamsburg was fiercely divided along ethnic lines: Polish, Italian, African-American, Hasidic Jewish and, as was most often said at the time, 'Spanish', referring to the Puerto Rican and increasingly Dominican sections. The white northern half was home to McCarren Park Pool, a site that exemplifies these divisions. The year the film *Los Sures* was released, the city closed the massive swimming facility, the largest of eleven pools built in New York City by the Worker's Progress Administration. Their decision was due primarily to complaints from older white residents about the people of colour from other areas that it attracted, the neighbourhood boundaries broken. Parks Commissioner at the time, Henry Stern was quoted on the closure: 'There were racial issues. The neighborhood was afraid of violence and that the police would be unable to contain it' (Short 2012).

The Latino subsection, Los Sures, could not really be called united either. A highway, the Brooklyn Queens Expressway built by Robert Moses, carves the

Fig 6: A map of the neighbourhoods of Brooklyn highlights the Los Sures section of Williamsburg. Design: Mike Dudek.

place in two, producing a psychological gap much more significant than the physical infrastructure itself. Early in Echeverría's film, we hear this referenced by a young man describing gang related violence: 'There's only three, three on this side. On the other side, there's more. On the other side, they got a lotta bodies.'

When UnionDocs started up in the neighbourhood in the early 2000s, these boundaries were still completely obvious, though more as an artefact of history than as a source of present aggression. What was most apparent and troubling, however, was the pervasive division between long-term residents and newer in-habitants. These two populations generally overlapped in space, but with few parks and public spaces available, they rarely intersected meaningfully. The sense of community that one sees so clearly in shot 212 from *Los Sures* seemed to me to have disappeared from many blocks. I saw people walking with blind-ers on, avoiding interaction with their neighbours or acknowledging the place they lived.

SHOT BY SHOT SYNTAX

A story has an author, is composed of 'slides' and is tagged with a shot number. Slides are either a few lines of text, a video, a foreground image, a background image, a highlight, or a streetview 'then/now comparison'.

Highlight: Some stories reference visible details in the shot. This tool logs an x,y coordinate indicating the specific point of the shot. However, shots are not static and locked off. As shot 212 reminds us, they pan, they zoom, they spin, they dolly. So in order to highlight the correct detail in the image, an x,y coordinate must be paired with a timestamp.

Street-view comparison: Along the way, and with the help of a young intern named Genesis Henriquez who knew the neighbourhood like the back of her hand, the exact location of each exterior shot was determined. With this knowledge, Google street-view could be used to approximate the angle of the original shot and produce a side by side comparison. On the front-end, this often appears as a simple 'Then & Now' interstitial between two author's stories. The feature had optional title and caption text attributes, so we also could use the comparison to extend a particular narrative or provide an anecdote about the site today.

Editing the loop: Stories sometimes refer to a very specific moment within the timeframe of a single shot, rather than a specific detail. For instance, many stories about shot 212 were focused on the interaction with the 'Beat Cop'. A loop editor function allows a specific portion of a shot to be designated to loop while the story was being displayed. Transitioning to a new story, a different loop displays or if none is designated, the full shot loops. This feature was used often, as it acts as a very seamless way of directing the user's attention.

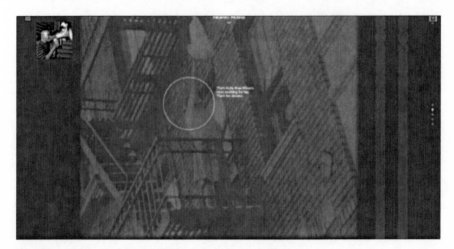

Fig 7: Example of a highlight in *Living Los Sures*: Shot by Shot.

Script highlight: Some comments and stories refer more to the character's dialogue than what could be seen in the shot. We contemplated adding a new editing feature, but then settled on a simple work around. We scanned the original typewritten script of *Los Sures*. Treating corresponding sections of the script graphically, we could highlight the spoken text that a particular story focused on. We then added this as a photo slide, offering an additional way to provide reference and connection.

FINDING AND FIXING THE FILM

From humble roots, UnionDocs has grown over the past ten years to become a bustling centre for documentary art with weekly screenings and events, intensive workshops and seminars, documentary productions, a collaborative studio fellowship, and an artist residency programme. The discovery of *Los Sures* came as result of these increasing activities, and the *Living Los Sures* project would eventually engage in one way or another with all sides of the organisation.

Following a UnionDocs screening of *State of Fear* in 2006, we learned that the director/producer couple, Pamela Yates and Paco de Onís, actually lived very close by. In passing, they mentioned a film made by an old friend that showed what the neighbourhood was like in the 1980s. We were instantly curious, and a few days later, they kindly delivered a bootleg VHS copy from their library. Watching the little-known film for the first time, I was blown away. In addition to being an emotionally compelling and expertly crafted piece of cinema, the film provided a window into a local history that was otherwise unwritten and inaccessible. We decided to connect to the filmmaker, Diego Echeverría, and arrange a screening of *Los Sures* as soon as possible.

From that point until 2010, UnionDocs would host a small screening or two of the films each year. We mainly worked with a low-resolution file digitised from that same bootlegged VHS, until we found a nice 16mm print at the New York Public Library. It turned out that this print, though in an openly circulated collection, was in fact truly precious. Elena Rossi-Snook, archivist at the NYPL's Reserve Film and Video Collection, received a grant to restore *Los Sures* and then searched dutifully across the country for the original elements or a better copy, only to find that the one in their possession was actually the single remaining version of the film in condition to be restored. We never imagined that a film with such historical significance for the city and for the Puerto Rican community, a film that was such an impressive example from early 1980s documentary could have been so overlooked and neglected. But it was. I am quite thankful that I did not accidently damage this delicate reel of plastic on the multiple occasions when I

Fig 8: Canisters and 16mm film of Los Sures during the restoration.

personally projected it for the public. In any case, just in time for the 30th anniversary of the film's premiere at the New York Film Festival, UnionDocs completed a beautiful 4K digital scan of the NYPL print. The re-release enjoyed a great deal of attention, a seven-week run at the Metrograph cinema, and sold out screenings at many other venues around town, such as the Brooklyn Academy of Music, the Museum of the Moving Image, the Brooklyn Museum, and MoMA's PS1.

89 STEPS

For a long time, we had hoped to connect to Marta Avilés, one of *Los Sures* five main protagonists. Searches and enquiries at local institutions, online databases and official routes to find her turned up little very. We were hesitant to walk around the neighbourhood with her picture from the 1980s and ask people in public. Nobody likes suspicious investigators. Finally though, as other routes failed, that is what we ended up doing. Our first stop was the bodega across the street from UnionDocs. The man behind the counter looked at the picture and without hesitation said 'Oh, yeah. That's Marta. She lives over on South 3rd at Keap Street.' The address was about a three minutes walk from UnionDocs.

When we met, Marta was at a crossroads. She was contemplating selling her apartment of forty years and leaving the neighbourhood in which she had lived most of her life. Among a few other factors, it was the six flights of stairs that she walked every day that prompted this difficult decision. Those 89 steps increasingly inhibited her plans to leave home and belaboured her breath upon return. Alison S. M. Kobayashi and I contemplated creating an update to Marta's story as part of the *Living Los Sures* project, but didn't feel excited about a straightforward short documentary about her situation.

During two Mozilla-sponsored hackathon opportunities – one in conjunction with HotDocs and the other with the Tribeca Film Institute's New Media Fund –

we were able to work with talented developers (first James Burns and then Bobby Richter) to make prototypes. We were in love with Marta's wonderful voice and her abilities as a storyteller and came up with a couple of guiding principles for the work. First, we hoped to a make a web doc that 'looked with' rather than watched the main character. We wanted to create the feeling that Marta's voice-over narration was dynamically aware of your choices and interactions, almost like she was looking over your shoulder or following you on a personalised tour. Second, we wanted the story to follow a linear structure, but offer a set of environments that presented simple interactions, each with a slightly different interface and goals that motivated the user to explore and problem solve. One advantage we had was that we were approaching this from the beginning as a web doc. Where many projects try to shoehorn traditional documentary materials into an interactive experience, we planned and recorded everything based on our design ideas. That might mean laboriously shooting the same scene from three contiguous angles, or shooting with an eye to create perfect looping video clips, or playing imaginative games with Marta in our audio interviews to get natural sounding commands that complemented the structure.

I felt pretty creative presenting Bobby Richter our concept of a dynamic voice-over narration that would respond to the user's choices. He responded: 'Oh, I get it. You mean like *Bastion*.' I looked blankly and shrugged. He then showed us a game-play clip from the independent developer Supergiant Games published about nine months earlier in which a voice narrates the player's action step-by-step in response to their choices. Of course, a video game company had already come up with and been celebrated for this little innovation. I was a bit deflated, but at least we were on the same page about the concept. The key now was to create a system that could play audio clips in a certain order, where parts of the narration could be skipped past or elaborated upon without unnaturally interrupting or cutting off the voice.

With a bit of funding from the National Endowment for the Arts and a commission from POV to join their first collection of digital projects, we attempted to build *89 Steps* (2014). Patricia Zavala, a creative developer recently graduated from New York University's Interactive Telecommunications Programme, joined Alison and me on the project. Bobby from Mozilla continued to provide technical oversight. Over a relatively rapid four-week push, we faced a lot of challenges. A downside to developing an interactive project on a relatively low-budget through multiple hackathons and concentrated sprints is that you can become protective of the progress you've made in previous pushes. Having moved between multiple developers and made shifts in content along the way, however, some of the baggage of earlier prototypes ended up slowing us down.

Also, the ability to test our ideas in the browser was pretty limited. The first scene in *89 Steps* is composed of eighteen looping video clips, one master background audio file, nine short background audio clips that are position-specific, and about twelve short narrative audio pieces. To control playback of this stack of content, we pushed the envelope of HTML5 audio with some new Javascript libraries (popcorn.js and howler.js). The result of combining these audio layers should feel seamless and natural, hiding the variability in the playback. When creating this in 2014, different browsers still required different file types for HTML5 video and audio. Cutting MP3s, OGGs, WAVs, MP4s and WEBMs of every audio and video clip multiplied the number of files we had to manage, increased the likelihood of confusion and mistakes and made the editing process and debugging much more tedious. There were a seemingly exponential number of variables. If a direction we tried wasn't working narratively, the effort required to try something else was truly daunting.

89 Steps doesn't function on mobile, but it has been very stable in the browser for the past two years. It has had hundreds of thousands of plays, and Marta's sense of humour and the creativity of the interface has garnered much positive response. Given the limits of our budget and the accelerated time to launch, we published the first four chapters of a planned nine. Instead, we concluded the piece with a short video that 'previews' the rest of the story. The intention was to return to the work with additional funding. Though we were successful with additional grants and benefitted from the theatrical and institutional distribution of the film from 1984, we ultimately decided to apply these resources to other aspects of the project. The difficulty of the development, the changes in the landscape of interactive (the fixation on VR, for one) and the audience's strong move

Fig 9: Still from chapter 2, The Stairs, of *89 Steps*.

to mobile, plus the great rewards that have continued to result from other aspects of *Living Los Sures*, all have factored into the realisation that we need to consider *89 Steps* complete as it is.

FROM LOOKING TO LIVING

To end at the beginning, it was 2010 when we kicked off a new thematic focus for the productions made by the Collaborative Studio, a programme for non-fiction media research and group production at UnionDocs that was just entering its second year. I named it *Looking at Los Sures*. The idea was to take Echeverría's film from 1984 as a starting point for a set of new short documentary projects to be made over the course of a year by twelve emerging artists who were supported by UnionDocs and guided by studio directors Jesse Shapins, Kara Oehler and myself. The project concept was, in many ways, a reaction to the results of our previous production *Documenting Mythologies* (2013). This inaugural work of the Collaborative Studio, which premiered at the Museum of Modern Art's Documentary Fortnight, was a collection of essay films edited into an omnibus feature inspired by Roland Barthes' famous book from 1957, *Mythologies*. Each short piece attempted to unpack an object that had obtained mythological status in society today. The concept was mostly a success, but I had the feeling that we were missing the opportunity to point the energy of this group of young artists towards a more complex interaction with their surroundings that might engender a greater investment in the politics of their work.

Projects in the collaborative studio are developed in a shared research and production environment, but also have an independent vision and process. That first year of the *Looking at Los Sures* focus, Laurie Sumiye and Andrew Parson made one of the strongest of the Southside Short Docs, an animated oral history called *Of Memory and Los Sures*. It accomplished our ideal for a collaborative studio film; first, because it was a result of the unique combination of the talents of Parson, who was more accomplished in radio, and Sumiye, who was an illustrator and filmmaker; and second, because the short played very well on its own, finding a prestigious premiere at BAMcinemafest, while also creating a dialogue with the original film and the growing pool of other shorts made for the project. Not all of the forty Southside Short Docs would realise a similar sweet-spot, but luckily quite a few did. Stories were told of the last remaining Latino social club in the neighbourhood, the fight against charter schools, the skills you could learn at the Moore Street Market, a man who looks after the neighbourhood's street cats, to more aesthetic explorations of the colours, sounds and motion of the place.

Of Memory and Los Sures benefited enormously from the relationship that the filmmakers established with the longstanding local community-based organisation, El Puente. They held extensive interviews with the founders, Frances Lucerna and Luis Garden Acosta about their experience growing up in the neighbourhood and creating what would become one of its most important organisations, a model for CBOs around the country. El Puente also opened doors to interviewing other long-term residents. This was a gift. Given the great divisions mentioned previously, gaining trust was a challenge for all the collaborative projects. Somewhat embarrassingly, UnionDocs had not yet truly connected to El Puente before this moment, but they became the gatekeepers to a more nuanced understanding of the local politics and culture, and helped shape the project's mission.

The following fall, happy with the films produced and with a feeling that we needed to go further, perhaps much further, *Looking at Los Sures* continued as a theme for the next round of fellows in the annual Collaborative Studio. We planned a more ambitious screening of the documentary from 1984, inviting local politicians and community stakeholders together as a way of creating a neighbourhood forum while introducing the new fellows to the project. We set up a meeting with Frances Lucerna of El Puente to see if she might be willing to be partner on the event and to become an advisor for the budding project. Early in the meeting she said, 'You mean that film we hate?' My jaw dropped. If Lucerna was against the film, there was little chance that our goals could be achieved.

It had been nearly three decades since she had seen Echeverría's film, but Lucerna remembered that the strong focus on poverty in the neighbourhood had angered her and some other long-term residents when it was broadcast. With so few representations of Puerto Ricans in the media, she saw the stories as stereotypical; a mother of five living on welfare, a young man turning to petty theft to support his family, an older woman clinging to religious traditions from her village. Where were the neighbourhood's entrepreneurs, the activists, the doctors, lawyers and others who demonstrated the Boricua 'fighting spirit'? It is a very fair critique, and over the course of the project we would hear it repeated by others. Luckily, Lucerna also saw the value of using the film as a vehicle to revisit and discuss history, and she agreed to work with us on the project. After a strong screening with over two hundred people and a very emotional discussion, Lucerna said that her opinion of the film had changed quite a lot, that the negative feelings had given way to seeing the stories as accurate to the individual's experience, if still not entirely representative of the community. Today, UnionDocs and El Puente are partnering on a pilot curriculum for youth that uses *Los Sures* alongside the expansive interactive project to speak to local issues, media literacy and documentary.

That screening changed something else: our title. *Looking at Los Sures* had emphasised the materiality of the film and the potential of this material to spark new projects. While many had told us, Los Sures as a moniker for the neighbourhood was fading, and some claimed the Latino portion of the neighbourhood was 'over', we saw how El Puente and others resisted this capitulation to gentrification. It was not inevitability as so many framed the conflict, but a question of will. Certainly many people were being forced out by rising prices, but for many others it was a decision. Luis Garden Acosta put it clearly: 'If people are not feeling like this is their community, then they won't feel like they have a future here' (cited in Nelson and Morales 2011). After that early screening, we saw how even through significant changes, the community feeling of Los Sures extends beyond the physical blocks. We understood that the project might be able to support this necessary sense of local pride and shared history, a mythology of another sort to document. Los Sures was no longer something that could be simply examined, it was something to be experienced and joined. Thus, Living Los Sures.

REFERENCES

Allen, Christopher *et al* (2014) *89 Steps*. Web documentary. Produced by UnionDocs; http://89.lossur.es/. Accessed 31 October 2016.

____ (2014) *Living Los Sures*. Expansive web documentary project. Prod-uced by UnionDocs; http://lossur.es/about-living-los-sures/. Accessed 31 October 2016.

____ (2014) *Of Memory and Los Sures*. Web documentary. Produced by UnionDocs; http://shots.lossur.es/#/0001. Accessed 31 October 2016.

Barthes, Roland (1957 [1973]) *Mythologies [Mythologies]*. Trans. Annette Lavers. London: Simon & Schuster.

Echeverría, Diego (1984 [2015]) *Los Sures*. Film.

Nelson, Katie and Mark Morales (2011) 'Brooklyn gentrification meets resistance from long-time Latino residents in South Williamsburg'. *New York Daily News*, 16 September 2011; http://www.nydailynews.com/new-york/brooklyn-gentrification-meets-resistance-longtime-latino-residents-south-williamsburg-article-1.957237. Accessed 31 October 2016.

Short, Aaron (2012) *The Politics of McCarren Park Pool*. New York: The Awl.

SOFTWARE AS CO-CREATOR IN INTERACTIVE DOCUMENTARY

Craig Hight

Central to interactive documentary is a strong emphasis on collaborative practice, whether this begins from the conception of a project, with how materials are gathered, or how collaborative relationships inform storytelling style and content. In the case of a webdoc, this might govern the structure of the site itself, either with interactivity defined as the opportunity for co-creating meaning with users, or in the ways in which a site is populated by users' content. This chapter addresses a different notion of 'co-creation' – one which is more pervasive within this form of documentary culture and more intimately derived from the nature of technologies used to create, develop and present interactive works.

The argument presented in this chapter draws from Software Studies, a comparatively new field of enquiry that Lev Manovich and others have championed (Fuller 2008, Kitchin and Dodge 2011, Manovich 2013). Within the software studies paradigm, software is the dominant cultural technology of our time – one which is fundamentally reshaping all areas of modern life and requiring all disciplines focused on contemporary society and culture to account for its role and effects. All contemporary media practices are now clearly embedded within and governed by various forms of software; from applications for everyday communication and media editing to social media platforms such as Facebook, Twitter and YouTube which provide a broader infrastructure of engagement, a set of 'givens' for how users can engage, participate and interact (van Dijck 2013). At an infrastructural level, the internet and worldwide web are themselves organised through software-based protocols (Galloway 2004) that govern largely automated processes that are rarely visible to everyday users, unless they fail. As discussed in this chapter, interactive documentary does not just operate in tandem with the software forms outlined above. Most stages of the development and implementation of interactive projects involve 'coded' practices in the sense that these are embedded within and increasingly no longer separable from, programming code. This fact contains a number of implications for the nature of interactive documentary itself.

A core premise of software studies is the need to move away from seeing software applications, platforms and infrastructure as 'neutral' tools (Fuller 2008: 16). Software is itself a cultural artefact, evolving within particular organisations which operate with their own specific discourses on the purposes and uses of their technology, with components that may have their own life cycle, but are also available to be recombined towards new ends (Berry 2011: 42). And most crucially software has *agency*: 'Software is written by programmers, individually and in teams, within diverse social, political, and economic contexts. The production of software unfolds – programming is performative and negotiated and code is mutable. Software possesses secondary agency that engenders it with high technicity. As such, software needs to be understood as an actant in the world – it augments, supplements, mediates, and regulates our lives and opens up new possibilities – but not in a deterministic way. Rather, software is afforded power by a network of contingencies that allows it to do work in the world' (Kitchin and Dodge 2011: 43–4).

This is important because many software applications (including those discussed in this chapter) foster other creative acts (Kitchin and Dodge 2011: 112). All forms of media production, including the design and implementation of interactive documentary, typically involve the strategic use of software-based media editors toward particular ends. The objects which interactive documentary designers create are themselves software constructions which users need to understand, navigate and engage with in particular ways in order to realise their purpose and agenda. A focus on the nature and implications of software provides one way of thinking through the cultural discourses that are embedded in programming code, together with the broader implications for users of how these discourses operate through the application of that code.

THE NATURE OF SOFTWARE: AFFORDANCES, INTERFACES AND PARADIGMS

There are key aspects of software culture which we need to first briefly outline here. Firstly, programming code needs to be understood broadly as engendering 'both forces of empowerment and discipline' (Kitchin and Dodge 2011: 10). Software applications and platforms are attractive precisely because they are designed toward increasing efficiencies and productivity, generating entirely new markets, and providing new forms of play and creativity. However, they also serve as 'a broad range of technologies that more efficiently and successfully represent, collate, sort, categorize, match, profiles, and regulate people, processes, and places' (2011: 11). This tension between 'empowerment' and 'discipline' offers a broad frame for understanding the layered and complex role which software plays at a variety of levels especially within networked media. At the more micro level, we need to be considering the manner and ways in which specific pieces of software work to both enable and constrain creative practices, such as those relevant to the production of and engagement with interactive documentary.

At the level we as users encounter an application or platform, our engagement is both fostered and constrained through the affordances that piece of software provides. An affordance 'is an action possibility or an offering' (McGrenere and Ho 2000: 6), something which might be provided by hardware or software. Affordances allow us to do particular things: to select, to view, to manipulate in specific ways. If we look at a software application as providing a set of these possible actions, then it is vital to map how these affordances appear within a specific hierarchy, with some made easily available to its users, and how they are more generally organised to support or constrain what users can use that application for. The interface for a piece of software embodies that hierarchy of affordances; these are the default tools we find most easily on the ribbons or drop-down menus of one of the Microsoft Office applications, or the buttons that are clustered together on a social media platform (such as Facebook's now expanded range of feedback buttons). At a more fundamental level, if we extrapolate from the set of affordances which a piece of software provides, we can start to see the underlying *conceptual* framework which an application or platform operates within.

As particular affordances become familiar to users and become naturalised to some extent within specific forms of practice, they can become associated with specific ways of thinking. For example, the repetition of cut, copy and paste as tools across a variety of pieces of a media editor has broader implications for how users conceive of the possibilities of creating content (Manovich 2013). When we look at a specific application, we need to analyse the ways in which it encourages particular ways of working through creative practices; the manner in which its design is informing and shaping how we imagine the creative possibilities for using that application.

Another closely related and fundamental facet of software culture, one which facilitates the transformative potential of coded practices, is automation. This enables aspects of a practice to be translated into algorithmic form, and hence opens new possibilities for augmenting and scaling up a practice. By combining different automated processes – sequentially or in parallel – software culture can start to exhibit practices that take on their own distinctive quality, including generating functions which in turn may also become naturalised for software users (Mackenzie 2006: 44).

Automated affordances are central to the seductive power of software environments and include everything from the semi-automated spell-checking function within word processing applications, to a range of more fully automated features of prosumer apps (and online systems) for creating media content. Our reliance on software-based automated functions are a key way in which we give some of our own agency to those software. I have written elsewhere of the example of Magisto, one of a number of automated video editors which use themes, styles and templates for generating edited video sequences from clips fed into them by users (Hight 2014). This is automation designed around the mimicry of professionally edited video content, offered as a service to those who want a user-friendly way of creating attractive, shareable and easily-digested highlights videos while avoiding the actual labour of editing.

There are a range of semi-automated tools typically provided by applications for building interactive content, allowing for the easy generation of timelines, creation of hyperlinks, embedding multimedia content, or using APIs (application programming interfaces) for surfacing content from YouTube, Google Maps and Wikipedia – as does, for example, *Timeline* (Knight Lab 2015). These provide an easy means of creating interactivity, but it is important to recognise that they are also a clear marker of how 'interactivity' has itself been conceived (and coded) in the design of these tools (as is discussed further below).

PERFORMANCE

Software Studies as a field is currently focused more on analysing the logics embedded within software applications themselves than building convincing models of how users understand and use the affordances of particular software tools within specific contexts (Hight 2015). However, it is obviously crucial that we recognise that all forms of software need to be initiated, to be 'run', in order to function. Programming code only becomes of interest when it is put into action by users (or perhaps by other software which has been initiated by users elsewhere). We can characterise users' encounters with software applications using a particular understanding of the notion of 'performance'. Drawing in particular from Brenda Laurel's work (1992), Manovich uses the term more generally to describe all of the ways in which we interact in professional or more everyday settings with software. At a fundamental level, we are collaborating with programming code when we engage with, respond to, or create content using an application or platform. But this is also the point where the 'empowering' or 'disciplining' possibilities of software are actualised. Generating digital content, as with any creative work involving software, involves human users in collaborative performances with a machine. A blank page in a media editor is in one sense a set of endless creative possibilities. However, the application also obviously informs and shapes what and how we perform options for navigating, editing and sharing content. In this sense, there is assumed to be a complex interplay between affordance and performance, which plays out in a unique way each and every time a user engages with any application.

For the field of interactive documentary, this notion of performance opens up new ways of conceiving of the creation, nature and implications of individual works. At some point in the development of their project, the designer and makers of interactive documentary strategically perform particular software tools in order to generate specific sets and hierarchies of affordances which constitute the work itself. These affordances in turn work to allow, foster and shape how users may themselves perform these works, presumably in the pursuit of a documentary experience (as Jon Dovey notes, 'the way a user discovers content, the navigational pathways they follow, will constitute the documentary experience' (2014: 27)). At each stage in this creative cycle, software (in various guises) is an actant in the manner in which forms of media content are generated, configured and made ready to be performed and engaged with by communities of users. Software is central to the production and distribution processes; helping to shape initial research, informing creative inspiration, facilitating communication strategies with collaborators (including subjects of the work), and crucially framing design choices including interactive strategies and the nature of any collaborative potential it promises.

For the designers of interactive documentary, then, one implication of a software studies approach entails a critical awareness of the nature of the (software) tools which are used to build interactive sites and applications. Interactive documentary is created through the performance of these tools, collectively tasked with creating a palette of documentary experiences which may be performed by targeted groups of users.

TOOLS

'The key for us is in the idea of "staging a conversation"; the documentary producer working online with Web 2.0 is called upon to "stage a conversation", with a user community, with research subjects, with participants, co-producers and audiences. The question for the documentary producer is how do we stage that conversation? How do we design the stage?' (Dovey and Rose 2013: 374) The choice of software tools – the applications which are put to use in, for example, developing a site, or application or game – is crucial to the nature of the interactive documentary generated by a specific project. Each tool provides set of affordances, a set of possibilities, as are for example listed on i-docs.org, which are strategically deployed to be performed by designers in pursuit of a specific set of projects. As outlined above, each tool embodies a particular conceptual approach to the creation of content, and while some replicate, simplify or semi-automate existing practices, others open new possibilities for imagining interactive documentary.

It should in fact be possible to chart the history of the interactive documentary through reference to the specific tools used to actualise each project. Once a tool is used to produce an exemplar of the conceptual possibilities it affords, other examples quickly follow. Jon Dovey and Mandy Rose have written of the emergence of new tools for creating these works, such as the now-defunct Popcorn Maker which encouraged the intersection of video and web content in new forms of spatial montage (2012: 164–7). Lev Manovich (2006) provides a partial template for this kind of genealogical work in his analysis of the role of Adobe After Effects in sparking the emergence of the language of motion graphics.

Let us take one example from the more user-friendly part of the spectrum. Racontr is an online system which provides tools to help build a number of interactive forms: i-docs, interactive videos, interactive illustrations, websites, serious games and what the Racontr site terms 'long forms'. The system is a WYSIWYG ('What You See Is What You Get') platform, providing helpful templates and the easy insertion of web-based features such as rollovers, hypertext links and embedded multimedia. Its creative paradigm is most obvious in its support for designers of interactive video (where the aim is to insert links to supplementary material for audiovisual linear narratives), but it also is exhibited in the types of templates it provides, and the specific exemplars, it gives of 'i-docs' and related forms. This is a system which assumes designers will use its tools to create narrative-centred interactive forms. Here, 'interactivity' involves adding functionality and layers to allow multiple pathways through content which is fundamentally story-based. These aspects of Racontr are important because they help to shape the nature of what is built using the system, including what functionality is provided for users to perform.

In contrast, let us turn to Adrian Miles' (2014a) analysis of the Korsakow system – a different tool used for developing interactive media. Instead of working to replicate the rhetorical and affective work of documentary film narrative, Korsakow demands a programming approach which prioritises the agency of the final (software) project: here, users function as a trigger for semi-automated forms of association. Users' encounters of (some, not all) Korsakow works are not intended to follow a carefully designed script but to set up the conditions and parameters for users to explore the pleasures of engaging with the combinatorial possibilities of audiovisual documents: 'Korsakow allows, and is premised upon, the creation of multiple, simultaneous links, that is relations, between the individual video clips that make up a K-film, and it is the simultaneous multiplicity of these relations that is Korsakow's most significant quality in the context of interactive documentary more broadly. [...] My elevator pitch would be that Korsakow is software for authoring generative, associative, and processual films. These films are complex, possibly autopoetic systems that rely on patterns of relation to emerge for author and users' (2014a: 209). It is important to the nature of Korsakow works that the designers will add a degree of complexity where they cannot know all of the possible outcomes of how their work might be performed (2014a: 212). The interplay between designer, user and the agency of the software itself is of a very different order to more carefully crafted narrative-centred interactive works which generate a limited set of possible pathways. As reflected in the ethos of Racontr, such works sometimes seem to be a limited step beyond the initial experiments with interactive non-fictional works on DVD formats which were deeply informed by the assumptions of cinematic forms of narrative and spectatorship. Examples of this might include Marsha Kinder's work on the Labyrinth Project (1997, ongoing).

The more complex and ambitious Korsakow works involve an explicitly co-creative practice between the user and software which involves playing with a far greater multitude of juxtapositional potentialities. Miles refers to the design process demanded by the Korsakow system as 'programmatic choreography', aimed at producing a 'dance between the programmatic, video, sound, author, user, and the processual logic of the computational' (2014a: 216). He likens the structure of the resulting real-time software-based performances as closer to musical forms of composition rather than narrativist creations (2014a: 218). The ability of Korsakow to make explicit the potential for co-creation with software ultimately provides a distinctive kind of 'documentary' experience. The user may be exploring material through a series of tangents, semi-random associational linkages and intended and unintended loops; all operations which would be confusing and even infuriating if the user were to encounter these as part of a promised narrative experience.

Racontr and Korsakow are just two among many new tools for developing interactive media forms. In a broader sense, the emergence and development of the possibilities for interactive documentary are symptomatic of the pace of evolution within this part of software culture. Interactive documentary designers are continually looking to strategically exploit the potential of new technologies, in order to engage potential users in the work of generating new forms of documentary experience. Software culture continually enables the pursuit of new ways of creating and thinking of media content. If we consider a very broad definition of interactive non-fictional forms to include everything from websites where users click through content, to sites where users make use of collaborative tools, through to more semi-automated and fully automated forms of engagement such as on gaming platforms, their common base is perhaps only that they feature software-based components being performed in real-time rather than allowing engagement 'with pre-defined static documents' (Manovich 2012).

A key reason why interactive documentary remains an experimental form (Aufderheide 2015) is that the basic set of technologies which are used to build these sites, applications, games and new software-based environments, are not themselves stable. There is yet to emerge within software culture an engine for media creation anything like the comparatively slowly mutating apparatus which underlies more than a century of feature film production. The combinatorial evolution of software culture, where new media components continue to be malleable with changes in the underlying architecture of platforms and operating systems, means that forms of software-based non-fiction continually take on new and unexpected inflections. Only some elements have become codified, such as the default possibilities for navigating through timeline or map interfaces, or an option to 'play' a site as a movie. What constitutes 'documentary' within this context is often familiar but also challenging the conceptual thinking of media designers (as well as rapidly outpacing the usefulness of theoretical tools developed for twentieth century mass media).

MAKING MEANING AND MAKING SENSE

A useful distinction to make within this environment is that between 'making meaning' which is possible through the spatial and temporal combination of any variety of media elements, and the more difficult strategic exercise of encouraging users to 'make sense' through their engagement with specific pathways through media fragments. As Craig Hight and Ramaswami Harindranath state: 'Within a digital ecology characterised by rapidly expanding social practices of documentation, including streams of visual and audio-visual material designed to be shareable within the algorithmic processes of social networks, documentary takes on distinctive new characteristics and roles. Within this environment of expanding ephemera, documentary retains its significance as a discourse and series of practices which "make sense" of digital materials which are aligned with reality, which carry the "ethical charge" of the real. Documentary is refashioned as a number of specific assemblages within networked media; as a curatorial imperative, a rhetorical template for designing pathways through online databases of everyday documents, a discourse to be applied into the design of multimedia sites, and an embedded logic within new forms of software tools available to an expanded continuum of practitioners' (2014: 177).

It is much easier to make meaning through the combination of any number of even disparate media elements, but making sense suggests aiming for an underlying coherence in the cognitive and/or affective experience of the user – something which remains an ideal for interactive documentary because of the common-sense assumption of most designers that the ultimate aim of any interactive documentary is to tell a story. This conceptual approach toward interactive documentary seems to be embedded in most of the tools built for interactive designers. Again, one exception is Korsakow.

Miles, in his excellent analysis of the Korsakow system (2014b), nicely summarises the ways in which this kind of software tool generates continuities and discontinuities with linear documentary forms. He returns to the 'granularity' of films, where each individual shot has a meaning in and of itself but can be combined through editing with other shots in innumerable possible sequences in order to create coherence for viewers: 'Cinema and interactive works share the common problem of being relational media that have a fragmentary deep structure. These fragments are small, understandable, parts that can be assembled into larger forms, generally considered to be the work proper. Cinema and interactive documentary therefore share the common problem: simply, how to make something whole from smaller fragmentary parts where, in both cases, these fragments are already whole' (2014b: 69).

Linear documentaries – that is, televisual and cinematic documentary – are required to 'make sense' in a deeply sequential, narrative way. They tend not to be accepted by funders, broadcasters, distributors (or audiences) if they do not conform to this paradigm. And the nature of the software applications used to create such media are inevitably coded this way as well. However much functionality is added to successive generations of digital nonlinear editors (DNLE), and despite the greater flexibility they allow to generate multiple versions of texts from the same material, these applications are still literally and conceptually organised around 'timelines'. The notion of 'editing' fostered by DNLE is an expanded variation of a well-established creative paradigm. Similarly, After Effects, as Manovich (2006) has detailed, allows for a more fluid 'remixability' of the techniques for creating animation, typefaces and moulding live action – the basis of motion graphics – but it still requires the marshalling of this expanded palette of affordances toward familiar sequential constructions.

Interactive forms have the potential to generate new possibilities for the engagement of users, by requiring the works to be performed by users. It is only then that a documentary experience is created, as users prompt a move from the 'virtual' set of possible linkages to the 'actual' set of materials which are generated through each user's encounter with an interactive form. Miles states that 'the difference of the database is not the possibility of different, or new sorts, of connections (literal, thematic, associative, disjunctive, temporal, atemporal) but the open multiplicity of these different connections being maintained as a structural possibility after the creation and distribution of the work' (2014b: 71).

Miles argues that the task of the designers is 'about choreographing the number and density of the possible connections available between granular parts' (2014b: 76). Different media elements might be arranged temporally or spatially as possibilities for action, but whether a user's performance works to 'make sense' of the various fragments contained within the interactive documentary is dependent upon the specific co-creative performance which she makes with the affordances the documentary provides. Korsakow is a software application which deliberately fosters, and even demands, a distinctive conceptual approach toward the design of documentary 'experiences' – one which moves us away from linear narrative form. The deeply processual and associative examples of Korsakow are certainly aimed at making meaning but not necessarily concerned with users' ability to generate sense out of their collective of materials.

There is a similar framework underlying Sandra Gaudenzi's conception of 'living documentary' (2013), where she focuses on interactive documentaries 'as relational objects, artefacts that link technologies and subjects and that create themselves through such interaction. My hypothesis is that an artefact that is relational in its core essence cannot be studied as a finite form but needs to be addressed through the complex series of relations that form it, and that it forms' (2013: 12). Gaudenzi has been particularly interested in the design of different strategies for the collaborative creation of content. She has outlined a taxonomy of the ways in which interactive designers might allow, and work to shape, forms of creative work on the part of users, with content which then accumulates from a variety of users to grow a site: 'When we speak about participatory documentary, we should specify that there are different possible moments of participation. The production life of interactive documentaries is, in most cases, split into four parts: preproduction (research and ideas); production (technical realisation of the platform itself, which involves coding, and production of some content); launch of the digital platform (often populated by little content); and user's content production. [...] In an interactive documentary there is therefore a distinction between the production of the interactive framework (designing the wireframe, coding of the website and the user interface) and the production of the content that is going to populate such interactive form' (2014: 142).

Her subsequent discussions focus on three key questions for designers which are integral to design and implementation of these kinds of interactive projects: 'Who is invited to participate?', 'What can the participant do?' and 'When is the collaboration happening?' (2014: 130). Perhaps missing from this discussion is an acknowledgement that these are all questions which are inevitably posed and enacted *through* software; that software needs to be acknowledged as an actant in this production life cycle.

Gaudenzi's examples, such as the sequence of *Highrise* (Cizek *et al* 2010) projects funded through the National Film Board of Canada, have at their heart a rich and deeply collaborative practice with the site's subjects and participants and with broader members of the research and design teams which drive the projects to fruition. At crucial stages of these projects, however, as (implicitly) outlined in the quote included above, these are also practices which are progressively embedded within programming code. And inherent to the design of affordances for collaboration are the possibilities and constraints enabled by the selection of software tools used to build a collaborative architecture. *Highrise* is still a deeply linear project, geared toward the objective of users making (a particular) sense of its subject. Interactivity is consequently defined within quite tightly prescribed parameters: what is available for users to perform is largely limited to a small set of operations for accessing and viewing/reading/listening to content.

WHAT ABOUT THE USERS?

So far I have outlined a still largely abstract set of ideas about the significance of software within the emergence of interactive documentary and its significance as a distinctive set of media forms. To reiterate: an interactive documentary form is not in itself a 'documentary' in the traditional sense, but it offers the potential for a documentary experience when performed by a user – and the nature of the performance/experience is intimately related to the design of the tools used to create it in the first place. Outside of the specific skills and conceptual inspirations which designers bring to the design of interactive documentaries, the key components of these performances are the set of assumptions *about* users which are embedded at the level of code, and the particular collective of attitudes, motivations, media experiences and other literacies which each user bring to their contingent, embodied performances.

Ultimately, this aspect of a software studies approach to interactive documentary implies investigating questions of users' agency and its cultural and political implications. Janet Murray defines [user] agency within interactive media more broadly as 'an aesthetic pleasure characteristic of digital environments, which results from the well-formed exploitation of the procedural and participatory properties. When the behavior of the computer is coherent and the results of participation are clear and well motivated, the interactor experiences the pleasure of agency, of making something happen in a dynamically responsive world' (2011: 410).

Unspoken here is the need to acknowledge the empowering and disciplining possibilities of various forms of software across the diversity of social, cultural, economic and political contexts in which that software is performed by users. A broad assumption underlying this approach is that the nature of the 'software literacies' which each user draws upon for specific practices effectively serve to contextualise their agency. I have written elsewhere in more detail on a tentative schema for software literacies, which can be understood to range from a basic skill in using a piece of software, through competency in trouble-shooting problems with an application, and ultimately to the ability to critique the affordances of applications and platforms and develop a critical literacy toward the broader role of software in shaping creative and communicative agency (Hight 2015: 71).

The growing literature on the persistence of a 'digital divide' highlights the range of factors which shape and constrain the participation of different user communities within networked media more generally. David Brake's (2014) overview of research into those user groups more likely to be active contributors to Web 2.0 media, for example, highlights how skewed these kinds of practices are towards a comparatively small percentage of users who are active contributors to collaborative media platforms, and an online population which tends to have greater resources, higher education and higher income. There are also some distinctive kinds of user groups across different countries, shaped inevitably by broader configurations of accessibility to networked technologies. These patterns also become more complex when researchers look to identify specific kinds of hardware and software tools which users are most competent and confident in using, which is still an area comparatively neglected within this research field (2014: 3–4). In a similar vein, John Horrigan's (2007) typology of ICT identifies ten different groups of (American) Web 2.0 users and non-users, ranging from the heaviest users (including those who did not have a great deal of access or resources), a middle range of distinct user groups who had access to lots of hardware and software but were nonetheless uncomfortable with the demands of extra connectivity, and groups in the lower end of the spectrum who were happy with a relative scarcity of information goods and services.

Ultimately, such research paints a picture of a rich variety of motivations on the part of users to engage in online and collaborative media, who have a wide range of resources and means to gain access to and use technology, and a similar variability in their willingness to explore the full affordances of connectivity within participatory media. These patterns grow more complex when analysed in relation to typical demographic groupings (such as across age, gender and ethnicity) and intersected with clear preferences for some tools over others and a lingering ambivalence toward the use of any new technology.

Obviously, this is a challenging environment in which to be designing interactive documentary experiences. Each project assumes the kinds of interactive strategies which might gain the attention and active participation of targeted users, and works to implement these into familiar but distinctive sets of interfaces and affordances. Empowering some groups of users inevitably marginalises others with differing motivations or literacies for specific kinds of interactivity. For a set of forms which are still experimental and lacking a demonstrably wide user base, this is an area which desperately needs greater empirical research.

Added to these challenges is a series of ethical concerns implicit in the forms of engagement afforded by an interactive documentary. How are users at this end provided agency and what are the implications of this? For documentary film-makers, ethical practices play out in their encounters with subjects and more especially in the editing room as audiovisual material is massaged into storytelling forms by framing and juxtaposing fragments of material in new ways (in Miles' terms, the point when the 'virtual' becomes the 'actual' documentary). The inevitable translation of any documentary-maker's encounters with topics and participants into something palatable and compelling for an audience is naturally fraught with ethical dilemmas. These take on more vexing permutations within interactive documentaries in part because meaning making is generated through users' co-creative performances of interactive works. Where documentary film largely works to predetermine a particular position which viewers take toward their human subjects, interactive documentary helps to establish a variety of new relationships – and especially those, both direct and indirect, *between* participants and other users. As this chapter has hopefully made clear, these are all relationships mediated by and through the software which is deployed and generated by each project.

REFERENCES

Aufderheide, Patricia (2015) 'Interactive documentaries: navigation and design', *Journal of Film and Video*, 67, 3/4, 69–78.

Berry, David M. (2011) *The Philosophy of Software: Code and Mediation in the Digital Age*. New York: Palgrave Macmillan.

Brake, David R. (2014) 'Are we all online content creators now? Web 2.0 and digital divides', *Journal of Computer-Mediated Communication*, 19, 3, 591–609.

Cizek, Kat *et al* (2010) *Highrise*. Web documentary series. Produced by Gerry Flahive, co-produced by NFB; http://highrise.nfb.ca/. Accessed 31 October 2016.

Dovey, Jon (2014) 'Documentary ecosystems: collaboration and exploitation', in Kate Nash, Craig Hight and Catherine Summerhayes (eds) *New Documentary Ecologies: Emerging Platforms, Practices and Discourses*. New York: Palgrave Macmillan, 11–32.

Dovey, Jon and Mandy Rose (2012) 'We're happy and we know it: Documentary, data, montage', *Studies in Documentary Film*, 6, 2, 159–73.

____ (2013) "This Great Mapping of Ourselves': New documentary forms online', in Brian Winston (ed.) *The Documentary Film Book*. London: BFI Press, 366–375.

Fuller, Mathew (ed.) (2008) *Software Studies: A Lexicon*. Cambridge, MA: MIT Press.

Galloway, Alexander R. (2004) *Protocol: How Control Exists After Decentralisation*. Cambridge, MA: MIT Press.

Gaudenzi, Sandra (2013) 'The interactive documentary as a living documentary'. Doc online 14; http://www.doc.ubi.pt/14/dossier_sandra_gaudenzi.pdf. Accessed 31 October 2014.

____ (2014) 'Strategies of participation: the who, what and when of collaborative documentaries', in Kate Nash, Craig Hight and Catherine Summerhayes (eds) *New Documentary Ecologies: Emerging Platforms, Practices and Discourses*. New York: Palgrave Macmillan, 129–148.

Hight, Craig (2014) 'Automation within digital videography: From the Ken Burns Effect to 'meaning-making' engines', *Studies in Documentary Film*, 8, 3, 235–50.

____ (2015) 'Software studies and the new audiencehood of the digital ecology', in Frauke Zeller, Cristina Ponte and Brian O'Neill (eds) *Revitalising Audience Research: Innovations in European Audience Research*. New York Routledge, 62–79.

Hight, Craig and Ramaswami Harindranath (2014) 'Documentary as sense-making', *Studies in Documentary Film*, 8, 3, 177–8.

Horrigan, John B. (2007) 'A typology of information and communication technology users', Pew Internet and American Life Project, 7 May; http://195.130.87.21:8080/dspace/handle/123456789/554. Accessed 31 October 2016.

i-docs.org (2014) 'Tools'; http://i-docs.org/2014/07/15/interactive-documentary-tools/. Accessed 31 October 2016.

Kinder, Marsha (1997) 'About the Labyrinth Project'. https://dornsife.usc.edu/labyrinth/about/about1.html. Accessed 31 October 2016.

Kitchin, Rob and Martin Dodge (2011) *Code/Space: Software and Everyday Life*. Cambridge, MA: MIT Press.

Knight Lab (2015) *Timeline*. Online Application. Co-produced by Northestern University and Knight Foundation http://timeline.knightlab.com. Accessed 31 October 2016.

Laurel, Brenda (1992) *Computers as Theatre*. Boston: Addison Wesley Longman.

Mackenzie, Adrian (2006) *Cutting Code: Software and Sociality*. New York: Peter Lang.

Manovich, Lev (2006) 'After Effects or the Velvet Revolution', *Millennium Film Journal*, 45/46, 5–19.

____ (2012) 'How to Follow Software Users'; http://lab.softwarestudies.com/p/publications.html. Accessed 31 October 2016.

____ (2013) *Software Takes Command: International Texts in Critical Media Aesthetics*. New York: Bloomsbury.

McGrenere, Joanna and Wayne Ho (2000) 'Affordances: Clarifying and Evolving a Concept', *Conference Proceedings of Graphics Interface 2000*, 15–17 May 2000, Montreal, 179–86.

Miles, Adrian (2014a) 'Materialism and interactive documentary: sketch notes', *Studies in Documentary Film*, 8, 3, 205–20.

____ (2014b) 'Interactive documentary and affective ecologies', in Kate Nash, Craig Hight and Catherine Summerhayes (eds) *New Documentary Ecologies: Emerging Platforms, Practices and Discourses*. Houndmills, Palgrave Macmillan, 67–82.

Murray, Janet H. (2011) *Inventing the Medium: Principles of Interaction Design as a Cultural Practice*. Cambridge, MA: MIT Press.

van Dijck, Jose (2013) *The Culture of Connectivity: A Critical History of Social Media*. Oxford: Oxford University Press.

2 METHODS

PREFACE

Sandra Gaudenzi

This section of the book explores how processes coming from storytelling, design, software and gaming are currently merging into new methods of production for interactive documentaries.

Ten years after *Journey to the End of Coal* (Samuel Bollendorff, 2008) – one of the first projects to be officially called an interactive documentary after being released on French newspaper lemonde.fr – i-doc production is still considered more a craft than an industry: a few pockets of expertise seem to have worked out their own production flows, but this knowledge is not widely shared. We are still in the exciting, but somehow chaotic, stage of the i-doc cottage industry.

It is within this context that this section of the book wants to bring forward some examples of successful methodologies, hoping to disseminate best practices and encourage sharing of production processes. For this, we have interviewed some renowned pioneers in the field, looked at future digital trends, selected case studies to observe how software and design methodologies might be applied to storytelling and focused on where, and why, creative tensions might arise in production teams.

Samuel Gantier and Michel Labour use the case study of *B4, Windows on Towers* to disentangle some of the tensions that can arise within web-doc production in the television environment, when 'real users' are not at the centre of the production process because the team players are referring to their own 'ideal users'. How can different professional backgrounds, interests and expectations result in weak design is the question at the heart of such investigation.

Sandra Gaudenzi, digs further into the cultural reasons for teams misunderstandings and clashes. She particularly analyses the difference in creative approach and expectations between the designers and filmmakers she has observed through her research project the *UX Series* and the professional training initiative *IF Lab* which she is involved with.

An interview with Lance Weiler, pioneer in transmedia and co-creation, reveals the origins and thinking behind the Learn Do Share methodology. How can design thinking help us create documentaries with better impact?

Through the case study of the POV Hackathons, Jess Linington describes in detail how agile software methodologies and multi-disciplinary teams can be used to spark new projects, promote cross-industry collaboration and push the boundaries of current digital storytelling.

Ramona Pringle shares her own experience, and best practices, in user testing while creating *Avatars Secrets*. How did constant testing help the team to stay focused and create a successful tablet narrative?

Finally, Ben Moskowitz questions what happens when social issue storytellers embrace techniques pioneered by the advertising industry: quantitative measurement, behavioural profiling and personalisation. He argues that adopting some practices of these 'watchers' can provide a strategy to subvert and critique them, and invites us to ponder potential ethical issues.

EVALUATING USERS' EXPERIENCES
A CASE STUDY APPROACH TO IMPROVING
I-DOC UX DESIGN

Samuel Gantier and Michel Labour

INTRODUCTION

Hundreds of interactive documentaries (i-docs) have been published on the Internet since 2005. Despite the apparent success of i-docs (Gantier 2012; Gaudenzi 2013: 247), it appears that a great majority of them do not keep their users beyond a few minutes.[1] How can one explain this? One response is that i-docs are particularly challenging as an emerging form, as they mix the language of documentary films with that of computational and interactive 'computerised media' (Jeanneret 2007). In effect, an i-doc is of a hybrid nature, which merges a graphic interface with an audiovisual flow (Gantier 2016). In this context, the aim of our study is to establish an i-doc user experience evaluation methodology.

To present the study, first an archetypal 'model user' drawn from the minds of professionals (filmmakers, producers, web coders, graphic designers, television broadcasters) involved in the designing of the i-doc *B4, Fenêtres sur tour* (Ribot 2012, *B4, Windows on Towers*) is portrayed. Second, we describe a novel tri-dimensional evaluation model. Third, in an empirical case study, we examine how two user groups experienced different viewing modes, some usability problems and the informational architecture of *B4*. Fourth, we examine how users sought to make sense of their i-doc experience. Finally, the gap between the 'model user' and 'empiric user' is advanced, along with recommendations to improve i-doc design.

1. ARCHETYPAL 'MODEL USER'

The study began when one of the researchers of this chapter, Samuel Gantier, was employed as a film editor on the six-month-long design of the i-doc *B4*. It provided an opportunity to observe how the design team imagined the archetypal 'model user' (Gantier and Labour 2015).[2] The identification of a 'model user' effectively crystallises a set of sociotechnical negotiations (Akrich 2006) and semio-pragmatic elements (Jeanneret and Souchier 2005), which conditions both the informational architecture and the interaction design of the i-doc and its 'film-interface'.[3]

1.1 Informational architecture of *B4*

B4 is an adaptation of the experimental novel of Georges Perec, *La Vie mode d'emploi* (2010 [1978]), which explores the fictional possibilities of algorithmic logic (see Hartje *et al* 1993). *B4* re-interprets Perec's exploration on how twelve inhabitants of a virtual twelve-storey inner-city block of flats feel about their neighbourhood. At the heart of the i-doc are 96 'documentary haïkus' of two to three minutes, totalling 180 minutes.

If one views, for example, six videos (for about fifteen minutes), and if one takes into account all the possible sequences of watching the haïkus, users have a choice of 667 billion different viewing paths. The *B4* architecture offers three navigation modes.

1. A *vertical* viewing mode presents a series of twelve characters in a specific haïku pattern. The mode is found by clicking on the columns of the virtual block of flats, or by clicking haphazardly on the décor.

2. A *horizontal* viewing mode focuses on each character of *B4*. Users click on the rows of windows of the building.

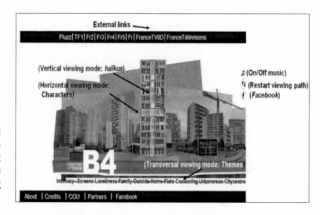

Fig. 1: *B4* informational architecture. Users can switch on or off the default background neighbourhood sounds of children playing and passing trains.

3. A *transversal* viewing mode offers the different themes of the videos. This is situated at the bottom of the screen.

1.2 Interaction design and user choice

During participant-observation of the *B4* design team, a central issue was deciding which actions should be system-driven, and which should be user-driven. This shows how, when viewing an i-doc, users are placed in a dialectical tension between the 'cognitive ease' of letting the i-doc system decide what is watched, and the 'cognitive effort' of letting users decide as 'spec-actors' (Barboza and Weissberg 2006) what to watch. User-driven decisions depend, however, on knowing what the options are.

Regarding the question of providing users with (choice giving) 'clickable' possibilities, Serge Bouchardon (2009) distinguishes between 'conventional engagements' (where the ergonomics of a system seek to increase the coherence of the narrative) and 'non-conventional engagements' (users do not find what they expect). According to Yves Jeanneret and Emmanuël Souchier (2005) when users find confusing on-screen features, they disengage.

In this context, the *B4* design team differed about how much leeway to give to users. Short of conducting tests to find out what users thought about the *B4* design, the in-team discussions focused around three key points.

1. The author-director and the graphic designer wanted to give users *minimal guidance*. Users were expected to discover in an open-ended, trial-and-error approach how the i-doc was organised *via* a series of non-conventional engagements (Bouchardon 2009).

2. The producer and development web coder pushed for a *semi-guided* user approach. They argued for visual decision-aiding graphics that would suggest how the videos were organised. They proposed that when a user clicks inside a window of the block of flats, the floors (horizontal line) and columns (vertical line) of the building simultaneously and momentarily light up to create an intersecting cross. This approach sought to reduce the users' cognitive effort as a way to limit disengagement.

3. The department director of France Télévisions Nouvelles Écritures (co-producer of *B4*) argued to embed established web design conventions. This design decision can be considered as providing 'conventional engagement' (Bouchardon 2009). It reinforced the decision to light up the horizontal and vertical lines of the block of flats.

1.3 Model User's viewing path

During the official launch of *B4*, its author-director created a 39-minute film focused exclusively on the *vertical* mode of viewing *B4*. The film represents an effective portray of a 'model user'. In this light, it would seem useful to compare the vertical viewing mode *B4* 'model user' to a data-based 'empiric user' inferred from a study of users' declared experiences.

2 EVALUATION OF USERS' EXPERIENCES

2.1 Research methodology

Focusing on user experience can highlight or diminish different aspects of an i-doc depending on the domain of reference (technological, ergonomical, emotional, cognitive, aesthetical, semio-pragmatic, etc). In interaction design, notably in the 'new documentary writing' domain, user experience is often described as 'an individual's perceptions of his/her interaction with a product, service, or environment' (Drouillat 2013).[4] For researchers such a description lacks precision, hence limiting its effective use. It is thus necessary to explain what is meant by 'user experience' in the *B4* context, namely concerning the evaluation dimensions.

Following the work on the metrics of interface usability (e.g. Baccino *et al* 2005) and multimedia documents (e.g. Huart *et al* 2008), the empirical analysis of *B4* users' experience was focused on the systemic[5] interaction of three dimensions (see figure 2):

1. *Viewing frame.* Given that i-docs are relatively ill-defined (Gaudenzi 2013: 26), viewers do not know what to expect or what to do. This can negatively impact on establishing the appropriate viewing 'frame' to enable users to adapt their interpretive 'belief system' to a document (Pignier and Drouillat 2005).[6] In this light, one hypothesis of our hypothetico-deductive study is that an i-doc viewing frame involves a simultaneous 'documentarising' (Odin 2011) and 'ludic' viewing mode (Genvo 2013).
2. *Usability.* This is described as the 'degree to which a product can be used by specifically identified users to attain a defined objective with efficacy, efficiency and satisfaction in a given context of use' (Bonnier 2013: 147). For an i-doc, usability can be seen as the extent to which a film-interface becomes meaningful for users in a given reception context.
3. *Sense-making.* This draws on the work of researchers like Brenda Dervin and Patrica Dewdney (1986), and more recently that of Michel Labour (2011). Sense-making research attempts to understand the construction of context-bound problem-solving constructs.

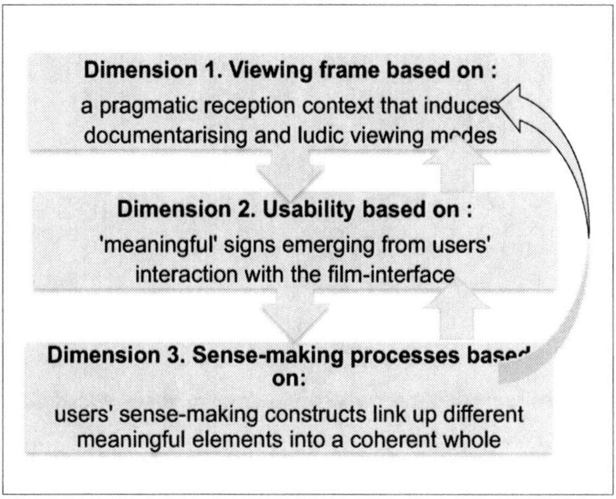

Fig. 2: The systemic tri-dimensional i-doc UX evaluation model. The model formally identifies three key interactive dimensions in an apparent top-down linear logic. In practice, however, the dimensions function as an interdependent emerging functional whole. An evaluation of i-doc usage should thus take into account the realities of actual use which go beyond formally identified 'dimensions' conceived for research purposes.

Dimension 1. Viewing frame based on :
a pragmatic reception context that induces documentarising and ludic viewing modes

Dimension 2. Usability based on :
'meaningful' signs emerging from users' interaction with the film-interface

Dimension 3. Sense-making processes based on:
users' sense-making constructs link up different meaningful elements into a coherent whole

Figure 2 summarises the tri-dimensional *B4* evaluation model based on interactive (via iterative loops) 'documentarising' and 'ludicising' viewing modes.

2.2 Working hypotheses

User experience evaluated	Underlying concepts	Working hypotheses
1. Viewing frame	Ludicising and documentarising viewing mode	H1: A successful viewing frame 'balances' the ludicising and documentarising viewing modes such that both emerge simultaneously.
2. Usability	Affordance and go-between signs	H2: Not grasping signs embedded in a film-interface creates problems of usability.
	Architecture of the informational and paratext	H3: The presence of decision-aiding paratexts increases the use of different viewing modes.
3. Sense-making processes	Sense-making constructs, Senselessness, Sense-making break	H4: The type of viewing mode impacts on sense-making processes.

Fig. 3: Hypotheses regarding users' experiences.

An advantage of a quantitative approach, like web metrics, is that it indicates the frequency and the duration of visits to i-docs. However, it is not enough to portray users' experiences. We contend that a qualitative and empirical experimental approach is also needed to understand how different users 'make sense' of i-docs. In this context, our evaluation was trialled in a pre-study that crystallised four working 'falsifiable hypotheses' (Popper 2007) of users' experiences, taking into consideration the three dimensions identified earlier (see figure 3). These hypotheses were tested by using a set research method.

2.3 Research method

In 2014, twelve users, aged from twenty to thirty years, were recruited on the basis that they had never met the researchers before the study, and were media and web literate. Users were randomly divided into two equal groups: A and B. The main difference between the groups was that only Group B received a decision-aiding 'paratext' (explicative text about a text) that explained the informational architecture of *B4* in the following way: 'The i-doc gives you the possibility of meeting twelve inhabitants of an inner-city block of flats. As you can see from the picture [see figure 1, above] you can view 96 videos in three viewing modes: Main characters mode, Type of films mode, Themes of *B4* mode.'

Before viewing *B4*, groups A (without paratext) and B (with paratext) were given the same verbal instructions: 'I would like you to discover the site *B4*. Have you already seen the web site? (If the answer is 'Yes', the user is asked to leave the room). Feel free to view the site in any way you wish. Afterwards, I would like to speak to you about how you viewed the site.'

Viewers spent about thirty minutes viewing the i-doc (see figure 4, below). In order to monitor users' viewing paths, a tracking software of users' clicks was installed on computers used in the experiment. After the viewing session, users agreed to fill in a self-evaluating Visual Analog Scale (VAS) questionnaire (preferences are indicated on a sliding scale of 0–100) and participated in a semi-guided interview about their *B4* experience.

3. EMPIRIC USER

3.1 Viewing frame (Hypothesis 1)

Documentarising viewing
Roger Odin (2011) defines 'documentarising viewing' as a user interpretative ('reception') skill that gives a text its 'documented value'. This rests on context-bound semio-pragmatic elements allowing users to infer the documentary value

of a text from its viewing situation. One function of the documentarising mode is that it allows users to establish who is responsible for the discursive and mood aspects of a text. In this way, users can symbolically question issues of 'identity of action and of truth' (2011: 56). The viewer is thus in a position to criticise the 'enunciator' (the one who appears to be responsible for the discursive and mood aspects of a text). In short, the credibility of a documentary is never guaranteed, as it involves a user's interpretative process: 'At the end the day, the i-doc says there is not one sole way of speaking about inner-cities. So I said to myself, why is there no inhabitant in a difficult economic situation in the films? Is this a deliberate choice of the film director? I wonder if the situation is not a bit distorted because the i-doc only shows more or less well-off inhabitants. In my opinion, the director should have shown what "really" exists, that is to say the socio-economic reality of the inner-city block of flats' (Gantier 2014a).[7]

Our study showed that overall, groups A and B accepted, without question, that the characters really lived in a Parisian inner-city. From this, one can infer that users successfully adopted a documentarising viewing mode in perceiving the inhabitants of *B4* as credible enunciators. In this sense, the *B4* characters and the users shared a common communication space based on an underlying 'agreement of trust' (Soulez 2004). This agreement is the outcome of a dialectic relationship between what the author states about the world and what the viewer thinks of the world. Guillaume Soulez describes this situation as the inevitable 'communicational challenge' of a documentary film director wanting viewer endorsement.

Ludicising viewing

For Sébastien Genvo, the idea of a ludicising mode involves playability, a ludic ethos, and a 'Model Player' that reinforces user involvement. By ludic ethos is meant 'a structure that seeks to persuade its user that "this is play"' (2013: 134) in echo to Gregory Bateson (2000: 178).

When users were asked to self-evaluate (using a VAS questionnaire) their ludic attitude when viewing *B4*, there was a 44 per cent difference between the highest (92 per cent) and the lowest score (48 per cent), with an overall average level of 73 per cent (see figure 5, below). This indicates that users' experiences of *B4* were in general playfully ludic. In this vein, it appears that the trial-and-error exploration of the film-interface provided some pleasure, notably concerning the parallax effect of the buildings and the random graphic animation of the i-doc décor.

Even if the trial-and-error mode is often encouraged in interactive media, it does not appear to trigger lasting user involvement (i.e. being 'engrossed, caught up, enthralled'; Goffman 1986: 345) with i-docs. This was illustrated in the analysis of User 11A's viewing paths. This user declared having adopted a ludic attitude level of 78 per cent, yet had not viewed a single video in its entirety. Given the limited time constraints of the viewing situation, the plethora of viewing choices and the absence of comment from the viewers about wanting to go back and relook at videos during the post-viewing interviews, it can be inferred that the determining factor appears not to be the 'ludic attitude', but the cognitive effort needed to understand the playability rules of an i-doc.

The effort required to grasp the three viewing modes of *B4* appeared to be high for users (see User 9B's comments, below). It was only once the informational architecture of *B4* had been assimilated that, according to a user, a ludic attitude became useful. 'I find the concept of a block of flats interesting but I did not answer "completely ludic" because it took me some time to understand how things work. I did not always understand the different categories. When I am on the Internet, I don't want to search how to do things. I prefer to have all that info quickly. I want to learn stuff, and searching how to understand how the site is built is too tedious' (Gantier 2014b).

Figure 4 summarises the degree to which users perceived the lucidity level of the film-interface. The overall result shows that the perception of playful ludicity was seen as relatively high (73.7 per cent), with only a three point difference between Group A (75.5 per cent) and Group B (72 per cent).

	Users	%
Group A (without paratext)	U2	70
	U5	73
	U6	89
	U8	79
	U10	64
	U11	78
	Average	75.5
Group B (with paratext)	U1	80
	U3	80
	U4	92
	U7	56
	U9	60
	U12	64
	Average	72
	Overall average	73.7

Fig. 4: Perceptions of the ludicity level of *B4*

3.2 Usability (Hypothesis 2)

In evaluating *B4*, the analysis of on-screen actions indicated how users perceived, understood and used the 'affordances' and 'go-between' signs (see figure 5) of the film-interface and attendant problems of usability.

Highlighted affordances

Donald Norman (2013: 10) defines an affordance as 'the relationship between the properties of an object and the agent's capacity to determine how the object could possibly be used'. The effectiveness of an affordance rests on informing users what possible actions can be taken without needing further guidance.

In the case of *B4*, after users click inside a window, the horizontal and vertical lines light-up as a momentary, yellow intersecting cross (see figure 1) as an intended affordance. The data show that 92 per cent of users did not see that the highlighted cross was a visual aid indicating the organisation of videos (see figure 5). In addition, 77 per cent of users did not grasp that the flashing cross indicated an entrance hall of the building that was clickable on what to watch, or not, as one of the test people stated: 'I saw the lighted sign, but it did not strike me that it could have been useful. I did not see it as something significant. For me, it was decorative' (Gantier 2014c).

At least two reasons can explain why most users did not click on the intersecting cross. First, when a user clicks on a video, a video player springs up in the middle of the screen, effectively blocking out the flashing light of the cross. Second, the lack of a label to explain the cross, differs from the logic of other parts of the film-interface that links the name of each character to a video, as User 5A's comments: 'I did not see the light in the hallway because the video player was in front of it. I didn't click on it probably because there wasn't a text to it. In the other windows, I know they were links because they had titles. When the lines flashed, I thought it was an animation – like permanent hazard warning lights at [French] railway crossings – that was not clickable. When I see a text that changes, I say to myself that something is clickable, but here it just flashed when my mouse was not over it, so I thought it was decorative' (Gantier 2014d).

Go-between signs

In the theory of screen writings ('écrits d'écran') of Yves Jeanneret and Emmanuël Souchier (2005), 'go-between signs' ('signes passeurs') are described as sign-tools (icons, words, buttons, etc) indicating what the viewer can decide to use. The go-between signs thus add a perfomative aspect to an i-doc. The design of such signs creates a dialectical tension between the graphic image of the sign and the norms of on-screen usage. In this way, clicking on an on-screen sign depends on

		Highlighted affordances		Instrumental go-between signs		
User	Win-dows	Inter-section Viewing mode	Entr-ance hall	Music on/off	Restart viewing path	*Facebook* sharing
1	Yes	No	Yes	No	No	Yes
2	Yes	No	Yes	No	No	Yes
3	Yes	No	Yes	No	No	Yes
4	Yes	Yes	No	Yes	Yes	Yes
5	Yes	No	No	Yes	No	Yes
6	Yes	No	No	No	No	Yes
7	Yes	No	Yes	No	No	Yes
8	Yes	No	No	No	No	Yes
9	Yes	No	No	No	No	Yes
10	Yes	No	No	No	No	Yes
11	Yes	No	No	Yes	No	Yes
12	Yes	No	No	No	No	Yes
Total Yes	12	1	4	3	1	12
% Yes	100 %	8 %	33 %	25 %	8 %	100 %

a user's capacity to make sense of the document as much, if not more so, as the ergonomics aspects of the text.

B4 users understood the go-between signs indicating the on/off soundtrack and the sharing with Facebook (see figure 1, middle right of the screen). However, 92 per cent of users did not grasp the 'Restarting viewing path' sign. In effect, users did not consider the option of changing viewing paths because they did not see how the film-interface was 'playable' in different ways.

The hyperlinks sending users outside of the i-doc (top of the *B4* screen, figure 1) were considered as confusingly graphically similar to other hyperlinks offering paratextual information inside the i-doc (see figure 1, bottom of the screen). This seemed to have disoriented some users. 'I thought that the thumbnails on top of the screen were the menus of Pluzz (catch-up TV). I was wondering why it had been placed there. I did not dare click on it because I didn't want to leave B4. I wasn't certain whether the menu at the bottom of the screen made you stay in B4, or not' (Gantier 2014e).

3.3 Informational architecture (Hypothesis 3)

For Group A, who had viewed *B4* without a decision-aiding paratext, 66 per cent used the *horizontal* viewing mode, compared to 100 per cent of Group B (with paratext, see figure 6).

For Group A the *vertical* viewing mode was 100 per cent invisible, whereas for Group B, 66 per cent of users used it in their alternative viewing paths. It appears

			Viewing modes		
		User	Duration	Horizontal	Vertical	Trans-versal
Group A (without paratext)		2	28'	Yes (24')	No	No
		5	27'	Yes (8')	No	Yes (13')
		6	33'	Yes (16')	No	Yes (20')
		8	31'	No	No	Yes (8')
		10	34'	Yes (15')	No	Yes (1')
		11	24'	No	No	Yes (1')
		sub-total	29,5'	4 (66 %)	0 (0 %)	5 (83 %)
Group B (with paratext)		1	33'	Yes (2')	Yes (32')	No
		3	30'	Yes (2')	No	Yes (7')
		4	33'	Yes (2')	Yes (7')	No
		7	23'	Yes (6')	No	Yes (14')
		9	29'	Yes (14')	Yes (2')	Yes (1')
		12	29'	Yes (2')	Yes (7')	No
		sub-total	29,5'	6 (100 %)	4 (66 %)	3 (50 %)
		Total	29'5	10 (83 %)	4 (33 %)	8 (66 %)

Fig. 6: Viewing modes of groups A and B.[8]

that Group B first needed to compare different viewing paths before opting for a vertical viewing mode.

The *transversal* viewing mode acted as a reference point for users, in what can be called a reassuring 'conventional engagement' (Bouchardon 2009). A problem with the transversal mode is that it repeated videos found in other modes, as User 8A's remarks: 'I would have liked to avoid the repetition of videos between those presented in the windows of the block of flats and those in the menu of themes because it was a right mess when you viewed the same video twice ... I wanted to stop viewing because I had the impression of having seen all the videos, or that it was not worth the effort of looking for videos not seen' (Gantier 2014f).

4. SENSE-MAKING PROCESSES (HYPOTHESIS 4)

Given that there are numerous viewing paths, *B4* users had to take a series of problem-solving decisions in choosing a given viewing path. The problem-solving process rests on a series of *coherence-seeking connections* of perceived meaningful elements (see figure 2) guided by users' preoccupations.

In the case of *B4*, users' central preoccupation was to explore inner-city 'togetherness' ('vivre-ensemble'). It led users to create information-seeking quests expressed in identifiable 'search modes'. These search modes allowed users to connect what they considered as meaningful elements into 'sense-making constructs' (Labour 2011: 96–9).

User	Examples of user sense-making search modes
U8A	Getting an overall view of the neighbourhood before zooming onto the block of flats.
U5A	Focusing on individual portraits.
U9B	Items of interest to young adults and children.
U12B	Discovering the intimacy of everyday life.
U6A	Items that may interest a given ('female') public about the North African urban spaces.
U11A	Curious about technical details.

Fig. 7: Sense-making search modes.

There are times, however, when the top-down and bottom-up dynamics of the sense-making process do not mutually reinforce each other (see figure 2). Users then find themselves in a 'sense-making break', or 'senselessness' situation.

Sense-making break

A break in the sense-making process (Labour 2011: 101–2) occurs when users can identify apparently meaningful elements but *cannot connect them up coherently* in terms of the perceived situation-problem (Goffman 1986: 345–77). This can incite users to look for new epistemological connections in order to resolve the problem-situation. The sense-making break leads users to re-frame what they perceive. This can accord with an author's wish to challenge how users see their world. However, attempts to question users' value system are challenging because users can disengage at any time, namely if they feel they are wasting their time, or if the task is seen as too arduous.

In this case, the *B4* author's intention was to change how people perceive inner-cities, as User 9B explains: 'There is an even bigger gap than I thought between the human warmth of inhabitants and the external environment of the flats. I've never lived in subsidised housing; I have always lived in a house in the countryside … I realised that beyond the cliché, people in inner cities had a story to tell. *B4* opened my eyes about something I had never thought of before. I said to myself that people are there because they escaped a war in their country, or they want a better quality of life over here. [...] There was an example, of a person who worked for a Member of Parliament. This surprised me, but it makes sense that not everyone is white in Parliament. I said to myself that when one takes the time to get involved in the inhabitants' lives, they are very different to what you see on TV' (Gantier 2014b).

Senselessness

Senselessness happens when users *cannot identify meaningful elements* (words, sounds, and pictures, etc) in a problem-situation (Labour 2011: 99–101). This can lead to a discouraging feeling of being in a dead-end, and disengagement can follow.

In the context of an i-doc, senselessness can be induced by disorienting (usability) problems that produce cognitive noise. Our data show that Group A (without paratext) declared a higher feeling of senselessness than Group B (with a decision-aiding paratext).

5. EMPIRIC USER AND MODEL USER GAP

The findings of the study, focused on four working hypotheses about a data-based constructed 'empiric user', show that:

- Users did indeed use a combination of ludicising and documentarising viewing modes when using the film-interface (Hypothesis 1 confirmed).
- Unclear or patently absent go-between signs and affordances effectively caused usability problems for many users (Hypothesis 2 confirmed).
- Users' ability to make sense of their viewing paths increased with the help of explicit decision-aiding guidance (Hypothesis 3 confirmed).
- Sense-making constructs were effectively personalised through a series of information-seeking quests linked to different viewing modes. The data showed that users' modified their initial viewpoints about inner-cities after having interacted with *B4* (Hypothesis 4 confirmed).

The comparison between the 'model user' and the 'empiric user' leads us to advance three key points in relation to lessons learnt for i-doc design.

First, if *B4* users deploy simultaneously a documentarisation and ludicising viewing mode, contrary to the author-director's 'model user', this did not encourage 'playability'.

Second, the archetypal 'model user' was aimed at encouraging an intuitive viewing of *B4*. This was not confirmed in the study. It turned out that most users needed to be provided with clear 'conventional engagements' (Bouchardon 2009). For example, in the film of the trial-and-error 'model user', the vertical viewing mode was promoted. Yet in our study, no user took the vertical mode unless they had been explicitly informed of its existence. In a nutshell, the design of i-docs could be significantly improved by giving users explicit guidelines about their informational structure.

Finally, our study revealed that senselessness increased when the viewing was conducted without an explicit decision-aiding paratext. The lack of such guidelines creates cognitive noise which hampers users' information-seeking quests.

CONCLUSION

A linear television (pre-production, production, post-production) model was used in the design of the *B4* i-doc examined in this study. This resulted in the i-doc being designed around a 'model user' based on the perceptions of the different author-filmmaker/graphic designer/producer/web coder/broadcaster involved in the i-doc design. However, the qualitative UX research approach of our study shows the gap between what the projected 'model user' should have experienced, and what the observed 'Empirical User' actually experienced. Given this, we propose an iterative user-centered design approach to ensure that empiric users grasp (sense-making) of the intentionality of authors is both fully experienced (usability) and taken seriously (viewing frame). Such an iterative design approach involves creating a user-validated prototype phase about the initial design (paper prototyping) before moving on to the implementation phases (dynamic prototyping).

One limit of the study was that it was conducted in a near-laboratory condition and not in a more natural viewing context. Future research could also compare very different i-docs as a way to improve i-doc design from a user perspective. More broadly speaking, a key challenge for emerging i-docs formats lies in evaluating iterative user-centred design. An example, of this approach can be found in the *Manifesto for Agile Software Development* (Deuff and Cosquer 2013) with its capacity to integrate authoring issues through self-organisation, team-work and flexible responses to change when improving i-doc design.

NOTES

1   There appear to be few reliable studies on this subject. The observation is based on professional grassroots practice.

2   The idea of 'model user' is inspired from Umberto Eco's (1985) concept of Model reader in his theory of textual cooperation.

3   Marida di Crosta (2009) defines a film interface as a series of hybrid objects found in the intersection between cinematographic fiction and video games.

4   See the interviews conducted by Sandra Gaudenzi; http://i-docs.org/?s=UX+series&x=0 &y=0. Accessed 31 October 2016.

5 A systemic approach involves circular causal relationships – *via* a series of feedback loops operating in different temporal frames – linking up different dimensions into a functional whole.

6 For Erving Goffman (1986: 345) a 'frame' organises 'meaning' and 'involvement', linked to normative expectations, such that 'participants will not only obtain a sense of what is going on but will also (in some degree) become spontaneously engrossed, caught up, 'enthralled'.

7 All of the interview extracts are translated from French.

8 Time given in minutes on an indicative basis.

REFERENCES

Akrich, Madeleine (2006) 'Les objets techniques et leurs utilisateurs : de la conception à l'action', in Madeleine Akrich, Michel Callon and Bruno Latour (eds) *Sociologie de la traduction. Textes fondateurs*. Paris: Presses des Mines, 79–199.

Baccino, Thierry, Catherine Bellino and Teresa Colombi (2005) *Mesure de l'utilisabilité des interfaces*. Paris: Hermès-Lavoisier.

Barboza, Pierre and Jean-Louis Weissberg (2006) *L'image actée. Scénarisations numériques, parcours du séminaire 'L'action sur l'image'*. Paris: L'Harmattan.

Bateson, Gregory (2000 [1954]) *Steps to an Ecology of Mind*. Chicago: University of Chicago Press.

Bonnier, Pierre (2013) *Utilisabilité. Le Design des interfaces numériques en 170 mots-clés: des interactions homme-machine au design interactif*. Agence pour la promotion de la création industrielle, Designers interactifs, Mov'eo et systematic paris-région. Paris: Dunod.

Bouchardon, Serge (2009) *Littérature numérique. le récit interactif*. Paris: Hermès/Lavoisier.

Dervin, Brenda and Patricia Dewdney (1986) 'Information seeking neutral questioning', *Research Quarterly*, 25, 506–13.

Deuff, Dominique and Mathide Cosquer (2013) *Méthode Agile centrée utilisateurs* [Manifesto for Agile Software Development]. Paris: Hermès.

Di Crosta, Marida (2009) *Entre cinéma et jeux vidéo. l'interface-film, métanarration et interactivité*. Bruxelles: De Boeck/INA.

Drouillat, Benoît (2013) 'Expérience utilisateur', in Isabelle Edessa *et al* (eds) *Le Design des interfaces numériques en 170 mots-clés. Des interactions homme-machine au design interactif*. Paris: Dunod, 57–9.

Eco, Umberto (2010 [1985]) *Lector in fabula. Le rôle du lecteur*. Paris: Grasset.

Gantier, Samuel (2012) Le web-documentaire un format hypermédia innovant pour scénariser le réel. *Journalisme en ligne*. Bruxelles: De boeck, 159–77.

_____ (2014a) 'Interview extract #12B'. Research unit DeVisu, University of Valenciennes.

_____ (2014b) 'Interview extract #9B'. Research Unit DeVisu: University of Valenciennes.

_____ (2014c) 'Interview extract #6A'. Research Unit DeVisu: University of Valenciennes.

_____ (2014d) 'Interview extract #5A'. Research Unit DeVisu: University of Valenciennes.

_____ (2014e) 'Interview extract #10A'. Research Unit DeVisu: University of Valenciennes.

_____ (2014f) 'Interview extract #8A'. Research Unit DeVisu: University of Valenciennes.

_____ (2016) Scénariser le rôle et le pouvoir d'agir de l'utilisateur: vers une typologie interactionnelle du documentaire interactif. *Entrelacs. Cinéma et audiovisuel*, 12.

Gantier, Samuel and Michel Labour (2015) 'User Empowerment and the i-doc Model User', in

David Bihanic (ed.) *User Empowerment: Interdisciplinary Studies and Combined Approaches for Technological Products and Services*. London: Springer, 231–54.

____ (2016) 'Scénariser le rôle et le pouvoir d'agir de l'utilisateur: vers une typologie inter-actionnelle du web-documentaire', Entrelacs Online. *Les enjeux des nouvelles formes audiovisuelles documentaires*, 13; http://entrelacs.revues.org/1840. Accessed 31 October 2016.

Gaudenzi, Sandra (2013): *The Living Documentary: From Representing Reality to Co-creating Reality in Digital Interactive Documentary*. PhD Thesis. Goldsmiths, University of London; http://research.gold.ac.uk/7997/1/Cultural_thesis_Gaudenzi.pdf. Accessed 31 October 2016.

____ (2014) *The UX Series*. Online video interviews; http://www.interactivefactual.net/ux-series/. Accessed 31 October 2016.

Genvo, Sébastien (2013) *Penser la formation et les évolutions du jeu sur support numérique* (Think formation and evolution of the game digitally). Post-doctoral thesis, University of Lorraine, France.

Goffman, Erving (1986 [1974]) *Frame Analysis: An Essay on the Organization of Experience*. Boston: Northwestern University Press.

Hartje, Hans, Bernard Magné and Jacques Neefs (eds) (1993) *Cahier des charges de La Vie mode d'emploi*. Paris: CNRS.

Huart, Julien, Christophe Kolski and Christian Bastien (2008) 'Évaluation de documents multi-médias. État de l'art', in Sylvie Leleu-Merviel (ed.) *Objectiver l'humain*. Paris: Hermès/Lavoisier, 211–40.

Jeanneret, Yves (2007) *Y a-t-il (vraiment) des technologies de l'information?* Villeneuve d'Ascq: Presses du Septentrion.

Jeanneret, Yves and Emmanuël Souchier (2005) 'L'énonciation éditoriale dans les écrits d'écran', *Communication et langages*, 145, 1, 3–15.

Labour, Michel (2011) *Média-Repères. Une méthode pour l'explicitation des construits de sens au visionnage*. Post-doctoral thesis, University of Valenciennes.

Norman, Donald (2013 [1988]) *The Design of Everyday Things*. New York: Basic Books.

Odin, Roger (2011) *Les Espaces de communication. Introduction à la sémio-pragmatique*. Grenoble: Presses Universitaires de Grenoble.

Perec, Georges (2010 [1978]) *La Vie mode d'emploi*. Paris: Hachette.

Pignier, Nicole and Benoît Drouillat (2005) *Penser le webdesign. Modèles sémiotiques pour les projets multimédias*. Paris: L'Harmattan.

Popper, Karl (2007 [1934]) *La Logique de la découverte scientifique*. Paris: Payot.

Ribot Jean-Christophe (2012) *B4, Fenêtres sur tour*. Web documentary. Co-produced by Mos-aïque Films and France Télévisions Nouvelles Écritures; http://www.francetv.fr/nouvelles-ecritures/banlieue-b4/. Accessed 31 October 2016.

Soulez, Guillaume (2004) '"Qu'y croire?": Le crédit de l'auteur dans la fiction, le reportage et le documentaire', in René Gardies and Marie-Claude Taranger (eds) *Télévision: notion d'œuvre, notion d'auteur*. Paris: L'Harmattan, 119–51.

USER EXPERIENCE VERSUS AUTHOR EXPERIENCE
LESSONS LEARNED FROM THE *UX SERIES*

Sandra Gaudenzi

In 2014 I started an online research project that I called the i-doc *UX Series*. My assumption was that for as much as i-doc makers understood the importance of putting the user at the centre of their creative process, they were actually not really doing it thoroughly because they lacked a design methodology.[1] Therefore, the idea behind the *UX Series* was to interview interactive design specialists and ask them if, and how, their methodology could be applied to the production of interactive narratives. Since my intention was to start a dialogue between two types of production practices, I asked seven renowned i-doc specialists to comment on each design, and also to invite a colleague of their choice to extend the debate through a series of Google Hangouts.[2] I wanted to check if, and how much, i-doc makers were incorporating design practices in their work.

In this chapter, the *UX Series* interviews will serve as substantive evidence to sustain my argument. Although they do not constitute a thorough quantitative survey, I believe these interviews provide a good indication of current production trends. The other evidence that will be used in this chapter is some recorded interviews that I gathered in 2015 while curating the !F Lab workshops – a series of labs aimed at initiating independent i-doc makers in digital methodologies. It is during these workshops, mainly attended by storytellers (people coming from film, documentary, journalism or photography backgrounds), that I observed how much novice i-doc makers are unaware of their own resistance to adopting design methodologies in their own work process. As we were doing some practical exercises, I realised that even if they are generally in accordance with the core principles of user centre design, they unconsciously stumble on all sorts of resistances when they have to put them into practice.

These emerging points of friction between design theory and i-doc production practice, made me want to investigate further. This chapter is therefore my attempt to reflect on such tensions, investigate their origins and, more importantly, dig into the assumptions behind each work practice. My hypothesis is that merging methodologies of work go beyond the practical adoption of new processes, touching upon core beliefs of individual responsibilities and power structures within a team that need to be addressed if we want them to change. The corollary of such a hypothesis is that these methodological tensions are currently holding back fledgling i-doc makers in an in-between creative zone that does not allow the form to flourish to its full potential.

MULTI-DISCIPLINARY TEAMS IN FILMS AND IN I-DOCS

Filmmaking has always been a team effort, with the length of most documentary credits showing just how multi-disciplinary filmmaking is. Although each documentary has a different budget, it would be fair to say that the minimum necessary team for a documentary comprises the roles of a director/journalist/narrator (the storyteller), a camera/sound/lighting person (the crew) and an editor.

More than a century of film production has allowed us to fine-tune the roles and responsibilities within multi-disciplinary teams through a methodology of production that uses both a process and a language common to all. Each member of the team knows what is expected from him/her and at which point of the process his/her competences are needed. In other words: for multi-disciplinary teams to work efficiently, a common process, language, division of roles and understanding of responsibilities need to be shared. The director, the sound mixer and the film the editor work together, but within an implicit canvas of responsibilities. Even if such roles can always be renegotiated, they are the result of a know-how that has established itself throughout years of praxis and that has now been culturally and collectively accepted.

As yet, this has not happened in the i-docs field. As i-docs are now reaching a certain maturity as a genre, some companies, and auteurs, have worked out their own methodology. A few names such as Upian, Honkytonk, Helios Design Labs, AKFN, Jam3, Touchpress, Kat Cizek, Brett Gaylor, David Dufresne, Ramona Pringle and Jonathan Harris will suffice to remind us that there is a growing knowledge on 'how to produce an i-doc', although these have not consolidated into an industry know-how yet. Some articles, such as MIT docubase's in depth analysis of *Do Not Track*'s production process (Tortum 2015) give us a glimpse of ad hoc methodologies used for single successful projects, but it is the consolidation to a shared industry knowledge that is still missing.

This chapter will not look at the pioneers of interactive storytelling, but rather at the creators that are entering the i-doc world carrying with them their linear production praxis. Those are the journalists, the photographers and the storytellers that would like to produce something interactive but do not know how to do so. These are the people that I have observed during the !F Lab training and to whom the *UX Series* was dedicated.

Back to basics: we know that an i-doc team will, at its minimum, need to comprise an author/narrator (the storyteller), a designer (with possible ramifications into the specialisms of graphic design, navigation design, user experience design, information architecture) and a developer (different coders might specialise in different languages and more than one person might be necessary). In a way, we are in a similar situation that filmmaking was in a century ago: a multi-disciplinary team in search of a work process and a common language. While we wait for a new generation of creative technologists to come through (content producers at ease in both software and design praxis) and naturally bridge this gap, it might be productive to spend some time pondering how methodologies coming from software, design and filmmaking are currently being merged together to create a better workflow for i-docs and why this might constitute a main issue for new entrants with linear film backgrounds. As Jason Brush, executive creative director at Possible, said in the *UX Series*, 'there is a process to follow to make films, and a process to do interactive design, but filmmakers do not understand design' (Gaudenzi 2014a). Ingrid Kopp, at the time of the interview director of digital initiatives at the Tribeca Film Institute, linked this lack of design sensitivity to the positioning of the user in the creative process. While commenting on the fact that the user is not taken into consideration enough in most of the projects that the Tribeca Interactive Fund has financed so far, she added: 'There are good reasons for that. Most people doing i-docs come from a filmmaking background, and in filmmaking you never refer to the audience as the user, so all of this is very new to them' (ibid.).

SOFTWARE AND DESIGN PROCESSES VERSUS FILM PROCESS

As noticed elsewhere in this book by Samuel Gantier and Michel Labour, the linearity of film and video as a medium affords a production process based on successive phases: pre-production, production and distribution. Using a term that comes from software development, Jason Brush refers to the film process in the *UX Series* as a 'waterfall process' – a process 'where everything needs to be perfect before moving to the next stage' (ibid.). It is indeed necessary to have shot all the rushes of a film before doing the final edit, and only once the final cut has been approved by the author, and possibly the commissioning editor, can the documentary be released.

But digital projects are code-based. They need to be tested, and debugged, several times before launch and this is why 'agile processes' are often adopted in software production.[3] Additionally, the fact that the final users will interact with an interface, rather than with code itself, places the users, and the quality of their experience, at the epicentre of the creative process. Siobhan O'Flynn reminds us that 'designing functional user-friendly interfaces and understanding both the design and perceived affordances and constraints of the digital technologies are essential for creating user comprehension and satisfaction' (2016: 74). The digital product relies on the collaboration of its user in order to exist: if the user does not interact with it, it stays dormant and does not move to the next stage. This is why design methodologies start by empathising with the user first, in order to map his/her needs, and then, out of such needs, start to ideate and sketch possible solutions that will lead to prototypes to be tested both technically and from a user experience point of view.[4]

The iterative cycle of incremental modifications that will eventually lead to a satisfactory user experience, is based on the assumption that a target audience has been preselected at the very beginning of the process. There is no such thing as 'one design fits all'. One of the responsibilities of a good designer is to observe and understand his user group to such a level of accuracy to be able to offer creative solutions. The creative moment for a designer is not focused on the expression of the self, but rather in turning user constraints into product solutions.

If we look at the production of an i-doc from a designer's point of view, it is clear that his role is first to identify who the i-doc is for, and then to propose design solutions – not only from an aesthetic perspective, but also from a navigation, interface, platform and system design point of view. The role of the designer is to create a user experience that reflects the aims of the project. As O'Flynn has argued, 'experience design aims to integrate the core concepts for the project across all elements of design' (ibid.). 'It is my job' says designer and Made by Many co-founder Isaac Pinnock 'to get [that] person to understand my product, and if they do not understand it then I have done something wrong' (Gaudenzi 2014a).

The interface (that the users interact with to frame their understanding of the piece) therefore becomes an essential conveyor of meaning: it positions users and dictates possible options. As leading interactive producer Alexandre Brachet says – 'the interface is content' (Aston and Gaudenzi 2012: 130). What users can and cannot do, and their intuitiveness of scope of action are, for the designer, as important as content (intended as text, graphics, video or sound) in the creation of meaning. In experience design one cannot be separated from the other.

I'd like to argue that an understanding of the role of the interface, and more generally of the interactive architecture of an i-doc, is currently a primary point of tension between i-docs designers and storytellers. This is particularly the case when the storyteller comes from a filming background and, more or less consciously, regards design as a frame through which to access video content, while video is the main carrier of meaning. By facilitating the !F Lab workshops, I have noticed that when filmmakers are the initiators of an i-doc, they tend to think of their video production first, and they will then hire a designer only once they have a clear picture of what they want from their project. But by doing so, they *de facto* cut out the designer from the concept phase of the project, and they therefore miss out on their knowledge of how to include the target audience's needs as a first step of the i-doc ideation.

By perpetuating the sequential (waterfall) production process (first do your research and clarify your concept, then step into production mode and hire your crew, finally brief them on what you want and direct the shoot and the editing), filmmakers seek to retain control of the authorial voice of their project. One reason for this might be that the satisfaction they get from their work is precisely in the expression of a personal and coherent view of the reality they want to portray. I would therefore say that the wish to express themselves through their creative work is often a second point of tension between the designer and the storyteller in i-docs production. Documentary films are good at expressing an authorial point of view. This might be where the pleasure lies – in making sense of the world through the process of filmmaking. Although pluri-vocality and co-authorship are possible in linear documentaries, i-docs have the potential to take it much further. The 'relational' (Gaudenzi 2011) nature of i-docs affords an authorial voice that can be more about orchestrating a debate/space/experience than expressing a point of view (Gaudenzi 2014b). As Patricia Zimmermann and Dale Hudson argue, 'thinking through digital media is also thinking *with* digital media' (2015: 19; emphasis in original) and embracing collaborative processes of thinking more akin to the network nature of the media, and of our world. Interactive designers are more used to thinking through digital media. They see their role as creative problem solvers, and possibly enjoy group questioning and observation more than self-expression; this is why they are essential in the i-doc team.

WHO IS THE I-DOC FOR? USER EXPERIENCE VERSUS AUTHOR EXPERIENCE

From a User Centred Design (UCD) point of view, without a target audience there is no design. The i-doc has to be designed for, and with, an audience in mind. Interestingly, although most i-doc makers I interviewed in the *UX Series* agreed with this statement, I would argue that very few were ready to fully accept its consequences. Designing for, and with, an audience means committing to an aesthetic, a platform and a language that best suit such an audience – even if these do not fit with the personal taste of the i-doc author. The question here is not to 'please' the audience, but to 'make sense' for such audience.

After interviewing some i-doc makers in preparation for Design Booster (the second of !F Lab's workshops), Made by Many's Isaac Pinnock was surprised at how many seemed to be producing for themselves: '[They are working for] an audience of one, rather than an audience of many. Obviously they want their work to be seen by many people, but it felt ... as if people were doing that classic thing of assuming that because they are interested in this therefore the way I want to consume this information is going to be the same as the people that I am targeting' (Gaudenzi 2015; recorded interview).

Miranda Mullingam, then executive director at Northwestern University Knight Lab, relates this pattern to the way storytellers and journalists are trained: 'We are trained as storytellers to have a good sense for interesting stories. But as we are trained at crafting and telling stories we are trained traditionally to think "I am the authority and I am going to broadcast this at you." And the most disruptive part with now having readers, viewers and users accessing our stories through digital connectivity is that it changes our relationship with them. We cannot just talk at people and assume that just because we have selected stories for them they will be interested in them' (Gaudenzi 2014a).

At the moment we are still in a phase where filmmakers who embark on i-doc production understand why they should create with, rather than for, a user but seem to resist committing to the implications of such methodology. Understanding an approach and putting it into practice are two very different things. Even experienced interactive storytellers, such as Bjarke Myrthu, who are convinced of the importance of user experience design in i-docs, can admit resistance to opening up their ideas to incorporate user feedback. 'I have not known a lot about the users in the projects that I have done' said Myrthu when interviewed (ibid.).

Why such resistance? Could it be part of the author's satisfaction comes from pleasing his/her own aesthetic sense, and that it is difficult to decide how much one should compromise to reach and make sense to an audience while still retaining the authorship of the overall message and form?

While facilitating Story Booster (!F Lab's first workshop), we ask i-doc makers to start by defining their target audience (the people they want to address) and the purpose of their i-doc (the shift or change they would like the user to experience). Both the choice of the platforms and the design of the product will then be influenced by such decisions. While having a tutorial with a participant coming from the documentary world who had proposed a project about the Female Gaze, I noticed that the author had chosen a target audience of 16–20-year-old girls. The rationale was clear: if one has to choose a target for such topic, it might be better to choose teenage girls who are still forming their ideas about the world, because they will become the women of the future. Although the educative argument for such a target group made perfect sense, I found that the author of the project was not ready to accept the consequences of her own decision: choosing a young target audience would lead the project towards an extensive use of social media platforms and, probably, to a design that would look 'teenagerish'. None of this was in line with the stylish website with handpicked filmmaker's videos that the author had pictured in her mind and described in her initial project treatment. The author had completed the exercise of choosing a target audience without fully embracing the process. While in theory selecting a target audience made sense to her, it seemed to me that it was challenging for her to accept the consequences of such a design process, as the author herself was not part of the target group she had selected, and therefore the aesthetic of her i-doc might not be pleasing to her.

THE ROLE OF THE USER

In their contribution to this book, and using the i-doc *B4* (Ribot 2012) as a case study, Samuel Gantier and Michel Labour argue that the heterogeneous decision-makers that participate in the creation of an i-doc (filmmakers, producers, web developers, graphic artists and television broadcasters) tend to create an i-doc geared at different 'model users', without really checking who the 'real users' are. In other words, when half adopting a user-centred methodology (in the sense of creating with a user in mind but without really getting in contact with such a user), decision-makers can be trapped by their own assumptions – assumptions that often derive from their different 'social worlds' (2015: 230). 'The inevitable preconceptions of the members of each member of the i-doc design team', they argue, 'will lead to a more or less conscious creation of a model user' (2015: 226). If different actors are taking decisions based on their own assumptions about different theoretical users, then it is likely that the final design of the project will be weakened by their contrasting ideas.

While agreeing with Gantier and Labour about the importance of involving real users in the design process, I would like to question why such players often keep producing for their 'ideal users' rather than their 'real users'. In other words, why adopting user-centred design techniques has so far encountered such resistance from filmmakers, broadcasters and journalists?

One could make a case that it is just a question of time, and that changing workflows in teams and institutions is a slow process. One could also point out that interviewing users and testing prototypes does involve a cost, and that small productions cannot afford the process. To these two valid explanations I would like to add a third one: that for many documentary makers there is resistance to the idea of testing their work.

If user focus groups have been used in television, this has predominantly been done when testing entertainment formats. Documentary makers have rarely been confronted with their audiences before production. To be controversial, one could argue that the *de facto* target audience for most linear documentaries is the commissioning editor. This is the person that needs to be convinced for the documentary to be financed and produced, not the audience. The film editor might act as a filter and external point of view during the creative editing, but they are still not speaking for the audience.

Within mainstream media production, the place where the user has consistently been put at the centre of the creative process is the world of advertising and marketing – ethnographical and participatory films being another exception, but they will be considered niche in this chapter. Before the creation of any advertising campaign, the client will define his target audience, do a competitive product analysis and, probably, establish his customer's needs. No documentary-maker wants to adopt methodologies that are somehow associated in their mind with selling techniques. A documentary is not considered by them to be a commodity, and diluting the voice of the author to please the audience would be seen as jeopardising its ethics and its *raison d'être*.

In his forward-thinking article 'The Interactive Documentary: A Transformative Art Form', former NFB chairman Tom Perlmutter noted that 'the importance of understanding and relating to audiences tends to elicit an almost offended reaction [from filmmakers]: "I am making my film. I am not going to be dictated to by what an audience wants. After all, this is art, not paint by numbers."' To which he comments: 'To take this attitude is to misunderstand profoundly what understanding audience means in an interactive world, where as creator you make the audience a collaborator in your processes. This does not invalidate the filmmaker as creator or auteur. It enlarges the notion of auteur. The new auteurs will understand that the relationship to audience as co-creators and collaborators is part of their medium of creation' (2014).

I'd like to add to Perlmutter's statement that 'pleasing' a user and 'testing' a product are not synonymous. In the world of interactive design, testing a product does not involve asking the users what they would like to have, but rather seeking to learn enough about their assumptions, existing knowledge and context of use, to make an informed decision on how best to communicate with them. This is a form of collaboration, as Perlmutter notes, although the decisions still belong to the designers. I'd like to use designer Isaak Pinnock's *UX Series* interview once more here: 'Even when a project is a labour of love, and you are doing it for yourself, unless it is true art and you do not care about what people think of it at the end, then it is incredibly wasteful to get to the end of the project and that is the only point when you test it. It will always be more beneficial, even for your own heart, to find out that you are going onto the right path... (Gaudenzi 2014a). Is it possible, therefore, to envisage the involvement of users as a source of creative inspiration rather than as a threat to creativity? Can the needs of the users be seen as one of the multiple production constraints that creatively shape a project? The third point of tension, then, between linear storytellers and designers, is the value they give to the user's input: it is seen as a dangerously pleasing attitude by the first and as a creative source of inspiration by the second. And the reason for this tension is based on the discordant interpretation of what to do with user feed-back: does it mean doing what the audience wants or using inside knowledge to better communicate the author's point of view?

Adopting a user-centred approach has consequences: it means accepting a bottom-up model of creation rather than a top-down one or, at least, a mid-way between the two. Such a creative model assumes that the author does not have a mental idea of what his project will look like before starting it – a position that is uncomfortable for people who are trained to sell a clear vision when pitching their documentaries. Embracing a user-centred methodology also means that platform, style and story architecture will largely emerge from the iterative design process between the designer and the user, and this clearly conflicts with the control that filmmakers are used to having. But if form, content and style are partially informed by the user, does this mean that all the main decisions are in the hands of the user? Can we see the user as part of the team? Where is the borderline between having the idea for a discussion, facilitating such a discussion, and making sense of it?

ROLES AND RESPONSIBILITIES – THE POWER BALANCE IN MEANING CONSTRUCTION

One of the consequences then of having multidisciplinary teams involved in the creation of i-docs is that authorship and production practices have to be re-negotiated within the team itself. These shifts in production methodology and creative control can be seen as both a blessing and a threat. On the one hand, teams can discover new ways of working together, giving technologists, designers and storytellers equal importance; on the other, tensions can arise around who gets the final say in decision-making, or simply who is responsible for what.

These tensions are further complicated by the increasing importance of the user in the creative process. As we have seen, UCD practices place the user at the heart of the development process, with their input guiding important creative decisions. What was already a difficult power negotiation between the storyteller, the developer and the designer, now becomes a sort of '*ménage à quatre*' with no clear boundaries and no predefined rules of conduct. Ultimately the roles and responsibilities within these four entities need to be re-negotiated. All the attempts to create new mixed methodologies of work touched upon in this book (LDS, hackathons, !F Lab etc) are moving in this precise direction. The RACI – Responsible, Accountable, Consulted and Informed – production model described by Brett Gaylor (2015) in his *Do Not Track* MIT case study (Tortum 2015) also provides a practical solution to distribute responsibilities and sign-off capabilities within a team. All of these are attempts to create new work-flows apt to rebalance the power of the forces at stake in a relational entity such as the i-doc. They are about redistributing roles (power) and responsibilities in the construction of meaning or experience in an i-doc.

What seems clear, is that the storyteller will have to loosen up the ownership of the form, functionality, style and, sometimes, content of their project. These will emerge in part through the iterative process of dialogue with the user and part will be in the hands of the aesthetic and technical creativity of the designer and the developer. What is left in the hands of the author is the intentionality of the project: its general story/idea, the choice of who it is aimed at and the delineation of its final purpose. I-doc storytellers are more *facilitators* than *narrators* and, together with a creative team, they are responsible for the coherence of the final user experience.

How to create a shift in the user – be this in terms of knowledge acquisition, affective response or tangible action in the world – is a process facilitated by a whole team. The power structures and the responsibilities within such teams are still looking for equilibrium and will probably have to be renegotiated on a case-by-case basis. As a rule of thumb, the designer might need to be more in charge of the iterative communication with the users, while the coder could take the lead in delivering a smooth experience; but ultimately they will have to work together and negotiate their responsibilities. The fourth member of the team is now the user: partly the source of the initial design, and of its iterations, but now also a player within the symphony that is an i-doc. The 'death of the author' is taking on a new shape. Paul Dourish, eloquent ambassador of the role of experience design, points out in *Where the action is* that 'design *reflects* a particular set of ontological commitments on the part of a designer, but it cannot *provide* an ontology for a user' (2001: 130; emphasis in original). We got used to the idea that it is the viewer that ultimately makes sense of a film, and that the editor and director do work as a team. We now have to agree to a change of power balance in the interactive narrative world and give their place to the designer and the coder – not to forget the software itself, as Craig Hight argues elsewhere in this collection.

The success of future i-docs rests on the capacity of teams to openly clarify their roles and responsibilities and, within them, to be able to work together towards a common goal. It is this internal dance that ultimately gives strength, coherence and meaning to a project. It has been the intent of this chapter, and somehow of this entire book section, to show how the redistribution of responsibilities is being renegotiated in the i-doc field as we write. I would want to argue that it is only through resolving the tensions between author experience and user experience that i-docs will truly come of age.

NOTES

1 The notion of User Centred Design (UCD) is normally attributed to Donald Norman. In his book *User Centered System Design* (1986) he states that 'from the point of view of the user, the interface is the system. Concern for the nature of the interaction and for the user – these are the things that should force design. [...] User-centered design emphasizes that the purpose of the system is to serve the user, not to use a specific technology, not to be an elegant piece of programming' (1986: 61). Nearly two decades later, in *The Design of Everyday Things* (2002), Norman updated his vision of UCD by stating that it is 'a philosophy based on the needs and interests of the user, with an emphasis on making products usable and understandable' (2002: 188).

2 All the interviews of the *UX Series* are available online at http://www.interactivefactual.net/ux-series/

3 In *This is Service Design Thinking*, Jacob Stickdorn and Marc Schneider define 'agile development' as 'an iterative methodology that allows projects to grow and develop over time, adapting around both the evolving needs of the clients, and the research materials the project may generate' (2011: 195). Agile methods are focused on quick response to change and continuous development, as first claimed in 2001 software developer's 'Agile Manifesto' (Beedle *et al* 2010). By working on short time-frame iterations, with incremental functionality, agile methodologies try to diminish the risk of errors: coding errors, but also functionality ones. This is achieved by continually test the product in order to align users needs and product functionalities.

4 The classic Design Thinking cycle, as described by leading Stanford University DSchool in their *Introduction to Design Thinking* (2010), divides the design process in five iterative steps: 1. Empathize (with the user), 2. Define (the challenge), 3. Ideate (possible solutions), 4. Prototype (start building), and 5. Test (within the real context of the user's life) – and then start again.

REFERENCES

Aston, Judith and Sandra Gaudenzi (2012) 'Interactive Documentary: Setting the Field', *Studies in Documentary Film*, 6, 2, 125–39.

Beedle, Mike, Arie van Bennekum, Allistair Cockburn, Ward Cunningham, Martin Fowler, Jim Highsmith, Andrew Hunt, Ron Jeffries, Jon Kern, Brian Marick, Robert Martin, Ken Schwaber, Jeff Sutherland and Dave Thomas (2010) 'Manifesto for Agile Software Development'; http://agilemanifesto.org. Accessed 31 October 2016.

Dourish, Paul (2001) *Where the Action Is: The Foundations of Embodied Interaction*. Cambridge, MA: MIT Press.

Gantier, Samuel and Michel Labour (2015) 'User Empowerment and the Model User', in David Bihanic (ed.) *Empowering Users Through Design*. Switzerland: Springer International, 225–47.

Gaudenzi, Sandra (2011) 'The i-doc as a Relational Object'; http://i-docs.org/2011/09/08/the-i-doc-as-a-relational-object/. Accessed 31 October 2016.

____ (2014a) 'The UX Series'. Online video interviews; http://www.interactivefactual.net/ux-series/. Accessed 31 October 2016.

____ (2014b) 'Strategies of Participation: The Who, What and When of Collaborative Documentaries', in Kate Nash, Craig Hight and Catherine Summerhayes (eds) *New Documentary Ecologies. Emerging Platforms, Practices and Discourses*. New York: Palgrave Macmillan, 129–49.

Gaylor, Brett (2015) *Do Not Track*. Web Series. Directed by Brett Gaylor, co-produced by Upian, Arte, ONF and BR. https://donottrack-doc.com. Accessed 31 October 2016.

!F Lab website (2015) http://www.iflab.net. Accessed 31 October 2016.

Norman, Donald (1986) *User Centered System Design*. New Jersey: CRC Press.

____ (2002) *The Design of Everyday Things*. New York: Basic Books.

O'Flynn, Siobhan (2016) 'Designed Experiences in Interactive Documentaries', in Daniel Marcus and Selmin Kara (eds) *Contemporary Documentary*. London/New York: Routledge, 72–86.

Pelmutter, Tom (2014) 'The Interactive Documentary: A Transformative Art Form – Policy Options'; http://policyoptions.irpp.org/issues/policyflix/perlmutter/. Accessed Accessed 31 October 2016.

Plattner, Hasso (2010) *An Introduction to Design Thinking, Process Guide*; http://stanford.io/1Lek2RR. Accessed 5 December 2015.

Ribot, Jean-Christophe and Kalid Bazi (2012) *B4. Fenêtres sur Tour*. Web documentary. Produced by France Télévision; http://www.francetv.fr/nouvelles-ecritures/banlieue-b4/. Accessed 31 October 2016.

Schneider Jakob and Marc Stickdorn (2011) *This is Service Design Thinking*. Amsterdam: BIS.

Tortum, Deniz (2015) 'Production Process of *Do Not Track*'; http://docubase.mit.edu/lab/case-studies/production-process-of-do-not-track/. Accessed 15 May 2016.

Zimmermann, Patricia and Dale Hudson (2015) *Thinking Through Digital Media: Transnational Environments and Locative Places*. New York: Palgrave Macmillan.

PUSHING THE CRAFT FORWARD
THE POV HACKATHON AS A COLLABORATIVE APPROACH TO MAKING AN INTERACTIVE DOCUMENTARY

Jess Linington

INTRODUCTION

The origin of the hackathon is within the software industry, with the first documented event hosted by OpenBSD – a computer operating system descended from Berkeley Software Distribution – in 1999 (OpenBSD 2000). Since then, the format has expanded beyond the software world and into other fields, with journalists, NGOs, universities and government agencies, including the White House, utilising variations of the model for various outcomes. 'In its most basic form, a hackathon is an intense, multi-day event devoted to rapid software production. Hackathon organizers invite programmers, designers, and others with relevant skills to spend one to three days addressing an issue by programming and creating prototypes' (Irani 2015: 5).

Within the interactive documentary field, there are established hackathons and labs – Tribeca Hacks (worldwide), POV Hackathon (US), Popathon (EU) – as well as recent additions to the scene such as Hackastory (EU) and the DOK Hackathon Leipzig (DE). The aims of these labs vary, with the model rooted in the software industry, but expanded to fit with the demands, skills and desired outcomes for i-doc makers. The key goal for Tribeca, for example, is to build new relationships between media artists, technologists and designers, whilst providing the opportunity to test new storytelling tools, hardware and platforms. This is similar to Popathon, which looks to create networking opportunities whilst facilitating open source digital storytelling. The POV Hackathon lab[1] – the focus of this chapter – sits in the space between these two: creative collaboration is a central aspect, but teams are also expected to create a working prototype, which is published online following the event.

The focus on this real outcome underlines the key aim of the POV Hackathon: to push the craft of interactive documentary and the field forward. Led by Adnaan Wasey, executive producer of POV Digital, the lab began in 2012 as a response to the 'virtually non-existent' interactive documentary industry at that time.

Wasey's professional background is within the software industry, and his experience there has contributed to the development and direction of the lab. 'There is a very deep-seated entrepreneurial culture [in the technology industry]. People are taking a lot of risks. There is also investment. I didn't see anything that was the equivalent of that in non-fiction. I was trying to merge some of these ideas together.'[2]

Based upon a long interview with Wasey, this chapter will seek to do two things. Part one will provide a blueprint of how to run a lab like this, based upon the POV model. This includes practical advice on the process: aspects such as location, budget and forming teams, based on the lessons learnt by Wasey and POV. Alongside this, it will explore not only the benefits of participating, but also the benefits for an organisation to run one.

Part two will examine the POV Hackathon's significance within the evolving model of interactive documentary production, answering the question: 'How does it move the craft forwards?' It will be argued that in being a response to a 'virtually non-existent' interactive documentary field, the lab is also a response to wider issues within the industry: to a lack of training, funding and investment, which stunts experimentation and production. This positions the model as an alternative means of investment – for both practitioners and organisations – beyond the funding of individual interactive documentary projects.

PART ONE: THE BLUEPRINT

AIM

The POV Hackathon brings together two worlds: non-fiction media-makers and technologists, who have little or no experience of working with each other before. The idea behind this fits under the umbrella of 'creative collaboration'; the pairings lead to the creation of new tools or new products that inspire other people to continue to make other new things in the same way – the broad aim of the lab.

The aim of the event itself is to create a working prototype for an interactive documentary project. This is an intense demand for two days of work and participants are acutely aware of that. However, by emphasising the need to make something tangible at the end – rather than presenting ideas – the model contributes to the field, falling inline with the overarching aim of the POV Hackathon.

The prototypes are released online through the POV website, often open-sourced, with in-depth documentation around the technology used, the concept of the project and the teams' skills. This culture of sharing, which only works if you have something to share, is about building the capacity of the whole industry. This process is not just about inspiring filmmakers and technologists, but equipping them with the code to actually make something.

BUDGET

The first POV Hackathon was done on a '$0 budget', with no specific funding allocated, aside from Wasey's internal allocation. In the following years, it has received some additional funding from the Fledgling Fund, the Knight Foundation and the MacArthur Foundation.

This external funding has not really changed the way the lab is run, they remain very low cost. But it has aided expansion, with nine hacks run across three cities – New York City, Los Angeles and Chicago – in the past four years. However, the priceless component that has allowed the POV Hackathon to flourish is the on-going support from Wasey himself and POV as an organisation. When the lab first started, this support not only meant a reputable institution was backing the initiative, but also the ability to run hacks in spaces owned by POV, staff available to work on the preparation process, and marketing to aid promotion. Having this in-kind support has meant POV has never had to charge participants to take part, something smaller or independent events may struggle to offer.

Despite the technical nature of the lab, the main cost is catering – although POV can't fund participants' travel or accommodation, they provide food throughout the weekend. Wasey eschews the traditional fast food and energy drinks that are synonymous with the all-night hackathon's in the tech industry. Instead, importance is placed on good nourishment: 'We want people to be fed well with healthy food. If anyone says anything about POV Hackathon, it's not about the prototypes. It's about the quality of the catering. That's a good thing. I like that. It means that people know that we treat them well, because it's all about them doing the best work they possibly can do.'

SPONSORSHIP & PRIZES

A route for gaining further support and giving participants an incentive to take part is sponsorship, which other events have embraced. POV have been offered various forms of sponsorship in the past but have turned it down, as it doesn't match up with their ethos. Most notably, many sponsorship deals involve a prize for a winner and nothing for other participants. The POV Hackathon follows the adage 'it's not the winning, it's the taking part that counts'. For Wasey, deciding winners and allocating prizes would upset the balance of pressure that is achieved, something that is explored in more detail later in this chapter.

Beyond this, it is also the *kind* of sponsorship that's been offered which hasn't been viewed as worthwhile for all participants. For example, cash for all the teams, which could fund the continuation of a project, or subsidise travel, is something that would be universally useful, particularly with the sparse funding available in the field.

LOCATION

The location of the lab is important for two reasons: the geographical location affects who can take part and the physical location – the space it's held in – endorses a particular environment that assists with collaboration and creativity.

The geographical location

POV have run labs in three major cities in the US: New York, Los Angeles and Chicago. Wasey explains: 'The idea is when we're in New York, we have a lot of New York-based media creators and technologists. When we're in LA, we have more of a tendency to have LA- or California-based or even West Coast-based media-makers and technologists. While Chicago caters for the Midwest.'

This means most projects are local to wherever the lab takes place. Although this can prove a barrier for those from further afield taking part, it can also help to cultivate a local community of media-makers and technologists who may work together in the future, assisting the development of the field in the USA. When considering adopting and expanding the model, pushing for a wider geographic spread, particularly in the Global South, could lead long-term 'hubs' of production creating interactive non-fiction work.

The physical location

Creating a conducive working environment is also important. The POV Hackathon has been run both within POV buildings and in external venues which have the 'right' environment.

Venue basics

It's widely understood that participants will bring their own equipment to a lab, such as laptops and cameras. But venue basics such as plenty of power outlets, open desks and good wifi are of paramount importance.

Fig. 1: Co-working space for POV Hackathon 5 at the Center for Social Innovation, NYC. Credit: POV/The American Documentary Inc.

There is a need for space; teams don't want to feel like they are on top of each other, but also need the ability to work in the same area, sharing a large table or desk. Explicit 'co-working' spaces such as the Center for Social Innovation in New York where previous labs have been hosted provide the desired environment. They have spent the past ten years refining their co-working model and provide large open rooms that are both functional, yet creative and inspirational.

Finding places willing to donate their space can appear hard, however there is value in them doing it. Hosting a lab like this – particularly one that is well documented – positions the space as somewhere where interesting things happen and demonstrates its support for the local creative community. Alongside this, they're opening their doors to potential new members in the process – which can lead to valuable long-term relationships and collaborations.

Inspiration

If organisations are looking to adopt the model, they shouldn't overlook their own buildings. Whilst an explicit co-working space can be inspiring for participants, so can a space within an established institution or organisation which may provide something different. Wasey mentioned that a technologist said he was simply inspired to be in the place where POV had been producing and showing documentaries for 25-plus years because it was not the environment they were used to working in.

TEAMS

The way teams are put together is vital to the success of the lab and Wasey believes the 'matchmaking' that POV do is perhaps the most valuable service they can offer participants.

Applications

Prospective participants go through an application process. Applications are submitted on a rolling basis, but are subject to the individual POV Hackathon deadlines. They are organised through two forms: 'I have an idea to propose' and 'I want to be part of a team'.

Submitted proposals should be a project that has not been made before, the idea may be old, but the prototype they make must be something new. 'The purpose of the lab is to push the field forward, and we can't push the field forward if we're doing something that's already been done.' Whilst that is a fixed requirement, other areas of the process are more flexible. Applications range from something that is an old idea that has never been fully realised to participants applying with an idea specifically created for the lab, with a plan of what could happen with it. The POV team are also not adverse to adjusting ideas that are submitted, modifying proposals that need work, or finding a kernel of interest within a vague application.

Pre-formed teams are discouraged from applying, although there have been rare cases where someone is already working with someone or someone has suggested that they work with someone. It's much more common to have teams of people that don't know each other, or at least haven't worked together before. Individual applications are also important for finding the right skills to actually fulfil the project idea. If applicants apply as a team, they may come to realise they don't possess the skills that match their ambitions and their prototype will not be successful.

Once an application deadline closes – usually a few weeks before the event itself – the POV team evaluate the submitted ideas. This is an iterative process of trying to understand what the ideas could be, how the prototypes could develop and what the team needs to make it happen. POV normally receive a good balance of applications from media-makers and technologists, demonstrating a demand from both communities to collaborate with new people and work on i-doc projects. This success could also be attributed in-part to POVs reputation – lesser-known labs may find it harder to engage with both communities.

Matchmaking

As previously mentioned, the 'matchmaking service' is crucial not only to the smooth running of the event but also the lab's impressive 100 per cent prototype success rate. The ideal number for a team is four; two media-makers – normally a filmmaker and producer – then a developer and designer. In some cases, there have been teams of two or six, but generally Wasey has stuck to the same format. 'You don't have to have every person from a film production on a team... You just need the people who can make the prototype.' By bringing these two fields together – media-makers and technologists – the lab is breaking down the limitations faced by both. For a technologist, the ideal team encourages new ways of thinking, allowing them to consider their role in storytelling beyond providing technical knowledge. Whereas for media-makers, communicating with technologists can bring their idea into reality, as opposed to just imagining what a project could be.

At the core, there needs to be a skills match: team members must possess the right skills to create the proposed prototype or a close approximation. Beyond this, team members may bond over other reasons – similar work in the past, having mutual interests or being connected through a similar industry. These additional factors can improve a team's relationship beyond the shared goal of creating the prototype and can lead to long-term working relationships.

Communication

When labelling two distinct groups – technologists and media-makers – there is an assumption that they might not share a common language when developing work. However in reality, the opposite is true: 'They gel as a team almost immediately. You see it every time, because they all realise that they are working towards the same goal. They are two groups of people, but they are both very creative groups of people.'

Despite this, there may be misunderstandings about what the other group is able to do, but this can be combatted by immediately adopting a clear and direct approach: 'Can we do this? Yes or no?' Often it is the media-makers who get the surprise, either thinking something might be very difficult for a technologist, but it can be done in thirty seconds, or something they think is very easy might take a week. These misunderstandings, however, are part of learning how to work within a multidisciplinary team – a vital skill for those wanting to make i-docs.

STRUCTURE

The overall structure is simple but effective and has not changed hugely since the first lab in 2012. This section explores the structure of the lab, from the planning through to the jury at the end, looking at aspects like creating the 'right amount of pressure' for participants.

Planning

Planning the POV Hackathon lab is a fairly rapid process, with each event working on a roughly three-month cycle: two months before POV announce the date of the lab; then there is about a month for people to apply; the teams are decided upon and then notified, giving them about three to four weeks to prepare mentally and logistically.

When teams are notified, they're only told they will be part of a team with most participants not finding out who they'll be working with until less than a week beforehand, discouraging too much advance work on a project. This is done for a couple of reasons. Firstly, doing a lot of work in advance isn't viewed as constructive when the lab format has been specifically designed to make this prototype a reality. Secondly, it isn't respectful of other participant's time. They are often senior professionals who have other jobs and lives and are not being paid to participate.

Key information such as the skills of their team members can be released in advance, so teams know they have the right people to make the project happen and some preparation may take place. Media-makers might collect or organise assets or export media in an HTML5 format so it is useful to the technologists, whereas technologists might decide what framework or library to use, or whether to start from scratch. On occasion, a proof of concept is put together to ensure that the proposed technology can work, but generally participants bring their assets to the lab and start from there.

Day one

There are no social events at the lab, such as a Friday night mixer to 'get to know each other'. This means participants show up on Saturday morning and are told 'It's time to work' – immediately fostering an understanding of what is expected from the lab.

POV Hackathons are fast-paced: thirty minutes is allocated at the start of the lab for a strategy session. This encourages teams to begin working on the prototype quickly, as you can see from the schedule below: teams can work overnight if they wish, with the space remaining open and snacks provided, but participants are encouraged to sleep, as the second day is more challenging. Overall, there is a focus on a healthy work ethic and striking a balance. Participants recognise the

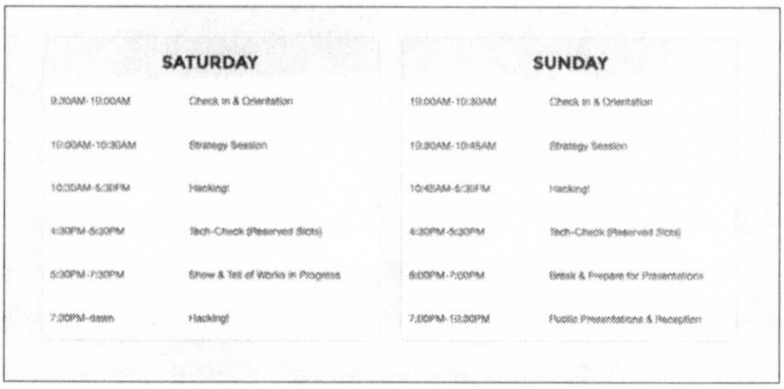

	SATURDAY		SUNDAY
9:30AM-10:00AM	Check in & Orientation	10:00AM-10:30AM	Check in & Orientation
10:00AM-10:30AM	Strategy Session	10:30AM-10:45AM	Strategy Session
10:30AM-5:30PM	Hacking!	10:45AM-5:30PM	Hacking!
4:30PM-5:30PM	Tech-Check (Reserved Slots)	4:30PM-5:30PM	Tech-Check (Reserved Slots)
5:30PM-7:30PM	Show & Tell of Works in Progress	6:00PM-7:00PM	Break & Prepare for Presentations
7:30PM-dawn	Hacking!	7:00PM-10:30PM	Public Presentations & Reception

Fig. 2: The schedule for the weekend. Credit: POV Hackathon website.

value of the lab for their project, so expect to sleep less, but not to the extent that they will harm themselves producing a prototype.

The day follows an iterative structure – a development concept borrowed from software industry, whereas a filmmaker may make a film, edit it and release it before moving onto the next project. The lab model encourages an iterative approach to a project from the start, involving plenty of feedback and changes to the project throughout the design process. Team members must adopt a degree of flexibility, being open to different ideas and criticisms and not allowing an idea to remain too fixed. This allows a project to develop in interesting and perhaps unexpected ways. Beyond the lab, this approach can be adopted for participants undertaking future i-doc projects.

Day two

The second day follows a similar structure to the first, starting again with a strategy session to allow participants time to plan the day in a coherent manner, factoring in the prototype launch and presentations at the end of the day.

The structure is designed to bring the right level – and right type – of pressure to get a good project finished in time. This is defined through the scope of work being just difficult enough: having to create a working prototype, but having the right team to do it, makes it an achievable goal. This is combined with the stress of presenting to both the public and a jury that may contain future funders.

Judging

The jury is an integral part of the whole structure for two reasons. Firstly, the jury members are carefully selected to give good, practical feedback from the perspective of storytelling, production or funding. 'It's not a case where someone is working in secret on a project for two years, they release it and they realise it has failed for some reason because the story doesn't resonate or something is

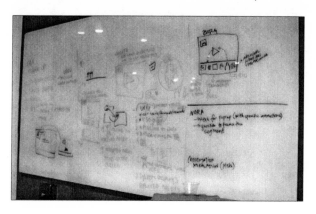

Fig. 3: A team's workings on a white board at day two of POV Hackathon 7 Credit: POV/The American Documentary Inc.

Fig. 4: Judges at the POV Hackathon 5. From left to right: Edwin Torres (Rockefeller Foundation), Ingrid Kopp (Tribeca Film StoryScapes), Brent Hoff (IDFA Doc Lab | NY Media Center). Adnaan Wasey is sitting on the far left. Credit: POV/The American Documentary Inc.

wrong with the design. You don't want to find those things out later, you want to find that out as quickly as possible', said Wasey. This is bringing in a concept from the product management world – risk minimisation. With every cycle of production, the project is reducing its risk of failure. Within the emerging field of i-docs, this is an important asset; you could be working with technology or code that hasn't been used for this purpose before, or treating a subject in a new and different way. Escaping the production bubble and getting expert, honest feedback is vital.

Secondly, the jury provides an anchor for the whole experience. Teams must present their prototype at the end and having a jury there, alongside an audience, gives that additional pressure to push teams to create something they are proud of and are willing to show publicly.

The prototype

The emphasis of the whole day is to make something real, something download-able or accessible online, which is published on the POV website. So far, the lab has achieved a 100 per cent success rate.

Creating a workable prototype has multiple benefits for both the participants and POV: by hosting them on the POV site, they provide a showcase for future events, they can be part of a portfolio for creative technologists and can be used by teams to pitch for funding to create the actual project. The ethos behind this is rooted within ideas from the entrepreneurial world, with a belief that publishing and sharing work is the most effective way to move a project forward.

Awards

There is no traditional 'jury prize' at the POV Hackathon. In its place is the 'Participants' Choice Award', decided upon by the participants. This decision arose in part from experience: 'At one lab, we gave two jury prizes and it was too much pressure, because [participants] were competing for a prize. I realised that people were trying to win, so we removed that, while keeping the right amount of pressure.'

The 'Participants' Choice Award' was also designed to give agency to participants. Only they really understand what they've been doing all weekend, so they choose who wins. By handing over the decision, the process, not just the project is taken into account when deciding a winner. For example, a project may not seem like it is the best to the audience or jury, but the participants know how far it has come since the start of the weekend.

PART TWO: THE POV HACKATHON WITHIN THE EVOLVING MODEL OF INTERACTIVE DOCUMENTARY PRODUCTION

OUTCOMES

Adnaan Wasey views the lab as the first cycle of a project, with the hope that participants will then refine and continue development. Although the lab is primarily run for experimentation purposes, POV have continued their relationship with some projects and participants. However, this ongoing relationship is viewed as something very separate from the lab and is not tied in with the overall aims but a subsidiary outcome.

POV as a platform

'Once the lab is over, then I wear a different hat and I'll think about "Are these projects worthy of funding for POV or other kinds of support?"' said Wasey. The 'support' from POV is not always direct funding, but can be in the form of creative assistance for a project to assist its development. This kind of support can be invaluable, particularly if funding is secured elsewhere.

At the time of writing, the following projects received direct funding from POV through the POV Interactive Shorts platform:

- *The Whiteness Project* (Dow 2014): an investigation of ethnicity and what it means to be white through candid perspectives on the polarising subject of race in America.
- *Empire* (Jongsma and O'Neill 2014): a global examination of the unintended consequences of Dutch colonialism pushes the boundary of what is possible online with web video that flips, spins, fragments and reconnects stories.
- *Unknown Spring* (Price amd Menon 2014): an exploration of post-nuclear di-

saster Japan weaves together art, artefacts and data to highlight the resilience of one survivor who has remained in Fukushima.

Although there was no mandate for these particular projects to continue working with POV, their development coincided with the creation of POV Interactive Shorts, which launched in 2014. As well as being at the right stage of production, these projects fitted in with POV's remit for the series or had the ability to make something that would work for it.

Despite these projects receiving this particular support, POV have continued to work with many of the people and projects from other labs. 'For example, we hired one of the developers who participated in a POV Hackathon, and have funded alumni to work on other projects that came after their POV Hackathon experience.' Wasey also continues to work informally with others, demonstrating the role the lab has to play in developing long-term networks.

Beyond PBS

Other projects that were developed in the lab have received funding or support from other organisations and achieved their own success beyond POV. The organisation UnionDocs started to create a tool in the first POV Hackathon, under the umbrella of the ongoing *Living Los Sures* i-doc project (Allen *et al* 2014). They came to the lab wanting to develop shifting navigational features that work creatively with video assets. From this initial development, the tool evolved into *Shot by Shot*,[3] an interactive experience that was released as part of the *Living Los Sures* project (discussed elsewhere in this collection).

Another direct offshoot was the project *Data Docs* (2013), which followed Wasey's cyclical ambitions for the lab by participating in two consecutive events. In the first POV Hackathon, they developed a concept through a prototype called 'Op-Video', which sought to re-imagine journalism for the digital age. Susan E. McGregor, Assistant Professor at Columbia Journalism School and lab participant explained the project development process: 'I was lucky enough to be part of the first Hackathon, and it was a really great experience. While our team shared a topical interest, our backgrounds and approaches were really complementary, which made it a rich and exciting learning process. The preparation help we got from the organisers was also incredibly valuable, and, I think, a key reason why we accomplished so much during the weekend. In fact, it was so successful that we continued to meet and develop the project in the subsequent months' (McGregor 2012). The second round allowed them to take on a new aspect of the project, *Data Docs*, which subsequently received funding from the Knight Foundation to continue development.

Lastly, an interactive counterpart for the linear documentary film, *Aatsinki: The Story of Arctic Cowboys* (Oreck *et al* 2013) was also developed within the first POV Hackathon. Entitled *The Aatsinki Season*, it had existing finance from the linear project and was able to go live online about three months after the lab.

In parallel to the experiences of other makers in the i-docs field, a project's lifespan is uncertain and varied. The outcomes for the projects from the lab are reliant upon so many different factors that there is no 'ideal' journey to follow. Along with the previous examples, which have all followed different, yet 'successful' paths, there are also a number of teams that are still working on projects without funding, but which could develop into something more concrete in the future.

THE PITFALLS

Creating the prototype is a solid springboard to start with, but it is nowhere near the end of a project. The real hard work is after the lab and participants must be aware of this. Wasey is keen that participants separate what happens during the lab, and the value of continuing the project. The intense development which happens over the weekend is unlikely to continue, as most participants have full-time jobs. This is coupled with the harsh reality of finding funding for a project, especially immediately. In contrast to the fast pace of the lab, the next steps will normally form a far slower process and in some cases, may never develop at all.

THE FUTURE

The POV Hackathon began as a response to a level of stagnation within the interactive documentary field, with the intention of moving the craft forwards. To do this, the model reflects the real demands of interactive documentary production, with collaborative working practices forming a central element. Technologists and media-makers are introduced, in some cases having never previously worked in a multidisciplinary team. These creative collaborations encourage cross-disciplinary communication and spur new working methods, such as iterative design practices. The skills picked up are vital to i-doc production, highlighting the different and varied needs of an interactive project to a linear one.

Alongside this, the POV Hackathon model is also a response to the sparse funding opportunities for interactive documentary makers. As a public media organisation, funding interactive projects on a continuous, individual basis is beyond their capacity and remit. However, by giving a space – both physically and mentally – to filmmakers and technologists to develop an idea, holds equal value for both the organisation and the field. It gives the time and skills to make an idea a reality, even if it that reality is a prototype. Allowing for the rapid development of ideas, the space to test and potentially fail and perhaps most crucially, providing good documentation of the process and adhering to open source practices, feeds into the advancement of the field as a whole.

Whilst i-docs remain on the fringe of the documentary world (although mainstream recognition is growing), there is not a well-trodden path for access to production skills, collaborative working methods or funding routes. This, coupled with outputs that vary hugely in terms of style, and success that is hard to quantify or measure, can make it hard for interactive work to be given the development it needs. The need for the lab space, even in a resource-rich country like the USA, highlights the difficulty of making work in the field.

Beyond the lab itself, having such a committed and ongoing relationship from a key industry figure like POV further legitimises the interactive documentary field as something important and worthy of investment – from the perspective of funders, commissioners and makers alike. The next step, to really push the field and the diversity of work made, is to expand the hack model geographically – something POV don't have the capacity to do. For this reason, Adnaan Wasey is keen to encourage others to adopt the same model, or indeed modify and build off it – allowing for the worldwide growth of interactive documentary labs.

NOTES

1   At the time of writing the name of the lab was the 'POV Hackathon' and is referred as either this, or just 'lab' throughout the chapter. It became the 'POV Digital Lab' in June 2016. More information and documentation about both the previous and upcoming POV Hackathon labs is available at http://www.pbs.org/pov/hackathon

2   All quotes are from a long interview conducted with Adnaan Wasey in 2015, unless otherwise stated.

3   *Shot by Shot* is one of four distinct projects that form the UnionDocs *Living Los Sures* project. It breaks the original 1984 documentary *Los Sures* (Diego Echeverría) down into individual shots – each of which contain their own story – and presents them back through an interactive interface.

REFERENCES

Allen, Christopher *et al* (2014) *Living Los Sures*. Expansive web documentary project. Produced by UnionDocs; http://lossur.es/about-living-los-sures/. Accessed 31 October 2016.

Dow, Whitney (2014) *The Whiteness Project*. Web documentary. Co-produced by KUDOS Design Collaborator and POV; http://whitenessproject.org/. Accessed 31 October 2016.

Irani, Lilly (2015) 'Hackathons and the Making of Entrepreneurial Citizenship', *Science, Technology & Human Values*, 40, 799–824.

Jongsma, Eline and Kel O'Neill (2014) *Empire*. Web Documentary; http://www.pbs.org/pov/empire. Accessed 20 October 2016.

McGregor, Susan E. (2012) *POV Hackathon: Know Your Hackers*. Op-video; http://www.pbs.org/pov/blog/povdocs/2012/08/pov-hackathon-know-your-hackers-joe-posner-op-video. Accessed 31 October 2016.

OpenBSD (2000) Hackathons; http://www.openbsd.org/hackathons.html. Accessed 31 October 2016. Images courtesy of POV/American Documentary. https://www.flickr.com/photos/povdocs/sets. Accessed 31 October 2016.

Oreck, Jessica, Mike Knowlton and Hal Siegl (2013) *Aatsinki: The Story of Arctic Cowboys*. Web documentary. Produced by Myriapod Productions; http://arcticcowboys.com/. Accessed 31 October 2016.

Posner, Joe, Susan E. McGregor and Lam Thuy Vo (2013) *Data Docs*. Web documentary; http://www.datadocs.org/POV2/. Accessed 31 October 2016.

Price, Jake and Visakh Menon (2014) *Unknown Spring*. Web Documentary; http://www.unknownspring.com/chapters_menu.html. Accessed 31 October 2016.

THE LEARN DO SHARE DESIGN METHODOLOGY
LANCE WEILER IN CONVERSATION

Sandra Gaudenzi

It is hard to give a specific title to Lance Weiler. Wikipedia describes him as a filmmaker but, on his own website, he shifts from 'a storyteller, entrepreneur and thought leader' to a 'writer, director & experience designer'. In the transmedia industry, most people would describe him as a pioneer in the field, or as a facilitator in collaborative storytelling, the initiator of the Learn Do Share (LDS) global collective and founding member and director of the Columbia University School of the Arts' Digital Storytelling Lab.

The reality is that Weiler does all of these things. He started as a cameraman in commercial shoots, moved into movie writing and production and then went on to experiment with interactive narratives by co-writing *Collapsus* (2010), directing the *Pandemic* experience (2011) and acting as experience designer on *Bear 71* (2012) – to cite just a few examples.

As a constant throughout his career, Weiler has pushed the boundaries of storytelling towards a more participative paradigm. In 2008, he started the DIY Days, an event aimed at mixing open collaboration, design and social innovation – which he later re-branded as LDS, a grassroots innovation engine and a combination of events, labs and peer production. What originally started as an experiment is now an established annual event that runs in twelve cities worldwide. The methodology that came out of it is freely shared through the LDS website, and has become an open resource for digital storytellers and social innovators.

LDS is one of the possible answers to the current need to establish new methodologies for working in fields such as digital storytelling, where multi-disciplinary teams are struggling to adopt a common creative process when working together. The lack of a shared language, of a transparent process and of agreed

Fig 1: Lance Weiler at LDS Laika's adventure workshop, 2014.

project aims are often acting as barriers to the success and clarity of digital projects. It is in this context that I have interviewed Lance Weiler: in the hope to connect the dots between the design process of an i-doc and its potential final coherence. What can we learn from the LDS methodology and how can we use it in i-doc production?

Sandra Gaudenzi: You started as a filmmaker, and gradually moved towards transmedia production. At which stage did you decide that a new methodology of production had to be adopted in digital projects? Tell us more about the background of the LDS methodology.

Lance Weiler: Well, I think that, in a lot of ways, I came up on film sets. I came up working in the commercial industry and working on music videos. I would always make many films. I always loved the collaborative aspect of being in a problem-solving situation. Film is incredibly collaborative. Even if it's a hierarchy at some point, it still is this amazing form where people can come together from all different disciplines, achieve a common goal, and are willing to problem-solve and just go with the flow.

When I started to look at my own work and, as a creator, think about the stories that I was telling, I was just looking at how things were rapidly changing. In some cases, initially, it was this idea that the physical forms were disappearing, like the physical media was eroding away, and market share was diminishing too for films. It was maybe around 2006 when I became frustrated with some of the industry systems that existed.

Why are we fighting against this permission-based culture all the time? There are all these new, amazing ways that you can reach people, tell stories and engage. There is a whole new audience that's going to be coming up and the way that they consume is changing.

I just started to think that I didn't feel like a filmmaker anymore. I don't feel like it defines me. I don't cut on film, I don't exhibit on it and I don't shoot on it much anymore, yet it defines me. I'm a filmmaker. I have this weird 'back and forth' with it.

Arthur C. Clarke says something like 'any sufficiently advanced technology is indistinguishable from magic'. I constantly feel that.

I started to become interested in this idea of including design methodologies in my work, and started to become interested in ways that I could embrace collaborative practice and ways that I could challenge and create work where I could R&D things.

Lyka's Adventure (2014) and *Pandemic* (2011) are perfect examples of that. A lot of my projects have long gestation periods or long development periods. A lot of people have a hard time with that. They want to move on to 'what's next', but I find I learn so much as I go along.

The opportunity to learn and then be able to share my learning made me want to shift my practice and through that maybe I can shift an industry. I guess design, for me, became this really interesting thing in my toolbox. It expanded what that toolbox was and the possibilities for what I could do, and it made me start to really think more about the *why*, which is funny, because it's something that I would do when I would write a screenplay. When I would write fiction, I would take the time to ask myself 'Why is this character doing this? Why? What does the character want and what does the character truly need?' Those were already design questions embedded in my writing process.

But then, there was this gap between my ideas and the realisation process of the film. And I started thinking: 'It can happen right now. It doesn't have to wait and gestate forever. It doesn't have to be perfect before it goes out.' At that time, these agile software methodologies started to come in, and all of a sudden people started speaking about rapid prototyping.

So all of a sudden, I started to fight against the perfection I had been taught in film craft and I started to realise, 'Oh, wow, this is like a twenty-first century rewrite. All I'm doing is just using different tools to write and to make something.' I think that's where it really started to open up in my mind and way to conceive my work.

SG: Would you say that what you call now the LDS methodology comes from you taking some processes from the design and software world and adapting them to the craft of storytelling?

LW: Yes. I would add two other terms: 'game mechanics' and 'experience design'. But especially 'collaborative design'. You could argue that there is user-centric design within software, because you design for users, but I'm more interested in not just what users do, and their behaviour, but in how they can become an invested participant in what the project is. The more invested they are in it, the further it can go.

Looking back I realised 'Wow, there's this whole other world out there, and there's another way to do stories.' So I started to bring those ideas together and mashed it up a bit to create what was then called the DIY Days.

SG: The DIY Days have evolved into what is now called LDS. Those are normally two days where people come together and participate in a creative process that is a bit like a hack with no software involved. Could you tell us how LDS works?

LW: Well, I think the idea with LDS is to experiment with collaborative design, first and foremost. You know, it's a reflection of the times; I've seen more and more with the work that I make that the audiences are their own storytellers, they're creating stories all the time.

And that, combined with certain changes in consumption, and the ability to mobilise in ways that it wasn't possible before, there's this real growth that's fascinating. It's incredibly chaotic, and it's really challenging. It's probably the area that's the most difficult, because you need to decide when you let something go, and when you don't; how much do you hold on to the process, and when do you let other people into that process?

And so, LDS became this really interesting way to explore open design, to create like a social sandbox, to bring in people from a variety of different, diverse backgrounds. It came out of this desire, that the development process is kind of broken for most content. It's a permission-based culture, for the most part, even though ironically we live in a time where the tools are considerably democratised. A lot of people are still hung up with the funding mechanisms, and hung up with kind of trying to adhere to different funding protocols, or schemes, or whatever they need to, and it's holding back exploration, it's holding back creators at a time where the tools are readily available.

So these events are a way to kind of spark collaboration between people, but it's also a way to continually iterate processes, and to experiment in a way that you have a group of people who come together, who represent a wide diversity of skills.

So it really came from that desire of not wanting to wait for things to happen, changing development processes, and saying, 'Can we use the event as a way to tackle challenges, and work towards impact?'

We are really addressing the mix between story and code, and those development cycles that are very different because the grammar behind it, the language behind it, the teams behind it, and the processes behind it are very different. They constantly butt up against each other, and create friction.

So a lot of the time we'll start with an immersive lab, and we'll bring together as many of the different stakeholders as we can. Then I'll come in with some design questions, I'll come in with some ideas that I have, some themes that I want to explore. But I'll really try to get a diversity of people. We might have a UX specialist, a data scientist or researchers. We might have mobile or web developers, designers. We might bring in people who are directly affected by whatever we're exploring, who are experiencing what we're trying to get at, or what we're trying to connect with.

Then we'll run through a process which is called EDIT (Empathy, Define, Ideate, Test) which mixes design thinking and some methodologies that Freedom Lab has developed, and that we've brought to the table too, as Learn Do Share. And we'll start with an 'Empathy' phase, and use that as a way to gain insight from the group.

We have a number of different ways that we do that. A lot of those are readily accessible through learndoshare.net where we openly explain in detail the process for others to follow it.

The EDIT process starts with empathy, where you're trying to really drill down and connect with the other people that are in the room with you. And then you start working on the design level by shaping a design question, and informing that design question.

Because the temptation is to just jump right in, and start to iterate, and try to come up with the ideas to solve the problem; but then you're going to get kind of lost, you're going to go away from where your core is.

And so, a lot of times, at that point, we'll shape the design question and use that as a filter, and the design question will usually have a multiple number of layers to it.

The design question is like a mission statement for your project. For example I could say that, for LDS, it is a quote by Buckminster Fuller that I will paraphrase like this: 'How do you make the world work for 100 per cent of humanity, in the shortest time possible, through spontaneous cooperation, without disadvantage to anyone or ecological damage?' Right there, there's like five different, four or five different major design questions, packed in that one thing.

But then, we'll use the design question as a way to always go back, and use it as a compass, almost. You know, 'Are we off course? Is this working for 100 per cent of people? Are we being cooperative in the way that we're doing it? Is anybody disadvantaged because of this? Is it ecologically sound?' So we have these filters that we can use.

So once you have that design question, then when you move into the 'Ideation' phase, the 'I' in the EDIT process, and you now at least have a collective reference that you can go back to, and that everybody recognises as the goal.

Then you just start to go through the ideation process with those various people who are in the room, and then you get into breaking into prototypes. We'll often go off and do really rudimentary paper prototypes. You know, we'll just try things, we'll test things, just quickly.

Some of that comes from agile methods of development or Scrum, and some borrows from Lean Startup and Minimum Viable Product, and all the buzzwords that are associated with that. But the core of it is that we are taking a group of really smart people from a diversity of backgrounds; bringing them into a time scenario, a pressure cooker almost; and using a number of tools to help mine the collective intelligence of the group.

I find that works really well, because you start to develop a common language. You bond with those people that you're working with. You meet them face-to-face. A lot of the teams that you end up working with now are kind of displaced, they're in different places, so you're looking at Google Hangouts or Skype chats. So it's nice to actually be in a room together at some point within it.

And then, you're kind of developing those core design principles that you're going to carry forward. Sometimes we craft stories around them. In some industries, there'd be a user journey. Depending on the project, it might be a learning journey, it might be a user journey. Whatever it is, our community journey, we will craft stories.

SG: So what is the final aim of the event?

LW: The goal of that immersive lab is to come out on the other side with a common understanding of where we're headed, and of what we're trying to build, so that the core of it is shared. Because a lot of times, I think projects will start from a creator having a vision of what they want to do, but then it breaks down as it goes, because of misunderstandings, as the grammar, the language, isn't there yet.

You say something to somebody, and they don't really understand it, you're talking past each other, and you think it's okay. But then all of a sudden, they go and they spend two weeks coding something, they bring it back, and it doesn't work.

Or you have people who code, and all of a sudden there's glitches, and then you're like, 'Oh my god, that's a beautiful thing. Can we play with that? Because I just found something in that that I didn't even know about.' But they would have never showed it to you.

So in a way what we are trying to create is a space in which you can collaborate.

SG: Problem solving could be a double-edged sword. If one gets the balance wrong, and uses too much of a design methodology in interactive storytelling, is there a risk that one ends up prioritising functionality rather than poetry? In the sense of adopting an 'app for a purpose' logic, rather than a 'story for the pleasure' one?

LW: In my experience, I think that the real opportunity is right in that tension. It's in that idea of, 'Okay, why do you think about it as an app? Why do you think about it that way? And why do you separate yourself from the story part?'

Because once you actually know how the app would work, or what you want the functions to be, it seems very natural that you could then start to shape stories, and that's where user journeys come from. But why can't you shape the user journeys to be something that's more emotionally relevant, and more powerful? Why can't you start to shift the story, and use that to drive what the product is? As opposed to having the product driving the story, do it the other way round: from the story to the product.

SG: Mixing story and product means mixing creative teams from the beginning. Is this something that you see happening around you?

LW: No, not enough. This is why we are doing LDS. I think that we need to invent new processes to communicate, so that we can really equally collaborate in a project. This means building a common knowledge, and also a common language.

A lot of times you'll find groups who are really comfortable with certain types of technology, or they're skilled in certain ways, and they kind of end up pushing you towards those solutions because those are what they're comfortable with, even if they don't mean to. So it becomes challenging for people who don't know that side to step into it, and it becomes intimidating, because there's a lot of places where it can go wrong. There are a lot of places where, all of a sudden, you're too far down a path, and you start making all these compromises that you didn't want to make.

For anybody who's working, whether they're doing a documentary or just telling a story, you know that it's about reducing those compromises to the vision of what you're trying to make. If you're trying to really drive impact, or create a message, you don't want to be watering it down, or creating a situation where you're not able to do something that you could really activate on, or that you could really make happen.

There's nothing worse than almost kind of getting there, and knowing the whole time that you could get there, but because you don't understand the technological side of it, you're like in handcuffs. You're seeing it, and it's almost like you're going over a cliff, and you're watching it, you're watching it, you're watching it, and you're kicking yourself, because you're like, 'I wish I understood that process.' So I think bringing the people together, developing that common language, and setting those goals and shared objectives, is really important.

SG: Would you say that the priority at the moment is in creating that common language for multi-disciplinary teams to work together?

LW: We are at the beginning. I feel like we're at this silent film point. They used to just shoot a stage, and the camera would be there, and the actors would just move in front of it. And then, one day, someone realised they could move the camera, take it outside, and they started to shape the grammar of what cinema is today.

I feel like right now, it's more compounded, because all of a sudden the audience can contribute with its work. We live in this really incredibly fragmented landscape, so it's really hard for creators. We are driven by platforms, formats and technology, and people have a really difficult time understanding how to use them. It's like a one-to-one relationship. They look at something like Facebook or Twitter, and they only see what they are told to look at. They don't see how they could take the data that comes from the device and use it in really interesting ways, or start open data initiatives, or how data can become a creative tool in what they do.

Data can be a tool for finding and telling of stories, as much as it can be a tool for measuring success.

So I think, in some ways, it's just a matter of experimentation. In a lot of the work that I'm personally doing, and what we're doing with LDS, is creating a space where you can experiment. It's really hard to find those places, although we really need them to move to the next stage of interactive language.

SG: We live in a world where technology is constantly evolving. How can we create a methodology of work that is not immediately going to be obsolete? Has the LDS format evolved in the past years?

LW: LDS constantly evolves. Multiple times, we've walked away from people wanting to give us large amounts to keep it in that format, because it was successful, but every time we keep evolving with the model. I think the process can be exported into so many other fields. Take education as an example. This is why we are working now to bring LDS into places such as Columbia University. To prototype the future of the university. Yes, it's almost like a lateral kind of structure, instead of a hierarchy. It's this idea of, 'Okay, I move to the teams that I need, when I need those teams.'

A university is by definition multidisciplinary. We are building out in a place where we can tap the talent all across the university, and by doing so we go across the silos. Because the silos in our society are indicative of everything. Those are all twentieth-century models.

SG: At the core of LDS is the belief that collaborative creation is a positive thing. Some people would strongly disagree and say that collaborative design dilutes the final product. Where is your belief coming from? Do you thing that collaborative work has more impact?

LW: A lot of documentary work raises issues to a group of people that already knows about them. But for me the real question is, 'Do you want this to go further than the people who do this or are victims of this? Do you want your product to help change policies? Do you want it to mobilise people? To go further?' I guess it comes down to what your goals are.

When I think about docs, I often wonder how so much money and resources can go into crafting something that's going to be on the screen, and then … it's gone. For me, using design methods and starting from the things you know you want to solve is more efficient. 'Why am I really making this work? How can I meet my design question with the project I am doing?' These are simple questions, but they are so critical. And they can only be answered with the collaboration of the people that are involved.

SG: So let's come back to the community of documentary-makers. If you had to illustrate why a methodology like LDS could help them in their creative process, what would you say?

LW: I would just say it's really easy to experiment with. It's something that can happen without a lot of investment, and it's something that you can just try. It might not be for everybody, and design is not the answer to all the ills of the world. But I think it is a way to give yourself an extension of your craft. It allows you to challenge the way in which you're thinking about approaching your digital productions.

As I said earlier, we are often too much driven by technology. Today, the latest flavour is VR so 'Oh, VR. I'm going to tell a story with VR.' Whereas, I feel like what is really needed is to take the time to understand the human experience of what we are trying to do. Then, you can figure out what the technology is.

I think that ability to understand how to work with other disciplines is something that design can help with. It helps you to make sure that you have a series of core questions, or principles, that you can always look at and say, 'Is that really solving what we said we wanted to solve? Does it really answer the issues we wanted to face?'

REFERENCES

Digital Storytelling Lab (2015) http://www.digitalstorytellinglab.com. Accessed 31 October 2016.

Freedom Lab (2015) http://www.freedomlab.org. Accessed 31 October 2016.

Learn Do Share (2015) http://www.learndoshare.net. Accessed 31 October 2016.

Weiler, Lance (2010) *Collapsus*. Interactive documentary. Directed by Tommy Pallotta, produced by Submarine Channel; http://www.collapsus.com. Accessed 31 October 2016.

____ (2011) *Pandemic 1.0*. Immersive storytelling experience. Produced by Lance Weiler; http://www.lanceweiler.com/portfolio/pandemic-1-0/. Accessed 31 October 2016.

____ (2012) *Bear 71*. Installation Co-creator. Interactive documentary created by Jeremy Mendes and Leanne Allison, produced by NFB Interactive; http://bear71.nfb.ca/#/bear71. Accessed 31 October 2016.

____ (2015) *Lyka's Adventure*. Experiential learning project. Produced by Lance Weiler; http://www.welovelyka.com. Accessed 31 October 2016.

____ (2016) Personal website; http://www.lanceweiler.com. Accessed 31 October 2016.

Wikipedia (2015) 'Lance Weiler'. https://en.wikipedia.org/wiki/Lance_Weiler. Accessed 31 October 2016.

TESTING AND EVALUATING DESIGN PROTOTYPES
THE CASE STUDY OF *AVATAR SECRETS*

Ramona Pringle

INTRODUCTION

With the widespread adoption of mobile touch screens, intuitive interactive functionality is literally at our fingertips like never before. This functionality enables narratives to be designed deep instead of wide, where audiences can explore the specific elements of a story that most appeals to them. But with this new emergence of interactive storytelling and user experience, how is the documentary production process changing?

Avatar Secrets (Ramona Pringle Productions 2015)[1] is an interactive documentary for the iPad. It is designed for touch screens to be viewed either in a 'lean back' movie mode, or in an 'interactive mode' with layers of rich media and additional features that let viewers dig deeper into its themes. Using *Avatar Secrets* as a case study, this chapter will examine how user experience can be devised as a component of the narrative from its inception.

Avatar Secrets was designed to bring the layered richness of a transmedia experience into one handheld device. Innovative features create an intuitive interactive movie experience that participants can dive deeper into as the story explores the complexities of human connection in the networked world.

Developed as an app, and utilising the media affordances of tablet touch screen devices, this i-doc intertwines a personal POV journey with layers of additional content including case studies, interviews and vignettes.

The main storyline follows the journey of the protagonist, after a series of personal misfortunes leave her unsettled and searching for meaning, and she ventures into the world of massive online games, to escape and to try and find answers. A virtual tourist in new terrain, she creates an avatar; even though her new avatar is just pixels and data, and even though it is her, she soon finds that her digital alter ego has a lot to teach her about levelling up, about this new world … and about herself.

As the true-life story progresses, *Avatar Secrets* examines and unpacks a number of contemporary issues and themes – from our ability to access information and the concept of the filter bubble, to the complex nature of human connection in a world where we are constantly digitally connected. Embedded inside the main storyline, these micro-narratives provide the audience with the ability to dig deeper into themes and issues, through related interviews, extended scenes and additional documentary storylines. Interview clips are interwoven through hyperlinks, into the main storyline, and are accessible through keywords and themes as a secondary access into the narrative.

The viewer can engage with as much or as little of the additional content as she wishes, digging deeper into thematic explorations, but able to return coherently to the main storyline at any time. Instead of using a branching path model, the user experience is designed so that the component parts always favour narrative cohesion; the timeline can be expanded to include additional perspectives and formats of exploration and analysis, or contracted for a condensed, more 'filmic' experience.

Designed to give audiences choices about how they interact with the media – either engaging with the main storyline in 'movie mode' for a lean back experience, or exploring the branches that divert from individual scenes in 'interactive mode' – *Avatar Secrets* brings the richness of a transmedia experience into one device, by integrating different stories, formats and aesthetics into one seamless experience.

INTERACTIVE FROM INCEPTION

Avatar Secrets was conceived, pitched and commissioned as an interactive project. The philosophy was that a complex story about digital media and how we connect should be told in an equally digital way.

The project was commissioned by TVO, a public media channel, with a mandate to educate as well as entertain. While this was a flagship interactive production for the broadcaster, it was still considered a documentary, with strong storytelling being the core of the project.

The design intent with *Avatar Secrets* was to tell an engaging, contemporary story with a compelling arc, and layer in interactive features and functionality to enrich the experience and add layers of analysis and additional content. Both the broadcaster team and the production team were committed to using interactive tools to enhance a compelling story and to give viewers more options with regards to how they engage with the narrative.

From the time *Avatar Secrets* was green-lit for development, the project evolved through a series of iterative phases and subsequent presentations in which interest in the subject matter and the approach to its execution was gauged. In these preview events and feedback sessions, the concept and premise was shared, the eponymous 'secrets' were presented along with the narrative, and early samples of media were exhibited. From this process, the initial premise was confirmed. The narrative strategy would be two-fold: to tell an engaging story, and to provide rigorous conceptual analysis through expert interviews and other interactive features. Based on this conceptual framework, user experience goals were established at the beginning of pre-production, influencing the functional design: it had to be easy, it had to be intuitive, and it had to give users the option to engage how they wanted to – either as a 'lean back' or 'lean forward' interactive experience.

Despite the ubiquity of mobile touch screen devices, even after identifying common best practices for user experience and navigation, ease of use cannot be assumed (Norman 2013: 226). As such, user testing and iterative design were established as tent poles of the development methodology; distinct components of the production were cyclically built, tested and revised (2013: 222). This way, user experience and design features could be imagined, prototyped and tested with representative members of the established audience, before a specific feature or experience flow was fully developed or realised.

While a traditional film may not be 'tested' on audiences until its near completion, the development of an i-doc is often more akin to the development of a new piece of software, whereby it is common not to know how a particular feature might function in use, until it is tested.

The development process employed in creating *Avatar Secrets* borrows from software development and agile production – a methodology that stresses early testing and iterative design that can be adjusted to account for feedback. This approach also emphasises knowing your user and building for him or her (2013: 8). Another concept that is prominent within the agile method is that of the minimum viable product (MVP), whereby the team identifies the smallest possible milestone that can be completed and shared for testing and feedback (Ries 2011: 77). Working within a series of iterative MVP's allows the team to test concepts or features individually, throw away ideas that don't test well, and make adjustments before integrating those features and testing the overall product. Not only is it beneficial for the development team to prototype feature by feature using this strategy, it also helps focus users who are offering feedback during a testing session (Warfel 2009: 91).

CONCEPT TESTING

While much of this chapter will focus on best practices for iterative design and testing in the creation of an i-doc, the notion of concept testing should also be addressed, as identifying audience interest in a story and approach to execution is a crucial component of the development process.

As a form, the i-doc, arguably more than any other format of documentary, relies on the engagement of the viewer. In many cases, the story only progresses if the user or viewer allows it to through overt interaction. Moreover, as a matter of discoverability, an i-doc is still likely to face more challenges with regards to finding an audience, as it lives outside of the traditional infrastructure of mainstream media; as such, the i-doc relies heavily on the audience as a means of distribution. In this respect, the i-doc may be a true media maverick. The best practices for audience engagement that are developed for these projects can also usefully inform online distribution. As legacy media seek to respond to a changing media ecosystem and evolving audience behaviours, they inevitably will have to adapt to the new attention economy.

What makes the issue more complex is that the i-doc – like the documentary film – is not always designed to be easy or entertaining; the intent of this format is often to educate or provoke. Balanced somewhat precariously between these two poles lies concept testing. For the creators of i-docs, there is more often than not a responsibility to educate as well as entertain, and the challenge is in identifying the often invisible line between 'giving the audience what they want' – what gets the first or fastest click – and engaging them in thought provoking subject matter as a tool for social good. In this framing, perhaps concept testing, for the i-doc creator, is not about the popularity of a given topic, but rather, the extent to which that topic can be made engaging, thought provoking, or novel through the unique approach to execution.

At the stage of concept definition, one of the first questions the creator of an i-doc will ask of him or herself is: 'How do you find a method of approaching a topic that people will engage with?' In this initial stage, it is valuable to test *approaches to a concept*, as opposed to testing just the concept itself. After all, for the i-doc, as was the case with *Avatar Secrets,* form and content are interwoven; the beauty of an interactive format is that how the story is presented or experienced is part of the story itself.

Moving beyond concept definition or ideation, the 'MVP' strategy whereby a testable product is created as quickly and efficiently as possible, can also be used to test the success of the approach to the content. The ability to test the execution of an approach through an actual interactive demo is vital, as creative intent and testable results may differ from the proposal stage to the prototype stage, based on skill, execution or other unanticipated factors.

With a successful i-doc, every technological feature, possible interaction, or interface element, should ultimately reinforce or enhance the narrative experience, and as such, as component parts of the user experience are tested and refined, questions relating to conceptual success – especially if and how specific elements impact the project's conceptual success – should additionally be asked of testers. This process will also help eliminate 'feature creep' or unnecessary clutter that might confuse users or detract from the intended experience.

While concept testing, or the testing of approaches to a concept, is most necessary at the early stages of a project, these considerations should be maintained throughout the production cycle.

THE PRODUCTION CYCLE

With *Avatar Secrets,* the production cycle was divided into pre-production, development (here, the term 'development' is used in the context of industry accepted terminology for the period before production begins, not to be confused with technical development), demo production and production.

The development process was open and public from the conception of the project. As the project progressed through development and production, different aspects of the concept design and approach were shared with the public, both at festivals and through the project's website. In keeping with the 'MVP' development approach, each presentation was unique and featured new content, allowing for incremental feedback on different aspects of the concept, content, creative approach, narrative structure and technical design.

i. Pre-production yielded paper prototypes, wireframes and mock-ups, as well as a narrative document outlining the linear story arc and branching content. The purpose of paper prototypes was to integrate storyboards (figure 1) and sample functionality, to communicate to testers, and notably to the broadcaster and other funders, how the experience would work, and how the interactivity would interplay with the narrative, with the ultimate goal of testing the overall concept and approach. Through photoshopped prototypes and wireframes overlaid on top of storyboards, these preliminary test groups were able to see how the distinct

Fig. 1: A sample storyboard from *Avatar Secrets*.

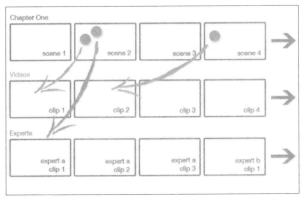

Fig. 2: Mock-ups were created to test the concept and functionality.

Fig. 3: Wireframe-style paper prototypes mapped out how distinct content pieces were related to each other.

media types would work together (figure 2), and where and how the transition points between the main storyline and additional layers of content would be accessible (figure 3). It should be noted that having the paper prototypes as a resource influenced the subsequent process of data collection and interviews, by informing how that content would be integrated into the overarching narrative scope.

ii. Development spanned approximately six months for the core team of six, including writer/director/interaction designer, creative director, animator, illustrator, videographer and iOS developer. This phase culminated with multiple iterations of a functional prototype, including what would become the underlying architecture of the i-doc.

As a final deliverable for development, the aim was to produce one of ten chapters from the final project in full. While the development process was iterative and broken into smaller component parts for the sake of testing, the cumulative result of this phase of production was a functional interactive demo that included most aspects of the final product.

This demo chapter served as a creative and conceptual proof of concept, whereby the aesthetic approach of transitioning between animated illustrations and live-action footage to evoke the transition between online and offline worlds was actualised, and the emotional immersion of the narrative could be tested. Functional testing involved specific questions such as: 'How do you move forward in the story?'; 'Do you know how to "unlock" additional content or change the play mode?' Conceptual testing involved more open-ended questions, such as: 'What is this chapter about?'; 'How did the interactive elements enhance or detract from the narrative experience?'

In this phase, the sketched prototype was adapted to XCode, the iOS development platform and media assets were prototyped to test content flow and functionality. Much of the technical logic of the project was established during this phase, resulting in a development 'bible' with regards to the component parts and their assembly. The interactive structure was compiled as a string of clips, sometimes called a 'string of pearls' approach – all of which had to be optimised for playback and maximum resolution. Any lagging would detract from the goal of a seamless 'movie mode' playback. Invisible cuts between distinct clips provided an opportunity to insert 'hot buttons' – hyperlinks to additional layers of content – at the appropriate time.

Because ease of use was a priority, a cross-section of touch screen experiences and media were examined ranging from e-books and magazines to i-docs to video players to identify the most widely adopted user experience strategies for scene progression, page turning or advancing, visual navigation and help guides. The elements of the user experience functionality that were identified based on this market survey of ubiquitous practices were tested during development. The ethos was that a user should not need a tutorial to be able to navigate the project interactively; functionality should be adopted from the most ubiquitous current standards, be it from e-books or digital magazines for features such as place markers or page progression, or video services such as YouTube for video player controls.

During this phase, multiple distinct features were tested. Testing was conducted with a selection of approximately a dozen men and women representative of appropriate demographics, 19–29, 30–40 and 40+. As a rule, in testing sessions testers were given the app to manipulate with little to no direction, observed interacting with the app, and then interviewed on their experience afterwards. Some testers reviewed the experience multiple times throughout the development and production process, while others were brought in towards the end of development phases to test unique features or the experience a whole.

It is worth noting that the usefulness of user tests is directly related to the granularity of focus at different stages of testing. This aligns with the 'MVP' methodology, whereby component parts of the experience are built and tested before testing the overall experience, as the most useful feedback will relate specifically to the feature in question and that singular aspect of the experience, while more open-ended questions about the experience can be used to refine the concept. As creators design specific features and interactions, it can be valuable to go back and forth between testing functionality and testing the concept, to ensure that each feature behaves as intended, while at the same time ensuring that a specific feature doesn't detract from the desired narrative user experience.

Examples of features tested during the development of *Avatar Secrets* include:

The timing of hot buttons: Hot buttons are animated overlays that indicate to the user that more content can be accessed by tapping the screen. Additional media is linked thematically to the content in a particular scene. The timing of when those buttons appears requires precision and purposefulness.

In the first iteration, the hot button indicating that there is available branching content would appear from the beginning of that scene. Unfortunately, when this was tested, it was found that people would tap it and get pulled away from the scene in the middle of an action or dialogue, resulting in a jarring 'cut' and also a distraction from the narrative progression.

On evaluating that first iteration, one suggestion was to delay the playback of the subsequent hyperlinked clip; however, doing so would remove the feeling of agency from the experience – even though the user would in fact be selecting the next scene, he would not be aware of his impact on the playback, because of the

Fig. 4: At the end of a scene (left) a hot button appears, which transitions to additional content (right) when tapped.

delay between input and response. (Norman 2013: 23). Because the media assets were designed to transition seamlessly – whether it be between two neighbouring scenes in the main narrative or between a scene in the main narrative and a hyperlinked layered asset, with the introduction of a delay – the awareness that their behaviour impacted the narrative progression would be eliminated. Ultimately, the solution was to have the hot button(s) fade up towards the end of the scene, around -2 seconds from the end mark, and pause the scene until the viewer swiped the screen to progress (figure 4).

Playback of a musical score: For the soundtrack to work successfully, there were several considerations to take into account: the track needed to be timed to correspond with the duration of the chapter in 'movie mode', but also needed to loop or expand to account for the expansion of the timeline if users opted to select and view varying numbers of additional clips.

Based on the nature of the interactivity, a user viewing the project in interactive mode would have a unique run time for each individual chapter depending on his or her behaviour, and the music track needed to account for this; instrumental cues and swells couldn't be integrated into the audio track, because there is no guarantee that the cues would align appropriately.

While a musical accompaniment is often scored to match a linear film, in the case of an i-doc, the score needs to be complementary but separate. With *Avatar Secrets*, we tested whether the music should fade low or off completely when a viewer diverts away from the main narrative. Based on testing this aspect of the design with multiple users, it was concluded that having a continuous music track helped to ensure that, as a scene transitioned from the main storyline to a branching sequence in 'interactive mode', the illusion of seamlessness that we aspired to was maintained. The music track helped maintain the illusion of seamlessness that we aspired to.

iii. Demo production followed the development phase. In keeping with the 'MVP' methodology of building tools as necessary during the production process, once the functionality had been tested within the prototyped sample chapter; the next undertaking was the production of a trailer. It should be noted that, at this phase, only 10 per cent of the final narrative had been produced, as the prototype was one chapter out of an eventual ten. Building a trailer for a project that was still being created served multiple purposes. Similar to the prototype built during development, the trailer multi-purposed to convey the content and execution style in an applied manner and as a tool to raise public, industry and media awareness.

iv. Production. The rigorous testing done during pre-production and development provided a framework for production. From a technical standpoint, there was a template for all members of the production team to reference when considering file size and compression, the ideal length of component clips, and how those clips would transition. Because the interactivity was considered from the inception of the project and the mechanisms by which the user experience is integrated with the narrative were tested early on, by the time the team was in full production mode, the technical architecture and work flow had been largely established.

While the 'MVP' development process is useful for an episodic structure, the same principles can also be followed in a more open-ended i-doc. The best-designed experiences use a 'less is more' strategy, whereby the interactions and choices are curated and part of the overall experience design. There is a temptation to add in functionality and features just because you can, but this 'feature creep' should be avoided as it can overwhelm the user and ultimately distract from the messaging, narrative and experience. No matter how fluid or borderless the experience is, in an i-doc there is an interplay between form and content whereby how the story is told or designed is part of the experience of the narrative itself, and identifying this intersection can help pinpoint a minimum viable product to test, iterate and scale.

In the case of *Avatar Secrets*, a large part of production entailed populating the digital infrastructure that had been iterated in previous phases. Once the framework for ten chapters had been fully populated, the second major phase of testing was initiated. By this time, testing examined the flow of content, and the logic of the experience. While the story had been mapped and storyboarded to include all of the layers of content and branching sub-arcs, there is a different user experience when engaging with time-based media than when reading through paper sketches, and testing this iteration accounted for affordance-based adjustments that could not be considered at an earlier phase.

For example, while the visual navigation was ideated during development, the feature could not be comprehensively tested until it was substantially populated with content. The visual navigation features a secondary mode of indexing sub-clips including interviews and extended sequences. At any point, the user can switch between engaging with the i-doc linearly and exploring branching content as it is revealed on screen through 'hot spots', or explore additional content through the visual navigation. Testing at this phase was set up to answer questions including: 'When a user leaves the main narrative and selects what content to watch through the secondary navigation, where does he or she return to?'; 'How deep "down the rabbit hole" can a user explore, through hyperlinked content?'; 'How does the user keep track of where he or she is in the storyline, while wandering down different paths?'

The interface and user experience is designed so that no matter how the viewer navigates through content, the experience feels seamless. Through testing, it was established that no matter how far users progress down a particular path or tangent, they can always return to the same spot they were in, in the linear progression of the main storyline. As Jennifer Tidwell states in *Designing Interfaces*, 'the best kind of commuting is none at all' (2010: 160). In the case of *Avatar Secrets*, keeping a darkened poster image of the current scene in the background at all times reinforces this 'way finding', while the user explores additional paths of content (figure 5).

The final round of testing was more comprehensive than previous cycles, with the intent of finding bugs or flaws in the experience that had not been previously identified. Because of the nature of the touch screen interface, any time the viewer wants to pause the experience, all he or she has to do is tap the screen. Once he or she does so, the i-doc rests in a paused mode in which all of the functionality is visible, including the lower visual navigation and buttons for the setting and

Fig. 5: When the screen is paused, the background image is darkened to highlight the navigation and simplify the user interface.

Fig. 6: A version of the interface was tested in which a wayfindig question mark was visible at all times. In a second version, which we ultimately chose, the question mark only appears when the screen is tapped and play is paused.

help pages. At this stage, when the focus of testing was on making sure that way-finding was clear and trouble shooting was easily accessible to users who might find themselves confused, certain stakeholders requested the addition of more on screen prompts or that on screen prompts be viewable at all times. This note conflicted with the established intent of creating an immersive full-screen experience with a clean aesthetic whereby navigational assets would only be visible when necessary.

The scenario that required testing was: if a viewer needs help, will he or she pause the screen? Using an AB approach, two versions of the experience were tested – one in which a small question mark hovers in the top right-hand corner of the screen at all times, and another in which the experience is full-screen without any overlays until playback is paused (figure 6). The second, full-screen version ended up being successful in user tests, allowing the project to remain faithful to the original desire for it to be full-screen, without any unnecessary distractions from the narrative experience.

BEST PRACTICES

Based on the way in which iterative prototypes were developed, tested and evaluated throughout the production cycle in this case study, the following testing and evaluation strategies and best practices have been identified, as they pertain to the creation of i-docs:

1. Test early. While it is common for films to do test screenings, and common for new software or products to be tested during development, i-docs present a unique case in which both the narrative and the user experience need to be considered for testing and evaluation.

There is a famous line in the start-up world: 'fail fast, fail often' (Babineaux and Krumboltz 2013: 32). While failure might not seem like an optimum goal to be aiming for, the premise of this statement is that bugs, flaws or errors in judgement should be found early so that they can be resolved early. For creators who come at i-docs from the world of traditional filmmaking, the idea of testing early can be hard to adapt to; even for a filmmaker who seeks input on a rough cut, she has still compiled a full product before soliciting feedback. With an i-doc, it can be a mistake to finish a full pass of the project, even in rough form, before seeking input or testing the user experience; a more efficient strategy is to identify what the smallest component part is that can be fully executed, to build it, test it, evaluate the feedback, incorporate notes in a revised prototype and continue to iterate in that loop.

While this is more challenging the less the project is bound to traditional linear structure, it is advisable to create a prototype, to be able to *show* instead of *tell*, in soliciting feedback. There is often a temptation in interactive works for the designer to walk the user through the experience, but this should be avoided in testing.

2. Build and test one feature at a time. A good strategy for testing and evaluating an i-doc is to build it in iterative steps. Once you have conceptualised the overall project, and the interplay between interactivity and narrative, start building features or component parts, piece by piece. In the prototyping phase, only build and test the pieces you are unsure about. It is common to feel that in order to give a test user an accurate demonstration of the experience, it needs to include every feature. However, the only features that need to be tested are the ones that are in question. Identify the pivotal or novel elements of your user experience and build and test those individually for evaluation. Creators may also find it useful to pivot between testing a specific feature and testing the success of the approach to the content.

It should be noted that the challenge in offering a guide for user testing i-docs is that the scope of what constitutes an i-doc is very broad; in some cases, it might be more difficult to identify a standalone UX component, and designers may find that the testable 'MVP' is nearly the project in its entirety. The purpose of testing is to collect as much feedback as possible to refine the output, so that the experience is as close as possible to that which was intended. The process of testing forces the designer, or director, to ask of him or herself 'What is this about? What do I want the take away to be? What do I want the user to think or feel?' and then ascertain, through an iterative process, how accurate the user experience is to the creator's intent. The more that specific components of the experience can be identified, the more granular feedback can be, which in turn can help close any gaps that might exist between the creator's intent and actual user experience, as that precise feedback informs not just what was experienced, but why and how.

3. Employ tools for testing. There are two predominant ways of testing elements of an i-doc to make informed design decisions: one is through a task scenario, which is used to gauge whether a user knows how to do a particular task within the experience, or what to do to achieve a particular goal. The other evaluation strategy is AB testing, where the tester is presented with multiple options or scenarios for comparison.

Task scenarios are particularly helpful within the context of i-doc production, as functionality that seems obvious to the creator may not be as apparent to the end user. It is common for creators to get excited about a new interaction at the expense of its ultimate functionality or usability. As 'cool' as a novel feature might be, if the user doesn't know how to use it to progress the narrative, the experience is flawed. Be empathetic with your users. Good design should make users feel empowered to explore and be curious.

AB testing is employed when a decision needs to be made regarding the user experience. Often AB testing is done with regards to aesthetics and layout. In many cases, a task scenario will be employed to test how different features, layouts or assets impact a given scenario. The user will compare their experience of completing a task within multiple versions of a design for evaluation purposes. In both task scenarios and AB testing, be mindful to avoid offering hints or describing steps. It can be tempting to walk a user through an experience, but the value of user testing is being able to evaluate unbiased feedback to strengthen the design.

4. Identify all stakeholder goals early on and test for them. There is the story you want to explore, and then, because of the nature of the i-doc, there is the way the telling of that story impacts the story itself. Various stakeholders – whether it is members of the creative team, the research team, the technical development team or broadcast and funding partners – will have distinct goals for the project, how it is built, and what the ultimate experience should be like for users. These goals should frame how the project is tested and who it is tested with. It is easy, during production, to nudge your goals from their original intent, based on how a project evolves, and while a project will naturally take on a life of its own, it is also important to identify the purpose of the project and who it is for, and test with that in mind.

5. Find the right balance between art and product design. I-docs are unique as they tend to sit somewhere between art, journalism and product design. The ultimate goal is often to tell an evocative story that educates and entertains, and to inspire empathy through triggering the viewers' emotions. The technologies we have at our fingertips give storytellers boundless means of transporting audiences into immersive worlds, and creating layered experiences that curious viewers can dig deep into. That said, there is a fundamental catch: a flawed user experience acts as a gatekeeper to narrative immersion. If a user is confused about how he is supposed to interact with the material, or what is required of him to proceed at any time, the entire experience is sacrificed. As such, even though the act of creation an i-doc is essentially an act of storytelling, it is essential that it be equally an act of good product design that acknowledges the user and his needs.

6. Less is more. There is a temptation when working within an interactive format to keep adding features. This 'feature creep' is a natural side effect of giving viewers or users increased control or agency over the progression of a narrative; more choice is better, isn't it? Not always. Too many purposeless choices can take away from the choices that will impact the narrative or user experience in a profound way. A well-designed experience gives users only the choices they need, and only the choices that will meaningfully enhance the experience. Too many options overload the screen and detract from the narrative. Establishing constraints, either technical or creative, will push you to make purposeful decisions as a designer as to how interactivity is integrated with the narrative.

CONCLUSION

What differentiates the i-doc from other documentary works or narrative forms is its interactive nature. By definition, an interactive experience relies on user engagement, which means that in order to gauge the success of the narrative in an i-doc, it is necessary to see it 'in use'.

Where a traditional linear form can be evaluated on its own, an i-doc requires user interaction in order to be fully evaluated. This makes user engagement an essential element of the i-doc – as important as other dominant elements of the form, including the narrative, themes, interface and technology.

Even when the production process has wrapped, to evaluate the ultimate success of an i-doc necessitates that it be played with, poked at, and put to use. User testing is an essential element of the i-doc design process, through every stage, to measure the success of the user experience, user interface and overall narrative experience, because it is the only way for a creator to truly judge whether the intended experience, themes and narrative(s) are conveyed as intended. Several strategies and best practices for how best to incorporate user testing into the i-doc design and development process have been included in this chapter as a guide for creators. Because the scope of what constitutes an i-doc is so broad, not all strategies will be suitable for all projects, but an appreciation and respect for the active role of the user or viewer and a philosophy of testing early and often are integral elements in any i-doc creator's design process.

As mobile touch screens become ubiquitous, interactivity can be integrated into narrative experiences like never before. But with this new emergence of interactive storytelling, the documentary production process has to evolve, too. In the brave new world of the i-doc, the user is an integral agent in the narrative experience, and as such, user experience needs to be considered from inception, through development and production. In a sense, the user is the creator's silent collaborator – the one who will bring the interactive experience to life once it is released to the public – and testing brings that user into the design process.

NOTE

1. Learn more about Avatar Secrets at www.avatarsecrets.com or download the app at App-Store.com/AvatarSecrets.

REFERENCES

Babineax, Ryan and John Krumboltz (2013) *Fail Fast, Fail Often*. New York: Penguin.

Norman, Donald (2013) *The Design of Everyday Things*. New York: Basic Books.

Pringle, Ramona (2016) *Avatar Secrets*. iPad/iPhone documentary. Produced by Ramona Pringle, productions in association with TVO. http://avatarsecrets.com/. Accessed 31 October 2016.

Reis, Eric (2011) *The Lean Startup: How Today's Entrepreneurs Use Continuous Innovation to Create Radically Successful Businesses*. New York: Crown Business.

Tidwell, Jennifer (2010) *Designing Interfaces*. Sebastopol, CA: O'Reilly Media.

Warfel, Todd Zaki (2009) *Prototyping: A Practitioner's Guide*. New York: Rosenfeld.

LOOK WHO'S WATCHING
WHAT STORYTELLERS CAN LEARN FROM PRIVACY AND PERSONALISATION

Ben Moskowitz

Internet video 'watches back'.[1] Like most web content, the majority of internet video is free for the viewer and subsidised by a form of lightweight commercial surveillance. So should social issue storytellers embrace techniques pioneered by internet advertisers: tracking, behavioural profiling and personalisation? Should documentarians take cues from the likes of Google and Facebook, which have grown rich by mining and analysing the personal information of their users?

Perhaps adopting some of the practices of these 'watchers' could empower documentary storytellers to create more intimate bonds with audiences. Examining the development of personalised and procedurally-generated web media – that is to say, media that adapts itself based on what it can learn about the user – may help observers and producers of documentary media to anticipate how the documentary form will evolve into the future. It may also reveal social problems brewing underneath digital life that future documentary storytellers will need to tackle subjectively.

FROM THE SPOKEN WORD TO THE WEB

To understand the significance of personalisation, we should first look backwards. In the oral tradition – in theatre and improvised performance – stories came alive for audiences in the moment of performance. Then, in the twentieth century, technologists developed technologies of mass communications: radio, television and movies. Stories could now be coded, broadcast and captured on magnetic tape, wax or plastic; they could be amplified to an audience ten, one hundred, or ten million times bigger than the storyteller could possibly entertain at a campfire, in a home, theatre or auditorium.

Although these capture and playback technologies enabled storytelling at scale, each viewing was a carbon copy of the others – performances and creative decisions snapshotted in time. The storyteller became a kind of ghost in a machine that mechanically reproduced the intent and initial performance of the storyteller.

Fixed as they were in physical media, stories became formatted, productised and based around patterns of consumption. Media consumers bought a standardised radio, TV set, record, laserdisc, VHS or DVD player. These technologies, which enabled large-scale playback and performance, also established baseline technology platforms and expectations for storytellers to work with.

The movement toward 'web-native' storytelling that has emerged since 2010 operated differently. For storytellers, the web came to signify a freely programmable space with no hard rules or creative constraints.

YouTube, the early standard-bearer of the web-native media world, presented an 'it just works' option for creators to publish their stories to a large and infinitely segmentable audience. This created space for low-cost experimentation and for producers to reach niche audiences, which in turn relieved some economic and creative restraints (Anderson 2006).

Yet in most other respects YouTube was not a departure from traditional publishing platforms, because the platform only hosted linear media. Although audiences could queue the content of their choice on demand, that content took the familiar box-form of a 'TV embedded in the web page': a rectangle with a play button. For many forward-looking storytellers, with inclinations to interactive and emergent media like videogames and hypertext, this was a limitation on creative freedom that drove them to depart from platforms like YouTube.

In many innovation centres, such as the National Film Board of Canada's interactive documentary programme, producers began to explore entirely new creative forms of media that would only be possible on the web (O'Flynn 2012). For a new wave of producers, the web itself was the platform.

This creative experimentation was enabled in part by the widespread and growing adoption of HTML5, the *lingua franca* of the web. By 2009 HTML, or hypertext mark-up language, had evolved way past its humble beginnings as a way of interlinking documents hosted at research institutions. Technologies under the broad umbrella of HTML5 and the web now enabled creators to interweave interactivity and audiovisual elements; to publish rich storytelling experiences online, freely available and just a Google search or Facebook post away. HTML5 was a far more robust development platform for interactive media than its proprietary ancestors like Adobe's Flash and Microsoft's Silverlight. It was free, well-documented and continuously generating new 'building blocks' like open source libraries for creators to quickly bootstrap their projects. HTML was the biggest standard publishing platform ever, with support in billions of connected devices – laptops, phones, tablets, TVs; even cars and refrigerators.

WHO PAYS FOR THE WEB?

It is useful to examine these developments against the backdrop of the prevailing economic model for web content. Financing a documentary is no easy task; financing an exotic interactive production is even harder. An early lament in the interactive media space was the lack of replicable models to pay for web-based productions, and the dearth of skilled interactive designers needed to execute them. But these were symptomatic of larger economic questions heralded by the web, including a very basic one: who pays for it all? Who pays for the Google searches, the maps, the social networking, and all those YouTube videos?

By 2016, there were more than four hundred hours of content uploaded to YouTube every minute (Statistica 2015). The democratisation of technologies for producing and sharing video created an explosion of content, which pressured media industries to find new ways to monetise. Faced with such a glut of content, many web media consumers chose 'free'. In fact, for most web users their entire content ecosystem was free. So most video-hosting platforms adopted the same monetisation schemes that paid for the rest of the web: data-driven targeting of banner and pre-roll advertisements, and selling data about user's viewing habits.

Who pays for the web? The simple, true and yet thoroughly clichéd answer to these questions is: 'you, with your data'. Throughout the course of each day in contemporary digital life, you passively generate a stream of personal data. This data can be mined for incredibly valuable insights about you. An analysis of your Google searches creates a trail of intent; an analysis of your email inbox establishes patterns of thinking; an analysis of your social network reveals who influences you the most. All of this data is processed and sold so that advertisers and others can better persuade you to take some action. It's not a secret. It's very well documented and explored in very good public interest journalism.[2]

For example: when you search for a bicycle on Google, or send an email about bicycles in GMail, that data accrues to a growing corpus of knowledge about you. The platform provider and its partners (in this case, Google and its AdWords customers) may analyse this data and infer that you're in the market for a bicycle. Google serves a lot of your content and so can rent your eyeballs to advertisers – you will become more likely to encounter AdWords advertisements and YouTube pre-roll ads which will attempt to persuade you to buy a bike.

There's plenty to like about this system, which ultimately shapes your entire media diet (not just your advertising diet; see Pariser 2011). Because of targeting and personalisation, you are less likely to see content that isn't relevant to you. And the things you use on the internet stay free. But there are many who fear the consequences of this system. Throughout years and years of just living and breathing on the internet, internet companies may begin to know more about you than you know about yourself. And they sell that data to firms on Madison Avenue, the world capital of advertising since the mid-nineteenth century – to people who have full-time jobs to figure out what kinds of advertising you're most vulnerable to. This does not begin to problematise how non-commercial actors – political campaigns, NGOs, governments – may use this same data to persuade you.

For Google and all commercial web services, the job is to stay competitive and relevant, and that means getting better and better at drawing insights and inferences from you, based on your data. At the time of this writing, it is commonly understood in the advertising industry that internet advertising platforms have a lot of room for improvement, even as they are growing in sophistication every day (Farahat and Bailey 2012). Although advertisers may not have a perfect ability to target and tailor persuasive messages today, the data needed for effective persuasion continues to accrue. There will be exponentially more of it stored and available to advertisers as time goes on. As a Google user, you can consult your Search History, or check your Ad Settings dashboard – where you can see what Google thinks it has learned about you based on your web and mobile activity. For many people, Facebook has an even better view of its users because a) users actually feed structured data about themselves to Facebook in the form of their social media profiles, and b) Facebook knows who all their friends are. This gives Facebook a certain edge in knowing how to persuade individual users, as well as the people who influence them.

For every one of us – even those of us who take pains to minimise the data we share – our data trail is growing. And the rate of acceleration is increasing with the mobile devices we carry in our pockets, which generate incredible rivers of intimate data, through myriad sensors on our smartphones. A prime example of this is location data. There's a lot that can be gleaned from analysing the patterns in your movements. To its credit, Google is very transparent about this – readers may want check their Location History dashboard for a sense of what data Google collects and stores.

The extent and social consequences of this data economy are not well understood. And there is even more passive data collection and inference happening 'behind the scenes'. For instance, Facebook like buttons (embedded in tens of millions of webpages outside of Facebook) and wireless beacons (such as Apple's iBeacons, physically installed in millions of retail locations) collect data continuously as we go about our day in the 'real world'. The proliferation of these and other technologies mean that average users are filling creeks and marshes of personal data on a daily, even hourly basis, mindlessly, just by surfing the web and walking around in public.

IS PERSONALISED STORYTELLING THE 'KILLER APP' OF WEB-BASED STORYTELLING?

The amount of data that a creative campaigner can collect about you, and the ability they have to deliver a unique message to you, is arguably what is most unique in the contemporary HTML5-and-apps world. The ability to tailor and deliver variations of a video to millions of specific individuals is starting to scale.

When creatives and technologists started experimenting with film on the web, many talked about interactivity as being as momentous to the technical vocabulary of filmmaking as sound or Technicolor in previous eras. New practices and heretofore-uncharted user expectations emerging in interactive media suggested a new montage moment which – like the cinematic renaissance led by Eisenstein, Vertov and Griffith in the early twentieth century – would inspire new generations of storytellers to explore the unique affordances of new technologies. The interactivity enabled by the web holds great promise as part of the storyteller's toolkit.

Interactive projects of the 2010–13 era exhibited familiar tropes, such as the incorporation of live data into stories, giving people things to click on, and generally building media products that were more interactive and participatory. The idea was to bring some of the characteristics of the web into film. For many creators making films more 'webby' defined the field of interactive storytelling.

An alternative analysis suggests that interactive storytelling is not ultimately a breakthrough in how most people experience documentary media. No interactive documentary production has yet begun to reach the scale or impact of a major, internationally-distributed documentary. Perhaps audiences will always be more comfortable with filmic experiences that don't demand full cognitive engagement (to 'lean forward') but rather invite the viewer to enjoy passively by 'leaning back'.

There is a case to be made that it is in fact personalised storytelling which will be the web's greatest contribution to the field of documentary. Why shouldn't storytellers be using all the techniques that have made the rest of the web economy work, and apply them to documentary film? After all, the most coveted talent and skills in the contemporary consumer internet and creative industries are wrapped up in data collection and data-driven persuasion.

How can a student or producer of documentary begin to think about the possibilities in personalised video? As an intuitive example, consider you're watching a video ad for Nike shoes, but as a fan of purple shoes you see the purple edition of the limited edition Air Jordans – the ones that you're more likely to buy. When Bob watches, they're yellow shoes – based on psychographic characteristics or purchasing preferences inferred from his data. When Alice watches, they're green.

The form and format here is visual media that, while still consumed passively, is nonetheless unique to each viewer. The viewer is not responsible for the interactivity of the content. Instead, the content adapts *itself* to their personality and profile. Machine learning and artificial intelligence are likely enablers of this kind of tailoring. If a computer can be fed enough data about an individual, it can do computationally-intensive pattern matching to guess her preferences. Shoes.com have already deployed a shopping experience based on this principle.

HOW TO DO PROCEDURAL STORYTELLING

Tailoring a piece of content to millions of individuals seems cost prohibitive, and is certainly infeasible to perform manually. Yet a number of works demonstrate that it is possible to generate an infinite number of creative permutations for a given commercial, documentary or episodic story.

How do you tell a story to a million users, individually? Of course, you do what people usually do when working at problems in scale: you use a computer. It is trivial to write a piece of software that dynamically and procedurally builds each scene, based on parameters set by the producer. Procedural media are like MadLibs, the classic interactive children's stories with missing words ('adverb', 'noun', 'city in Europe') that must be provided by the reader. Personalisation can be accomplished by creating a narrative system which includes variables that will be dynamically filled to complete the story.

A producer assembles all the creative assets in advance, along with methods for incorporating live assets that will need to be queued, composited and served to the viewer just in time. These live assets can come from other platforms on the web, such as Facebook, Twitter, Instagram and other data sources for instance, a film can incorporate the viewer's photos or demographic data. Some of the parameters or pieces of the recipe can be comprised of things that a computer can *infer* about a user, from readily available online profile data to passive data that users generate.

This 'runtime' approach – to borrow the language of computer programmers – is a different paradigm from producing a single, finally-rendered and gold-mastered cut in the editing suite. It can generate, on demand, a unique version of the same media for each viewer, millions of times over.[3]

It sounds complicated – and at a creative execution level, it certainly is – but at the same time, it's quite straightforward. Fundamentally, an interactive producer needs only three things:

1. Identity: a method to identify the user, such as Facebook or Google login (which may also authenticate the user and explicitly grant permission to access her data);
2. A client programmable medium: a framework such as HTML5 and JavaScript, which enables the producer to script out the unique adaptations that will present themselves to the viewer, based on what can be inferred from her identity;
3. Elbow grease: the creative patience to design, test with users, optimise and repeat until the programme is performing well at delivering a seamless, personalised experience for many unique users.

TVs are dumb and can only deliver a finished, 'flattened' product that's experienced the same way by every viewer. But a client application like a web browser has access to a user's identity and can do something about it. Through the web, a programmable medium, the producer of an interactive story can project their intent across space and time, know a bit about who's watching, and act on this information to tell a unique story for each viewer.

The following examples will argue that the fundamental difference between a TV and a web browser is that the web browser knows who you are.

PROCEDURAL STORYTELLING EXAMPLES – EARLY INTERACTIVES

Chris Milk's *The Wilderness Downtown* (2010) is a landmark work in this area. It is representative of a genre of interactive media that might be called 'powered by profile'. In this genre, the storyteller uses personal data from the viewer to turn that viewer into the protagonist of the story. *The Wilderness Downtown* is an early exemplar of an emotionally significant use of interactivity, a web-native story that merges form and function and would literally be impossible on any platform but the web.

The piece – a personalised music video created by Milk for the indie rock outfit Arcade Fire, under the aegis of the Google Creative Lab – was designed as a creative showcase for the emerging HTML5 platform, as well as the creative utility of Google's Maps API.

Before watching the music video, the viewer must first 'enter the address of the home where you grew up'. This information is stored for later as the video begins to roll. In the music video, street view images of the individual viewer's child-

Fig. 1: User address entry for *The Wilderness Downtown*.

hood home are interspersed with dramatically cut video of a young person running away, evoking both nostalgia and escape from adolescence. Aaron Koblin, creative partner of Chris Milk in the production, explained the approach in an interview: 'We wanted to push the music video beyond a traditional made-for-TV experience, to something truly made for the web ... the real kicker for this project though, was to make something data driven and customisable, but at the same time incredibly personal to each individual user' (Ford 2011).

Though the viewer must supply this information at the outset, it's nonetheless a surprising and aesthetic enhancement on a music video that makes it feel much more personal.

Later work in the creative industries worked to make this magic a bit more seamless. *Take This Lollipop* (Zada 2011) is a notable example, being both a showcase piece for the 'powered by profile' genre and a comment on the darkness underlying the public availability of our personal data.

In *Take This Lollipop*, the viewer is coyly offered to take a metaphorical lollipop – evoking a sinister gift of candy to a vulnerable child – by logging in with her Facebook account. In the next few minutes the viewer is introduced to a sweaty,

Fig. 2: In this music video, street view images of the individual viewer's childhood home are seamlessly woven into the edit.

Fig. 3: The viewer is confronted with a creepy antagonist that's **stalking her own, live** Facebook profile.

twitching man crouching in a dimly-lit basement, his face illuminated by a computer screen. The viewer hears his keyboard keys clacking and sees the twitch of his eye and upper lip. Suddenly, this creepy basement-dweller is revealed to be perving on the viewer's actual Facebook profile, clicking through her profile pictures, seeing her wall interactions with her friends, even finding and mapping her home address. This social media violation fades on a scene of the basement dweller slamming his car door and speeding away with a photo of the victim posted on his vehicle's dashboard. The use of seamless personalisation here serves to underscore the dangers of posting too much personal information about oneself on the internet.

MEDIUM AS MESSAGE

This kind of storytelling is impossible without actionable data about the viewer at the time of viewing and that data is available only because of the underlying structure of the web economy. As a result, the technical tropes enabled by personalised storytelling offer producers the opportunity to comment on the nature of personal data and online privacy itself. In the early 2010s, a wave of documentary media, ad campaigns and experiments emerged that used personal data to recursively explore these issues and their social consequences.

Do Not Track (Gaylor 2015) is a seven-part episodic interactive web series about online privacy. It explores how targeted advertising became the internet's business model, what it means for privacy and the media, and how people can take back control of their data. To do so, it makes use of the same tracking technologies and practices it places behind the filmmaker's lens. In fact, the header of *Do Not Track*'s homepage proudly proclaims: 'Guess what? *Do Not Track* IS tracking you. And we use cookies to do so.'

Each episode of *Do Not Track* is a short, personalised vignette that keeps the viewer engaged through personalisation which helps to make the subject of the

Fig. 4: Each sequence of *Do Not Track* customizes itself according to **variables unique to the individual user.**

documentary less abstract. In the opening scene, for instance, a Mac user logging in at 9:00am in New York might see: 'I know right now that this is the country you live in. I know that it is a nice morning. I know that you're on a Mac.' A PC user, a Belgian, and a night owl will each have a different experience in just that sequence. The number of permutations for the whole series means that each viewer will have their own unique experience.

To produce the series in this fashion, Brett Gaylor and Paris-based studio Upian had to innovate in both form and approach to production. One notable innovation was the idea of 'state-based storyboards'. This accounts for the fact that in each sequence, there are variables unique to the individual user as explained in this case study: 'Interactivity is communicated through state-based storyboards, where a user does not merely arrive at a timestamp, but also has several variables attached to that timestamp based on decisions she or he made previously as well as on aspects of personalisation. [...] "Fail states" on the storyboard convey scenarios when things do not go as planned (e.g. a viewer's Facebook page does not reveal enough data about the person to proceed with personalisation). The script also has additional labels to mark different types of media. These labels offer a convenient vocabulary for writing interactive documentaries' (MIT Open Documentary Lab & McArthur Foundation 2016: 90).

A video sequence was to be produced soup to nuts, in the traditional fashion, in multiple languages for each release region. A text sequence included interactive personalisation via information that users provide themselves. A real-time sequence mixed data the user has previously provided, as well as data that the *Do Not Track* site collected from the user's IP address – such as the user's location, operating system, and other available data.

In Limbo (Viviani 2015) goes even further by asking: 'Will your data outlive you?' The interactive documentary prompts you to authorise eight different data sources: your name for a Google search, access to your webcam, your geolocation, Twitter, Facebook, LinkedIn, Instagram and Gmail. Personal data from these services is interspersed and intercut with a contemplative film about memory and forgetting.

Karen (Blast Theory 2015) is an experiential art mobile app for Android and iOS. Designed to get viewers thinking about their intimate relationships with their mobile devices, it presents itself as a virtual life coach named Karen (played by actress Claire Cage who is quite convincing as we later find her character teetering on the edge of an emotional breakdown).

Karen asks the viewer progressively pointed and more personal questions, as might an overeager life coach. Over time, those questions become uncomfortable and Karen herself less professional. Behind the scenes, the information and choices the user supplies affect the narrative. At the end of experience, viewers are invited to make an in-app purchase (for $3.99) to access an extensive psychological profile compiled by Karen.

As Frank Rose (2015) opines on the profile of the app in the *New York Times*, 'few software characters offer the peculiarly ego-boosting appeal of adapting themselves to the user. This makes *Karen* an intriguing tool for exploring the knotty relationship between digital personalisation and human solipsism.'

Digital Me (Gaudenzi 2014) takes a lighter approach toward awakening the user's consciousness of their relationship with technology. *Digital Me* enables a Socratic dialogue with a mirror-image, virtual self that is composed from artefacts from the viewer's digital footprint. Sandra Gaudenzi explains her motivation for the project as follows: '*Digital Me* is you. It is the you that is created daily through your digital activity. The more you post, the more you are creating a representation of yourself that has its own life. And it stays there forever. [...] I have always been intrigued by the notion of the self, and the digital world seemed to offer an extra layer to the complex beings that we are: a layer that we tend to ignore because it is not tangible' (BBC Taster 2014).

WHAT ARE THE RAMIFICATIONS FOR DOCUMENTARY AND SOCIAL CHANGE MEDIA?

Many forms of documentary media are activist, agenda-driven or persuasive. Most aim to persuade or inform ('I need you to believe that climate change is important', or 'I need you to believe that the Flint water crisis is a national disgrace'). What would it mean to apply these personalisation techniques to documentary and how can interactive producers make social issue storytelling more persuasive? For a start, producers can use insights and identity specific to each viewer to modify the edit and present a more persuasive narrative. We can consider a few common tropes that might emerge:

- Motion graphics – Producers might show viewers personalised statistics to put their own experience in broader context. A simple widget that reports on the minimum wage in the viewer's state could be animated into a more filmic narrative about income inequality, which would presumably make for more relatable and engaging viewing.
- Scene selection – Producers might play with narrative structure by affecting scene order depending on who's watching. In a documentary about steelworkers, imagine there's a specific subject who deeply clicks with 15% of viewers and strikes as a very sympathetic figure. But 85% of viewers can't stand him, get distracted and tune out. In a conventional documentary, there's a hard creative choice to be made. Perhaps it's possible to have it both ways?
- Voice-overs – Producers might lean on computers for help with narrative voice-overs. Dynamically generative scripts may be read by modern synthetic voice synthesis in lieu of people in a recording booth. Could computerised narrators customise the script and address viewers directly, increasing the emotional and persuasive power for that demographic? Alternately, might producers automatically select from a number of pre-recorded voiceovers? What if the relevance of an online story could be broadened by recording multiple master narratives with diverse narrators, and selecting the narrator most appropriate for each viewing? Perhaps some viewers will respond better to an elderly Asian woman narrator, whereas others will stay spellbound by a 15-year-old narrator?

There are immense creative possibilities to be explored.

OBJECTIONS AND CRITIQUES

Some say that this production style is technically unfeasible and won't work. In fact, there is plenty of prior art – this chapter only scratches the surface.

Others worry that personalised media requires the auteur to cede authorial control. These ideas are especially offensive to the conservative, old guard of documentary filmmakers who already regard the web suspiciously because it has thoroughly disrupted film finance and distribution. To these traditionalists, targeted and procedural media may represent a kind of creative disruption – personalisation fails to respect the basic bonds between creators and audiences, and also the ideal of an auteur labouring toward a perfect, fixed artefact that is shown to a captive audience in a darkened theatre. But it can be argued that procedural storytelling offers even *greater* authorial control. In a sense, procedural and personalised storytelling enables an evolution from 'one-to-many storytelling' to 'one-to-one storytelling with many people'. Personalisation, in theory, offers even finer-grained control of the message and experience for an individual viewer.

There is also a question about intimacy. Could computer-enhanced narratives ever truly feel as intimate as finely tuned works? Won't these stories fall somewhere within the widely referenced concept of the 'uncanny valley', and feel somehow disingenuous or hollow? This is a question that can only be answered through years of experimentation. New storytelling technologies have awkward gestations as creators grapple with their craft and application. On the other hand, what could be more intimate than data?

Others express fears that personalised storytelling – particularly the practice of quietly tailoring media to someone based on their personal data – is, on some fundamental level, manipulative and wrong. Should the sophistication and seamlessness of personalised storytelling significantly improve in coming years, the ethics of personalisation may be something the field will need to seriously grapple with. Audiences must be aware that something is tailored, because they generally expect that they are watching the same thing as everyone else. Imagine a water cooler conversation about a film that was different for each viewer; producers should be obligated to telegraph to people when personalisation is happening behind the scenes. Could unchecked personalisation represent a new frontier of propaganda and a threat to people's 'cognitive security?' (Hill 2014)

We can look to developments in the media industry as evidence that we are moving closer to practical and effective personalisation. In 2015 the BBC R&D lab made public through its Visual Perceptive Media project that it is testing TV shows that adapt to the viewer's tastes and personality, as they announced online (BBC Research and Development 2015). In press materials, the lab paints an interesting picture of a new media frontier: 'Imagine a world where the narrative, background music, colour grading and general feel of a drama is shaped in real time to suit your personality. This is called Visual Perceptive Media and we are making it now in our lab in MediaCityUK' (ibid.). Project lead Ian Forrester describes the effort as 'rethinking our notions of media as a solid monolithic block' (2015). The BBC R&D lab has also worked with Julius Amedume (film director and writer) to explore the links between personality and affect. Colour grade and music were explored, along with shot choices, which 'we felt were most achievable' with today's technologies (ibid).

Today's artificial intelligence can defeat grandmasters in Chess and Go. It is not unreasonable to expect that the next generation of big data, neural networks and artificial intelligence will be adapted to discern and cater personalised storytelling content to individual psychographic profiles.

WHY PERSONALISATION MATTERS

Personalisation is likely to become even more magic and less detectable. Today's storytellers have access to webcams and emotion recognition routines that can read the viewer's face and detect her emotional state, as does for example Microsoft's API as one of many. If a BBC documentary on endangered species leaves a viewer insufficiently moved, perhaps the documentary should adapt its colour grading and music until it finds the right emotional knob? If a war documentary is too brutal-ising for a particular viewer, perhaps the documentary should read the viewer's expression and skip the footage where the bomb goes off in the marketplace?[4]

The consequences of personalisation could be quite dark if such techniques were to be applied ubiquitously or unethically. An experimental study in 2004 delivered tailored political ads to test subjects. In the ads served to the test group, presidential candidates' faces were subtly blended with facial characteristics of the viewer (Bailenson *et al* 2008). It turns out that if you show someone a political ad for George W. Bush, with their own facial characteristics blended in, they are more likely to want to vote for him (or any candidate, for that matter).

Advertising that uses personalisation for this kind of subliminal effect could be quietly deployed across social media in a not-too-distant future – and is not too far removed from the data-driven persuasion and targeting techniques employed throughout the web economy today.

This issue is more important than who pays for those free internet services, and is bigger than the present discourse around internet privacy. Many interests,

Fig. 5: An early online video advertisement tailored to the specific viewer.

not just advertisers, will be using targeting and personalisation to exploit people's individual cognitive biases and weaknesses. This has significance for public opinion across nearly every social issue imaginable. This is the brave new data-driven world into which we are headed.

The art, artifice and consequences of personalisation are interrelated. The responsibility to explore the social consequences of personalisation and algorithmic persuasion will fall to journalists and documentary storytellers – and they will be up against much better resourced commercial and government interests. 'Privacy itself' is emerging as a social issue, and it affects all other social issues.

All of this provides ample reason for public interest storytellers to reflect on what they can learn from the privacy debate. No matter what the issues they choose to tackle, learning about the web economy will help documentary storytellers to better identify, reach and persuade audiences in coming decades. In other words: storytellers shouldn't just keep an eye on the watchers, but also take a good look at who's watching their documentaries – and create documentaries that watch back.

NOTES

1. Where a single word or phrase is put in quotes, it indicates a term commonly used within the industry, a convention used throughout this chapter.
2. Notably by Julia Angwin and her privacy investigative team at the *Wall Street Journal*, which was a finalist for a Pulitzer Prize in the category 'Explanatory Reporting' in 2011.
3. Media philosopher Gabriel Shalom explores related 'just in time' principles from computer game design, including sprites, sound design and rendering: https://vimeo.com/14604303. Accessed 31 October 2016.
4. Relatedly, MIT researchers have demonstrated that it is possible to detect a person's heart rate by analyzing subtle frame-to-frame variations in webcam videos; http://people.csail. mit.edu/mrub/vidmag/. Accessed 31 October 2016.

REFERENCES

Anderson, Chris (2006) *The Long Tail: Why the Future of Business Is Selling Less of More.* New York: Hyperion.

Bailenson, Jeremy *et al* (2008) 'Facial Similarity between Voters and Candidates Causes Influence', *Public Opinion Quarterly*, 72, 5, 935–61.

BBC Research and Development (2015) 'Visual Perceptive Media. Personalised video which responds to your personality and preferences'; http://www.bbc.co.uk/rd/projects/visual-perceptive-media. Accessed 31 October 2016.

BBC Taster (2014) '*Digital Me* inside story – If you do not trust yourself, who can you trust?', http://www.bbc.co.uk/taster/projects/digital-me/inside-story. Accessed 31 October 2016.

Blast Theory (2015) *Karen*. Mobile app. https://play.google.com/store/apps/details?id=com. blasttheory.talktome&hl=en. Accessed 31 October 2016.

Farahat, Ayman and Michael C. Bailey (2012) 'How effective is targeted advertising?', *Conference proceedings of 21st international conference on World Wide Web* (WWW '12), ACM, New York City, 111–20.

Ford, Rob (2011) 'The story behind… *The Wilderness Downtown*'; http://www.thefwa.com/ article/the-making-of-the-wilderness-downtown. Accessed 31 October 2016.

Forrester, Ian (2015) 'Visual Perceptive Media gets people talking'. Blog post, posted 22 December; http://www.bbc.co.uk/rd/blog/2015–12-visual-perceptive-media-gets-people-talking. Accessed 11 October 2016.

Gaudenzi, Sandra (2014) *Digital Me*. Web documentary. Directed by Sandra Gaudenzi and co-created with Mike Robbins of Helios Design Labs for BBC Taster; http://www.bbc.co.uk/ taster/projects/digital-me. Accessed 31 October 2016.

Gaylor, Brett (2015) *Do Not Track*. Web Series. Directed by Brett Gaylor, co-produced by Upian, ARTE, ONF and BR. https://donottrack-doc.com. Accessed 31 October 2016.

Hill, Kashmir (2014) 'From Tinder Bots To "Cuban Twitter", Welcome To "Cognitive Hacking"', *Forbes*, 17 April; http://www.forbes.com/sites/kashmirhill/2014/04/17/from-tinder-bots-to-covert-social-networks-welcome-to-cognitive-hacking. Accessed 31 October 2016.

Milk, Chris (2010) The Wilderness Downtown. Personalised interactive music video. Directed by Chris Milk, produced by B-Reel, co-produced by google, music by Arcade Fire; http:// www.thewildernessdowntown.com/. Accessed 31 October 2016.

MIT Open Documentary Lab & McArthur Foundation (2016) '*Do Not Track*. Turning Pulp into Prototype with Agile Documentary', in William Uricchio, with Sarah Wolozin, Lily Bui, Sean Flynn and Deniz Tortum, *Mapping the Intersection of Two Cultures Interactive Documentary and Digital Journalism*. Boston: MIT Press; http://opendoclab.mit. edu/interactivejournalism/Mapping_the_Intersection_of_Two_Cultures_Interactive_ Documentary_and_Digital_Journalism.pdf. Accessed 31 October 2016.

O'Flynn, Siobhan (2012) 'Documentary's metamorphic form: Webdoc, interactive, transmedia, participatory and beyond', *Studies in Documentary Film*, 6, 2, 141–57.

Pariser, Eli (2011) *The Filter Bubble: How the New Personalised Web is Changing What We Read and How We Think*. New York: Penguin Press.

Rose, Frank (2015) '*Karen*, an App That Knows You All Too Well', *New York Times*, 2 April; http://www.nytimes.com/2015/04/05/arts/karen-an-app-that-knows-you-all-too-well. html?_r=0. Accessed 31 October 2016.

Shalom, Gabriel (2010) 'Hypercubist Manifesto – Pecha Kucha Berlin'. Vimeo video, posted 31 August 2010. https://vimeo.com/14604303. Accessed 11 October 2016.

Shoes.com (2015) 'SHOES.COM & Sentient Technologies Unveil Visual Filter – the World's First AI Shopping Experience'. Blog post; http://www.sentient.ai/news/shoes-com-sentient-technologies-unveil-visual-filter-the-worlds-first-ai-shopping-experience/. Accessed 11 October 2016.

Statistica (2015) http://www.statistica.com/statistics/259477/hours-of-video-uploaded-to-youtube-every-minute/. Accessed 11 October 2016.

Viviani, Antoine (2015) *In Limbo*. Web documentary. Directed by Antoine Viviani, co-produced by ARTE, and NFB; http://inlimbo.tv/en/. Accessed 31 October 2016.

Zada, Jason (2011) *Take this Lollipop*. Interactive horror short film and Facebook app. Directed by Jason Zada, co-produced by Little Monster and Tool of North America; http://www.takethislollipop.com/. Accessed 31 October 2016.

3 HORIZONS

PREFACE

Judith Aston

This section looks at future directions for interactive documentary, on the one hand in response to technological developments and on the other in response to wider social, cultural and political circumstances. It has been edited taking a broad view of interactive documentary practices, and with an interest in how they might be responsive to changing circumstances across both space and time.

William Urrichio begins by looking back in order to look forwards. After making some general observations about antecedents to i-docs, he focuses in on algorithmically-generated documentaries, as a form that is genuinely new. In so doing, he raises important questions about the meaning of agency when computers are able to respond to human interventions in ways that can be invisible to the untrained eye.

Nonny de la Peña continues by reflecting on her unique and influential work in virtual reality, which looks at documentary through the lens of immersive journalism. She questions the centrality of the uncanny valley thesis to documentary and virtual reality design, suggesting that the key to creating a sense of presence lies in allowing viewers to match their physical movement to the imagery inside their headset.

Judith Aston takes the debates about immersion in a different direction by looking at the role of live performance within interactive documentary. She makes the case for emplaced interaction as a new paradigm through which to look at i-docs, one which challenges the ubiquity of screen-based culture and which gives centrality to the shifting contexts of time, place and occasion.

Paolo Favero provides a cross-cultural perspective, by focusing on his fieldwork in India and looking at how i-docs play out in that cultural context. In so doing, he makes a case for taking an expansive view of i-docs, which accommodate inclusive, participatory and multi-modal experiences, created in response to specific and localised needs.

Arnau Gifrau picks up on this by looking at emerging interactive documentary practices in Latin America. He makes the point that being such a large area sharing the same few languages opens up a large new market for interactive documentary production and consumption, which has much potential to connect local projects with historical representations.

Finally, Jon Dovey looks at interactive documentary from the perspective of Gartner's hype cycle and media in perpetual transition. He suggests that interactive documentary is here to stay, the task being to continue the long, patient and slow work of building institutional infrastructures, developing audiences, and making a culture within which it can continue to evolve.

THINGS TO COME
THE POSSIBLE FUTURES OF DOCUMENTARY... FROM A HISTORICAL PERSPECTIVE

William Uricchio

History can be a great teacher, if only we put the right questions to it. At a moment when the documentary form continues to diversify, driven equally by changes in technological possibility, user expectation and media infrastructure, history might seem to provide a strange ally. After all, the challenges posed by such new developments as interactivity, live documentary and virtual reality, to name but three, seem to have few precedents. And yet, or so this chapter will argue, we might benefit by taking a closer look at the past and seeing what lessons can be learned. Continuities can reveal long-term sites of cultural fascination; they can help us to anticipate patterns of popular reception; and they can relativise the shock of the new. A somewhat less obvious benefit of the rear-view look also helps to demarcate that which is truly distinctive, even if temporarily camouflaged within the terms of the already familiar. This chapter will draw from the past as a way of reflecting about the future, speculating about the implications for documentaries yet to come.

Let's begin with an example of continuity and end with an instance of the disjunctively new. Some 250 years of efforts evident in the panorama, stereoscope, 3D film, and today's Google Cardboard, yellowBird and Oculus Rift, all underscore a long-term fascination with evoking a sense of immersion in the world around us. They point to a tension between re-presentation (depicting something that exists elsewhere and/or elsewhen) and evocation or even experience (making something felt, 'as if being on the spot' to quote Robert Barker's 1787 patent for the panorama). This long history of precedents offers a vantage point from which to assess on-going preoccupations with Virtual Reality (VR) and to anticipate future developments.

Strategies deployed by mid-nineteenth and early-twentieth century documentarians, evident in their use of 'new' technologies such as photographic and filmed panoramas, suggest similar interests in evoking experience rather than merely representing it and in exposition rather than analysis (Uricchio 2011a). We might frame some of the (as of this writing) latest VR iterations in terms of a long-term fascination with presence, immersion and 'being there' – conditions that images of the real world support more immediately than images of fictional worlds whose rule-sets first have to be established and rehearsed.

On the other hand, history can also help to sort out the disjunctive and truly new, demarcating their contours and suggesting their possible implications. So, for example, the increasingly important roles played by algorithms in domains such as image recognition software, narrative generators and taste recommendation systems all suggest a fundamental break from the forms of agency that have structured the representation systems of the past. As they slowly penetrate existing media elements – from cameras to 3D capture systems – they are often retrofitted to feel familiar and do their work with minimal disruption. And yet, if we look carefully, we can see that something like algorithmic processing intrudes upon and fundamentally reorders the old binaries of maker and artefact, of artefact and viewer, disrupting our representational traditions even while on the surface appearing consistent with them.

After making the case for using historical precedent as a rear-view mirror to help with the orientation process, this chapter will look ahead to consider the possibility of algorithmically generated documentaries, and briefly consider algorithms' roles in VR – roles that require disaggregating different technological strands of VR: one, as noted, familiar; and one quite new.

REFRAMING THE DOCUMENTARY

Before continuing, a few words are in order regarding the term 'documentary'. Deployed variously as a style, a genre and a representational claim, the term harkens back in a narrow sense to a simple genesis, namely its invocation by John Grierson in 1926 to describe Robert Flaherty's *Moana* (1926). That generative reference has proved to have its share of complications, relegating the previous three decades of reality-based film production to the rubric of 'non-fiction'; implicitly shackling the documentary project to narrative; and predicating the documentary form on intentions, treatments and associations. Even if occasionally applied with trepidation to the films produced between 1895 and 1925, the term seems stretched to breaking point when used to describe reality-based representations that took place before the appearance of the film medium. And yet, somewhat asymmetrically, the post-war period has seen the concept applied to non-film media forms, starting with television (which initially exhibited filmed documentaries and later produced its own on tape and even live, in the process embracing the new medium's expressive capacities). So too digital media, at first a convenient distribution platform for film and video and now a site of innovation as documentary-makers explore the new capacities for interaction and user participation available to them. And we have a rich history of documentary as a radio-format, on the pages of illustrated magazines, and even as theatrical events. These uses may have brought considerable richness to the larger documentary project, but they also invoke the film tradition as analogy. Curiously, this pattern of reference and media agnosticism is rarely applied retrospectively, before Grierson's 1926 comment.

My point is not to go down the rabbit hole of deconstructing the term documentary, although the *Oxford English Dictionary* offers plenty of earlier invocations by the likes of Jeremy Bentham and Thomas Carlyle (using the term to mean, respectively, 'of the nature of or consisting in documents' and 'evidential').[1] Suffice it to say that for the English-language film world, Griersonian medium-specificity is hard-wired into the bibliographic reference system thanks to the *Film Index* (Leonard 1966) which used the term 'documentary' almost exclusively for post-1925 non-fiction film entries and deployed various cognates for pre-1925 counterparts, but not the term documentary. Today, when 100 per cent analogue film productions are an endangered species and digital platforms have blurred the lines between media forms, it doesn't seem like much of a stretch to extend the documentary moniker to a robust spectrum of digital forms; but somehow it seems a step too far to look beyond the historical Griersonian horizon for precedents relevant to today's situation. 'Documentary' is a term that has grown elastic with time, but the closer one comes to its point of origin, the more restrictive are its uses.

Documentary, whether narrowly or, as I prefer, broadly construed, has a certain advantage over its more pointedly fictional counterparts. The role of technique in much of the fictional domain is doubly tasked: it must assert itself as an appropriate expressive form and meanwhile, it must quickly convey the rules of the fictional world – is it a world where wizards have powers, or a time when man and dinosaur co-inhabit the earth? By contrast, documentary's world is generally known. It may be unfamiliar or even unsettling, but there is often no need to establish the rules of physics, or the sequence of natural history, or power of magic wands. Freed as they are from the burden of basic world-building, documentary's makers consequently can have greater stylistic latitude. Or said another way: they can turn their focus away from world-building to the task of *world-revealing*.

The actuality claim, while stylistically liberating, encourages a focus on *what* is represented, on whether it is accurate, and on whether the film's argument has proved to be transformative. This serves to reinforce documentary's functionalist agenda, whether social change or armchair travel, suggesting a form primarily of interest because of what is shown rather than how it is shown. Form and content enjoy a deeply symbiotic relationship, of course, but in the world of documentary, they also enjoy a strictly hierarchical one in which form is in the service of content.

Yet it is precisely documentary's innovative formal tradition that has enabled it to take on radically different realities and to deploy radically different approaches to explore them. And, as just suggested, the documentary tradition's development and deployment of technologies and techniques has gone on to infuse the larger media culture. From this perspective, today's interactive, immersive and participatory developments in documentary demonstrate that innovation and experimentation continue. And, as an added value, we can expect to see these innovations extending beyond documentary's boundaries, where they serve as harbingers of things to come in the double-tasked world of dramatic fiction.

BACK TO THE FUTURE

Today's media buzzwords come backed by deep histories of practice. Take the term 'remix'. Enabled by an abundance of source material and user-friendly tools for the cutting-and-pasting of digitalised text, image and sound, remixing seems to be a condition born of the digital era. In its wake have come challenges to long-held notions of authorship, textual integrity and stability. These questions are familiar from the world of i-docs: what is the nature of the users' (re-mixers') textual activities – collaborative authorship, textual hacking or a radical form of textual navigation?; is there a hierarchy of authorship, perhaps giving primacy of place to the originating creator of the interface and textual database, and secondary credit to those who make choices within them?; does the creation of a through-line and text from a sea of possibilities constitute the defining creative act?; what are we to make of a radically reconfigurable set of textual possibilities – or better said: of the fundamentally unstable text?; and are shared textual experiences and intersubjectivity things of the past?

While these challenges are part of the digital condition, in fact they have been historically posed by the photo-collages that thrived in the 1920s Dada movement and after (Hannah Hoch and John Heartfield's remixing of found photographs come to mind); or by early Soviet compilation films (Esfir Shub's *Fall of the Romanov Dynasty,* 1927); or in mass-marketed pre-glued books designed to aggregate the user's clippings from newspapers, calendars and product packaging

(Sears sold the *Mark Twain* brand). The practices of fragmenting texts and reassembling the shards to make a new one, or indeed, selectively combining elements from a meta-textual environment into a new and unique text, go back to the origins of the book itself, with the commonplace book instantiated in fifteenth-century Florence with the Zibaldone or hodgepodge book and codified by John Locke in his 1685 treatise on the methods for their construction.

The questions provoked by interactive documentaries and their attendant textual remixing have, it turns out, been with us longer than we remember. And yet these early remixing practices peacefully coexisted with the realm of the traditionally authored text, neither posing threat nor generating anxiety. If anything, their long marginalised traces are only now visible thanks to the challenges wrought by their digital counterparts, exacerbated by new copyright regimes and an intensified scale of production and distribution. However, with a little perspective, many of the disruptions enabled by today's technologies – at least with regard to remixed textual systems – can be seen in the light of precedent. These long-term practices suggest an as yet unwritten history of textual production, a spectrum between fixity and malleability, between the canonised texts that we institutionally perpetuate and the far more diverse and eclectic remixed and dynamic texts that have always been there. The history of authorship can also benefit from this tradition, with historical precedent restoring a sense of respectability and creativity to practices like textual hacking.

MIT's Open Documentary Lab and the International Documentary Festival Amsterdam's DocLab joined forces to map this fabric of precedents and conceptually related practices in a web-based project called *Moments of Innovation* (2014). Organised on terms such as 'interactivity', 'immersion', 'locative' and 'participatory', the project traces the long history of endeavour by linking ongoing developments in interactive documentary with pre-digital actuality-based antecedents. As with the remix, the point is not that we have seen it all before, but rather that we can benefit from remembering that many of the uncertainties and even crises provoked by today's changing regimes of representation have ample conceptual precedents. These precedents open up alternate through-lines to our received histories of textual engagements, alerting us to the range of techniques that can be deployed for particular expressive ends. Precedent, in this sense, can also inform and enrich today's documentary deployments, predicated as they are on a new generation of networked digital technologies. What we have learned from the past, together with the affordances of these new technologies, can together create possibilities for greater accessibility, new strategies for meaning creation, and an opportunity for bringing publics together in innovative ways, both with one another and with the issues of the day.

THE UNPRECEDENTED

As scholars such as Brian Winston (1986) have amply demonstrated, even the most innovative technologies and techniques can be traced back to earlier developments of one kind or another. Nevertheless, as Thomas Kuhn (1962) argued with his notion of scientific paradigm shifts, we know that cultural framing and our ideas of causality can change radically; and the history of technologies, from the Bronze Age to the Information Age, suggests that quite dramatic shifts in production and the material affordances of technology also take place from time to time. Unprecedented change, in other words, is possible, even if historical continuities of one kind or another underlie them. History's power at such moments derives less from underscoring continuities than it does from accentuating difference and letting the contours of the new be appreciated without stuffing them back into existing categories. Historians, both in this scenario and in the one discussed in the previous section, have a precarious task: they can easily overlook precedents by hewing too closely to the norms of the day; and conversely, they can try to inscribe the truly new within well-worn categories, in the process missing its radical potentials.

Looking ahead to possible futures for the documentary form, particularly at a moment characterised by widespread access to digital cameras, pervasive connectivity and a culture of audiovisual production, algorithms loom large as a factor that can help to generate and navigate stories, in the process, redefining interactivity. Of course, algorithms as instruments for calculation are not new, going back at least as far as Euclid, but their conditions have changed significantly. And their changed conditions align with those facing documentary makers: ever-accelerating processing power (Moore's Law), ever-more pervasive networked connectivity and an ever-richer data environment. In this setting, despite their continuities with the historical past, algorithms have demonstrated unprecedented capacities including the ability to identify and sort data and transform them into stories. Particularly at a moment when, to use but one measure, some four hundred hours of video are being uploaded to YouTube *per minute*, or 65.7 years' worth of video per day (Bower 2015), we require new organising systems to make material findable, let alone functional in a documentary sense.

At one level, the use of algorithms to help with this task seems commonplace. By initiating a Google search, we deploy configurations of many hundreds of thousands of algorithms to find our particular needle in a haystack. From the perspective of the human initiator, such an act is trivial. Moreover, we probably shrug-off the carefully calculated advertisements that also appear on our search page. And unless we take active steps to mask our identity, we don't usually have to ask Google to give us results in our language or that relate to our geographical location. A Google search page, including advertisements deemed relevant, stands as an algorithmically composed text, as a responsive text interacting with, on one hand, some notion of the user's profile and needs, and on the other, a massive data set. Beyond entering a search term and pressing 'enter', human interaction is not required (although active intervention is required if one wishes to circumvent these new deployments).

In microseconds, algorithms can search, filter and order results; and meanwhile control for language, location and marketing profile. One may describe the resulting text, the search page, as interactive, even though the interaction that occurred was undertaken by programme elements on behalf of the user rather than by the user. That is, the process of curating and presenting selected elements from an ocean of data reveals quite intricate interactions (including micro-auctions among possible advertisers) that construct a unique text. While these actions 'converse' with the user's previous behaviours, and while the result of human-designed programmes, the interaction takes place in a 'third' space beyond that of the user and the data set.

For a hint at what this might mean for moving images, we can look to Guy Maddin, Evan Johnson, Galen Johnson and the National Film Board of Canada's *Séances* project (2016). The individual instantiations of the project are algorithmically assembled, or as the project's website describes it: 'In a technical feat of data-driven cinematic storytelling, films are dynamically assembled in never-to-be-repeated configurations. Each exists only in the moment, with no pausing, scrubbing or sharing permitted, offering the audience one chance to see this film before it disappears.'

Maddin *et al* are in dialogue with the ephemeral character of early cinema and its emotional registers of loss. But for our purposes, the shots and intertitles are configured within certain rule sets and designed to cohere, rather than just existing as arbitrary assemblages of clips from the larger project's environment.

The algorithmic sorting and arranging carried out by Google searches for purposes of information relevance here takes the form of narrative plausibility, even though *Séances* lacks a Google search's personalisation and made-to-measure specificities. As such, *Séances* offers an early moving image instantiation of something that is currently flourishing in print journalism, where companies such as Narrative Science generate unique on-the-fly stories for news organisations and individuals alike, producing dynamically generated and personalised texts from large bodies of structured data. Since 2012, Narrative Science and its peers have been a growing presence in beats with structured data such as sports and finance, where their algorithms can quickly convert data into publishable stories (Podolny

2015). They have made inroads not only into the newsroom, but as well into such niche markets as reporting on Little League Baseball, a sport for children that rarely receives press coverage and yet includes millions of proud parents who are eager to share news of their offspring's successes. Authoring algorithms can produce a barrage of stories that rework the basic information of a particular game to fit the needs of its individual readers. In this word-based journalistic setting, narrativisation and personalisation combine.

One scenario for future interactive documentaries derives from these processes. Like the examples just discussed, in this setting, interactivity is a textual condition enabled by algorithmic rule sets and data about the user, rather than direct user activity. Users can have a 'sit back' experience, even though it is one uniquely crafted for (and, in a sense, with) them. Imagine a further step, namely enhancing today's existing storytelling algorithms with taste prediction, where the kind of story we see is informed by the calculated extrapolation of our profile, our behaviours, and the anticipation of our desires. The predictive capacities of Pandora's algorithms with music, Amazon's with book recommendations, and Netflix's with film and television programmes show that the state of the game is well-developed, suggesting that such a move is imminent. Imagine combining these narrativising and personalising capacities with image recognition software, a sector that has enjoyed huge advances over the past two years.[2] This is a precondition for image-based stories (unlike Narrative Science's word-based work) and, as processing strategies in this space continue to develop, they will enable far more creative use of the vast image archive available online and growing at a formidable rate. Finally, imagine arming these various processes with the verification software increasingly deployed by journalists seeking to distinguish fact from fiction in user-generated content (Shorenstein Center 2015). Together – and indeed 'together' is the way that most algorithmic ecosystems are deployed – we can see that the conditions for the production of a radically new kind of (documentary) text have reached a tipping point.

This scenario for personalised documentary production represents a relatively new direction in our relationship with media. The text is configured for us, on the basis of information about us, but without our active intervention (and sometimes, despite it). One might describe this as a 'responsive text' since the ordering of textual elements is both dynamic and corresponds to the system's notion of our preferences. Yet it appears to the user as a stable, fixed text. Should we consider this an example of interaction? With algorithmic assembly, the users need not do anything – they are simply offered a text that feels familiar in its old-school solidity and fixity (no clicking or navigation needed). 'Interactivity' occurs at the programme level, where the text is constructed from pre-existing textual elements and organised on the basis of information gleaned about the user and the textual bits themselves. The process of interaction is occluded from view and rendered into an 'automatic' process.

These developments are already with us, and while they have certain affordances, such as bringing customised documentaries to viewers who prefer to 'sit back' rather than 'lean forward' to navigate their way through an interactive documentary, they raise deeply troubling questions regarding agency, control and ultimately, governance. Seeing that something is coming down the road is different from welcoming it; our task is to see and be prepared, developing critical strategies for assessing and using these new possibilities.

RETHINKING INTERACTIVITY

How might this future scenario fit within our notion of interactive documentaries? To the extent that our definition privileges the text-generating interaction between the user and the pre-authored textual environment, then – recalling the uses of history mentioned earlier in this chapter – historical examples might help to show that this is a long-standing practice. We could look to nineteenth-century serial authors such as Wilkie Collins, tracing the slow interactions with his reading public that resulted in significant changes between serialised chapters and the final novels. Or we could look to the long-term development of various versions of the Bible, finding interactions between interpretive communities and the various textual components that are included or not, or sequenced in particular ways (Uricchio 2016). One might argue that deploying the term 'interactivity' in these settings is a semantic game: other terms could be deployed with equal or better effect to describe these user/text relationships. But the use of the term helps to underscore a common set of behaviours binding today's 'point-and-click' notion of digital interactivity to both historically precedent and algorithmically emergent forms of interactivity. The larger point is that the appearance of textual stability in no way precludes the role of interactivity as a generative process.

Interactivity in our current generation of computer games and interactive documentaries relies on real-time behaviours of the 'cause-effect' variety. Each use of the control interface results in a textual change. But if the term refers to a condition of user-generated textual change and multiplicity, then we can challenge the relevance of several characteristics associated with interactivity. Consider temporality: the real time 'cause-effect' notion of interactivity, I've suggested, can be complemented with temporalities of textual production that are glacially slow (the Bible) and quicker than our fingers can click (algorithmic narrative generators). Consider agency: the individual pointing-and-clicking subject can be complemented by the creative intervention of collectivities (from religious interpretive communities to reading publics) and, controversial though it is, by the work of algorithms (informed by passively generated or actively collected data).

These examples suggest that the term 'agency' is changing. The term's historical antecedents seem clear enough, yet for some, the attribution of agency to non-human actors seems a step too far. And yet this is precisely the change in language – and condition – heralded by today's algorithmic regimes (Uricchio 2011b). Shifts in the meaning and site of agency have appeared in posthumanist discourse (Moravec 1998; Hayles 1999) and in Actor Network Theory (Latour 2005) in reference to non-human actors. Non-human agency has been invoked by the computer industry ('intelligent agents'); and is taking statutory and legal form with self-driving cars and auto-piloted drones. Behind these manifestations is a larger shift in the modern (fifteenth century to the present) subject/object relationship that underpins our philosophical systems and was emblematised by Martin Heidegger's 'world-picture'. As that relationship gives way to an algorithmic intermediary that selectively repurposes multiple subjectivities and the data of the world, we must expand agency's meaning … or create a new term. The algorithmic mediation increasingly evident in our search, navigation and finance systems, and even in our construction of citizenship and policing, brings with it new dangers (when it is shackled to the power dynamics of the past) and affordances (where it can harness collective ideas and behaviours). But algorithms are neither inherently dictatorial nor amplifiers of the self: they are tools that herald an age of radical contingency. They stand between the subject and object, requiring that we rethink the long-held assumptions of the modern era regarding the construction of the self, certainty, agency and ethical responsibility.

In many of today's digital environments, interactivity leads to textual encounters that tend to be ephemeral and fleeting, although they have consequence (a score in a game, the 'completion' of a documentary) and are capable of being forensically recovered or even recorded in some way. However, the environments from which users carve texts tend to be much more permanent; for example, the data set and interface design that constitute a particular version of a documentary are fixed as intellectual property and distinctly persistent relative to the text-producing interactions that one has while exploring it.

The implications for documentary are significant. If the move from the traditional linear documentary to the i-doc turns in part on shifting agency from an all-controlling author to interaction between the author (as creator of the data set and interface) and the user (as a navigator and constructor of text), then the algorithmic processes just-described shift agency in another direction altogether: to the interactions between a rule set and machine-readable data (Hoelzl and

Marie 2015). The rule sets (algorithms) are in some senses arbitrary. They may be systematic, but they exist as constructions at a distance from the notions of visible evidence that documentary-makers have long relied on. The same can be said of data sets: rule-bound constructions that have expanded from the world 'out there' to included selected behaviours of the human interlocutor.

This represents a dramatic shift from our past encounters with representation. Claims regarding the image's indexicality notwithstanding, we have a rich cultural and institutional tradition of 'reading' film and photography, as well as a legal tradition of accepting certain images as evidence. Rule sets and machine readable data, by contrast, are far more abstracted entities and are only beginning to find evidentiary status in the culture at large (and that, problematically, as debates over such practices as predictive policing suggest).[3] In other words, the anxieties that today's 'point-and-click' interactive documentaries have evoked around traditional sites of authority (of author, of argument, of text) play out in quite different ways when algorithms and machine-readable data enter the picture. Rather than giving form to an experience through the collaboration between creator and user, in this new setting, the designers of the rule sets and definers of data ultimately shape the range of possible user experiences. This deferred and abstracted agency, increasingly common in the organisation of our social lives, requires an active critical framework if we are meaningfully to incorporate it into making stories about the world.

This algorithmically-induced reordering of agency and therefore authority can also be seen in a quite different and emergent area of documentary production: virtual reality. As a term, virtual reality is a claim, an ambition and a material ensemble that papers over two quite different technologies. On one hand, 360-degree-video conceptually replicates the late-eighteenth-century panorama. It is essentially a fixed, pre-recorded video asset in which the user can interact, directing attention where she will. In this sense, it invokes many of the same possibilities and challenges of 'point-and-click' interactive documentaries: the user works in tandem with the creator of a textual environment to explore and construct a text. While fixed in terms of visual and sound assets, the user has extensive latitude in assembling these elements.

On the other hand, 3D capture technologies essentially use data and algorithms to generate textual worlds on demand. Rather than traditional photographic or videographic optical information, these systems use lasers or photogrammetry to generate a fine point cloud of measurements, information that can take numerical form. These measurements have been deemed to have indexical status, as evidenced by their use by insurance companies, engineers and the police. These data points, in turn, need to be re-assembled and put into motion, and that is the work of algorithms. But because, as noted earlier, these are essentially constructed rule sets, they are in a sense arbitrary. If the point cloud reference to an object must behave the same as that object in the real world – say, subject to the laws of gravity – that behaviour has to be programmed. In other words, although the data points may have a clear correlation to things in the world, their behaviours must be constructed, and with this, 3D capture systems encounter the same dilemma as was just discussed with algorithmically constructed narratives. Agency shifts from being a human-centric affair, and turns instead on the algorithmic constructions of human, rule set and data interactions.

While by no means perfect, the correlation between 'point-and-click' and algorithmic stories on one hand, and the two VR systems (one 360-degrees and fixed and the other algorithmically generated) on the other, is nevertheless good enough for parallels to stand out. The interactivity enabled by 'point-and-click' documentaries, like that of 360-degree VR, has deep historical precedents. The technologies obviously differ, but the implications for user interactions with a fixed domain of sound and image assets, collaborative creativity and challenges to traditional notions of authorship and textual stability are similar. By contrast, algorithmic story generators and 3D-capture VR both introduce a third element into the creator/user binary: a procedural, programming element. While authored in its own right, the algorithmic rule set intermediates between machine readable data and the user, constructing a view of the world that even if indexical in the detail (the data points) is simulated and contingent in its operations.

CONCLUSION

So where does this leave us? We understand and have made good use of historical precedents to help ground the operations of new technologies that in fact hew to old behaviours. Linking today's digital remixing back to the commonplace book, or 'live documentary' to the work of silent film era 'explicateurs', or 360-degree VR systems to the panorama, all offer us fresh and generative readings of the past as well as insights into our latest iterations of these endeavours. But history can also help to distinguish aspects of our media practice that are indeed new, and by so doing, alert us to the need for fresh and critical thinking about their operations and implications. This chapter has sketched two scenarios of likely relevance to the future of the interactive documentary: algorithmic storytelling and 3D-capture virtual reality systems. As noted, algorithmic storytelling has made significant inroads in the world of print journalism; and developments in taste prediction, image recognition and image verification systems are making rapid progress. VR documentaries using 3D-capture systems such as Karim Ben Khelifa's *The*

Enemy (2016) and Oscar Raby's *Assent* (2014) are also appearing with greater frequency.

At one level, these future developments fit well within the expanding contours of the documentary. They make good use of documentary's ability to explore new forms, and with them, new expressive possibilities. Transitional phases tend to be retrospective, with new technologies and techniques tasked with serving old agendas. But we can also expect considerable innovation as our makers grow more familiar with the possibilities of the new.

But on another level, these algorithmic developments pose challenges. As noted, despite appearing fixed in form, these constructions are not only dynamically responsive and unique, but arguably interactive as well. On a terminological level, one can make a historical case for interactivity, but it requires challenging our assumptions regarding the concept's assumed temporality and agency. 'Family resemblances' rather than fixed definitions may be the way to go, opening up new ways of reading old practices – Collins' writing process or the Bible's textual evolution for example. At the same time, these new algorithmic forms exacerbate the anxieties already at play in the shift from traditional notions of author, reader and text (the linear documentary) to the possibilities of collaborative authorship and instable texts that characterises the 'point-and-click' notion of interactive documentary. They displace authorship and agency to a culturally unfamiliar space, that is, to algorithmic rule sets and metadata characteristics of machine-readable data.

'Unfamiliar' is perhaps an overwrought term in this context, since algorithmic agency plays an increasingly important part in our digital lives, where its manifestations in our searches, social networks and navigational systems is routine, despite their profound implications for governance. But for our textual systems, our critical encounters with seeing and re-presenting the world, their implications are deeply profound and they are the site of critical interrogation, as demonstrated by Brett Gaylor's *Do Not Track* (2015) and Sandra Gaudenzi's *Digital Me* (2015).

The reordering of the concept of agency common to these future systems does not fit easily with the notion of the subject as it has developed in the West since the fifteenth century. New wine in old bottles, the implications of this new order of things are not immediately evident. They have been deployed in most aspects of our social lives, and their routine appearance in the world of documentary, like media generally, is already in process. Our task is neither to lament the passing of the old nor grow frantic over the emergence of the new, but rather to assess carefully and critically their capacities and implications for documentary practice and representational literacy more broadly.

NOTES

1 According to the OED (1827) J. Bentham, Rationale Judicial Evid. I. i. iv. 54 Documentary evidence...' and (1843) T. Carlyle, *Past & Present* i. iii. 25: 'It is an authentic fact, quietly documentary of a whole world of such.'
2 For a sense of the progress in this sector, see Imagenet Large Scale Visual Recognition Challenge http://image-net.org/challenges/LSVRC/2015/. Accessed 31 October 2016.
3 For example, see Maurice Chammah, 'Policing the Future, The Marshall Project', 3 February 2016; https://www.themarshallproject.org/2016/02/03/policing-the-future#.tlOncNt0i. Accessed 31 October 2016.

REFERENCES

Bower, Bree (2015) 'YouTube Now Gets Over 400 Hours of Content Uploaded Every Minute', *Tubefilter,* posted 26 July; http://www.tubefilter.com/2015/07/26/youtube-400-hours-content-every-minute/. Accessed 31 October 2016.

Chammah, Maurice (2016) 'Policing the Future – The Marshall Project', posted 3 February 2016. https://www.themarshallproject.org/2016/02/03/policing-the-future#.tlOncNt0i. Accessed 31 October 2016.

Flaherty, Robert (1926) *Moana*. Film.

Gaudenzi, Sandra (2014) *Digital Me*. Web documentary. Directed by Sandra Gaudenzi and co-created with Mike Robbins of Helios Design Labs for BBC Taster; http://www.bbc.co.uk/taster/projects/digital-me. Accessed 31 October 2016.

Gaylor, Brett (2015) *Do Not Track*. Web Series. Directed by Brett Gaylor, co-produced by Upian, Arte, ONF and BR. https://donottrack-doc.com. Accessed 31 October 2016.

Grierson, John (1926) 'Flaherty's Poetic *Moana*', *New York Sun*, 8 February 1926.

Hayles, Katherine (1999) *How We Became Posthuman: Virtual Bodies in Cybernetics, Literature and Informatics*. Chicago: University of Chicago Press.

Hoelzl, Ingrid and Rémi Marie (2015) *Soft Image: Towards a New Theory of the Digital Image*. Bristol: Intellect.

Khelifa, Ben (2016) *The Enemy*. VR experience. Co-produced by Camera Lucia, NFB, Dpt. and Nouvelles Ecritures; http://theenemyishere.org/#team. Accessed 31 October 2016.

Kuhn, Thomas (1962) *The Structure of Scientific Revolutions*. Chicago: University of Chicago Press.

Latour, Bruno (2005) *Reassembling the Social*. Oxford: Oxford University Press.

Leonard, Harold (ed.) (1966 [1941]) *The Film Index: A Bibliography. Vol. 1: The Film as Art*. New York: Arno Press.

Locke, John (1706 [1685]) 'A New Method of a Common-Place-Book', in *Posthumous Work*. London: Churchill.

MIT Open Documentary Lab and IDFA DocLab (2014) *Moments of Innovation*. Web project; http://momentsofinnovation.mit.edu. Accessed 31 October 2016.

Moravec, Hans (2000 [1998]) *Robot: Mere Machine to Transcendent Mind*. New York: Oxford University Press.

Podolny, Shelly (2015) 'If an Algorithm Wrote This, How Would You Even Know?, *The New York Times*, 7 March; http://www.nytimes.com/2015/03/08/opinion/sunday/if-an-algorithm-wrote-this-how-would-you-even-know.html. Accessed 31 October 2016.

Raby, Oscar (2014) *Assent*. VR experience. Produced by VRTOV; http://oscarraby.net/wp/assent/. Accessed 31 October 2016.

Shorenstein Center on Media, Politics and Public Policy at Harvard University (2015) 'Tools for Verifying and Assessing the Validity of Social Media and User-Generated Content'. Posted 2 April; http://journalistsresource.org/tip-sheets/reporting/tools-verify-assess-validity-social-media-user-generated-content. Accessed 31 October 2016..

Shub, Esfir (1927) *Fall of the Romanov Dynasty*. Film.

Uricchio, William (2011a) 'A "Proper Point of View": the panorama and some of its early media iterations', *Journal of Early Popular Visual Culture,* 9, 3, 225–38.

____ (2011b) 'The Algorithmic Turn: Photosynth, Augmented Reality and the State of the Image', *Visual Studies*, 26, 1, 25–35.

____ (2016) 'Interactivity and the Modalities of Textual Hacking: From the Bible to Algorithmically Generated Stories', in Sara Pesce and Paolo Nolo (eds) *The Politics of Ephemeral Digital Media: Permanence and Obsolescence in Paratexts*. London: Routledge.

Winston, Brian (1986) *Misunderstanding Media*. Cambridge, MA: Harvard University Press.

TOWARDS BEHAVIOURAL REALISM
EXPERIMENTS IN IMMERSIVE JOURNALISM

Nonny de la Peña

INTRODUCTION

'In fact it is real. It isn't fiction.'
— Words penciled by a patron in a book after experiencing *Project Syria*

In June of 2014, we installed *Project Syria* (de la Peña 2014a), a computer-generated virtual reality journalism experience which recreates scenes from the Syrian civil crisis, in the Tapestries Room at the Victoria and Albert Museum in London. The set up was far from elegant, especially in contrast to the sumptuous centuries-old, ornately hand-sewn communication antiquities hanging on the walls. Eighteen scuffed black boxes, second-generation motion-tracking cameras created by a company called Phasespace, were connected to each other through a long string of Ethernet cables. These were mounted on eight heavy, durable tripods, creating an approximately fifteen-by-twenty-foot boundary box that demarcated the space where users could walk while wearing virtual reality goggles.

The installation was not advertised by the museum. This meant that visiting patrons, hailing from all parts of the globe, had not anticipated the exhibition and were alerted to the experience only by a sign outside the entrance to the Tapestries Room. On entering, they would find a strange scene of someone walking around in heavy goggles, a duct-taped box like contraption covering their eyes and bright red lights mounted like a Christmas-bulbed antenna above their head. Given such unfamiliar and tenuous-appearing apparatus on show, visitors had to be somewhat daring to try out the *Project Syria* virtual reality journalism experience.

Figs. 1 and 2: *Project Syria* in the Victoria and Albert Museum's 'Tapestries Room' – June 2014.

Project Syria is based on factually documented events; first a moment in Aleppo when a mortar shell hits a crowded city street and then a type of virtual reality infographic that shows a rapidly growing refugee camp filling with children. Computer-generated imagery recreating these scenes, informed by video, audio and photographs, plays back in a game engine synchronous with the powerful sounds captured at the time. While attempts were made to mirror the physical world episodes as closely as possible, the reconstruction had little financing, resulting in low-fidelity digital characters and buildings.

Despite these limitations, and the strangeness and complexity of the set up, numerous V&A patrons felt compelled to write comments in the *Project Syria* guestbook. In fact, at the end of the five-day exhibition, 54 pages of extraordinary and emotional responses filled the guestbook in an outpouring that a museum curator called unprecedented. Remarks consistently exclaimed how 'real' and 'immersive' the experience was and how they felt as if they were 'actually there' with one distinct comment noting: 'This was a very difficult piece to experience (as a Syrian whose family is still living in Homs). Although I felt the piece was inappropriate at first, I have certainly changed my mind after experiencing it first-hand. It is important for the world to bear witness to the situation in Syria and this is a powerful and effective way to do that...'

What is it that makes something like *Project Syria* so visceral, commanding such powerful commentary from its audience? Can it be considered non-fiction or virtual documentary? And what about the concept of the 'uncanny valley', accepted by many within immersive design as a guiding truth, that digital characters can cause a creepy sensation if they are situated in the supposed computer-simulated purgatorial state between 'friendly low-fidelity' and 'real enough' (Mori 2012). Should journalists and documentarians allow the ideas behind the uncanny valley to direct their approach when they create immersive journalism experiences in virtual reality?

REFLECTING ON THE UNCANNY VALLEY

Over the past eight years, I have been using virtual reality to explore and depict non-fiction stories, drawing in particular on human rights issues to frame the narrative structure. Utilising my more than twenty years as a working journalist to help guide the flow, I have now constructed multiple experiences, which have been exhibited around the world. This has allowed me to observe, record and survey thousands of people's reactions to full immersion in embodied virtual reality that rely on the believability of the story. In my previous publications, I have referred to this structure as 'embodied digital rhetoric': 'In fact, we have a *plastic presence* that allows for "injection-moulding" into different spaces or different body forms. People can actually feel as if they have been transported to another place or that they inhabit a different body. [...] This is not to say that participants entirely forget their physical world whereabouts or completely detach from the environment in which their bodies actually reside, but this secondary connection can be intense. Importantly, these sensations of presence can only be achieved if the changes in the virtual environment happen in real time, that is, if the viewer participant is allowed to move freely while the digital environment changes visually and aurally in exact keeping with gaze, location and body position (jumping, squatting, bending, etc). This combination of virtual reality tools, including goggles and fast computer graphics, invokes a fully immersive experience that takes advantage of our plastic presence. By using both body and the *kairos* of a real time delivery to create an empathetic connection, a new embodied digital rhetoric emerges for framing persuasive arguments' (de la Peña 2014c: 314).

The feeling of being actually situated *on scene* is crucial to the audience accepting that they are bearing witness to a non-fiction event that parallels a physical world occurrence. My pieces allow the audience to remain who they are when they travel the story by using a virtual reality system that requires no avatar, no controllers, and nothing but natural human motion to give an experience without costume and without pretence. It is my belief that this manifestation of 'oneself', akin to being present in the natural world, allows the stories to be communicated in a uniquely visceral manner. In rhetorical terms this would be considered to be a persuasive device. This sensation remains true even though there is a duality of presence: participants know that they remain in the physical location where their body resides but they also feel at the exact same time as if they have been transported to the environment where the scene is unfolding.[1]

My argument is that by combining virtual reality technologies with strong storytelling techniques, profound and visceral experiences can be offered to audiences, as exemplified by the reaction to *Project Syria* at the V&A. Yet the 'uncanny valley' is often used to dismiss the use of CGI representations of humans within non-fiction virtual environments, due to worries of alienating the audience and thereby diminishing the power of the narrative. I wish here to suggest otherwise, having come to the conclusion that there is much evidence to suggest that the 'uncanny valley' thesis, focused originally on real-world robots, should not be applied to immersive virtual reality. For me, a better way forward is to concentrate more on gaining a deeper understanding of behavioural realism and feelings of presence in this medium, as these offer greater insight into inducing a connection or disconnection for audiences.

It is important to note that in the last decade a variety of studies have reflected on the validity of the 'uncanny valley'. They have focused mostly on how techniques used in cinema can create a sensation of the eerie, giving the viewer the feeling that a character is creepy and scary. The belief is that the presented character strikes the same chord as an unhealthy human whose physical or mental deficits signal that they perhaps should be avoided. Yet researchers most often point to specific manipulations, such as unnatural eye or limb movements, as causing the uneasy sensation rather than the appearance being just short of lifelike to pass and therefore inducing the classic definition of the 'uncanny valley' (Brenton *et al* 2005). Moreover, other studies trying to ascertain a definitive 'uncanny valley' have often fallen short, leading a reviewer who surveyed the field to write: 'One essential question to ask is just whether there is enough evidence to say that the uncanny valley exists? Surprisingly, the answer is equivocal' (Pollick 2010). While I would agree that immersion can break in virtual reality, I have found that it was not actually an eeriness that caused problems, rather it is when 'realism was not matched with behavioral realism' (Brenton *et al* 2005: 2).

This chapter uses three of my pieces – *Project Syria* (2014a), *Use of Force* (2014b) and *Across the Line* (2016) – to explore what behavioural realism looks like and how it can support or devolve immersion through its effect on 'response-as-if-real' (RAIR) (Slater 2009). It also addresses what I have been calling a 'duality of presence' (de la Peña 2014c), which offers an approach to understanding why an audience reports that something *feels* as if what is happening is real while still knowing it isn't *actually* real. This is something that I see as aiding the acceptance of non-fiction work without sensations of the uncanny, which will increase in relevance for designing non-fiction as consumer headsets, which allow kinetic experience, become more commonplace.

At the start of the 2013 fall semester, Elizabeth Daley, the Dean of the USC School of Cinematic Arts, brought Klaus Schwab, the executive director of the World Economic Forum, for a visit to experience *Hunger in Los Angeles* (2012). This work, which premiered in January 2012 at the Sundance Film Festival, reconstructs an actual crisis when a diabetic man, waiting for a meal in a long line at a food bank, falls into coma because his blood sugar drops too low. The piece is now considered to be the first positionally-tracked virtual reality journalism experience that allowed the audience to walk around the scene as the events unfolded. It was built with little funding and neither volumetric capture nor 360-degree film cameras set-ups were available at the time. Instead, three-dimensional models were created from photographs of the street and surrounding buildings, while the virtual avatars were programmed through the use of motion capture, almost entirely through donated labour. Like *Project Syria*, the characters and environment can seem cartoony when viewed in a 2D video or photographs but, when experienced in virtual reality, the piece creates a strong sensation of being present on scene.

In fact, for Klaus Schwab, like so many others who experienced *Hunger in Los Angeles*, the impact was instantaneous. After removing the headset, he immediately enquired about the possibility of creating a piece about the Syrian refugee crisis using the same technology for the following January's World Economic Forum meeting. After several months of negotiation, a $35,000 budget was set and work began in earnest to gather the necessary images and audio to act as the fundamental scaffolding upon which to build something appropriately reflecting the horror and chaos that has turned so many Syrians into displaced refugees.

The goal of the piece was to offer audiences a sensation of being *there* when the events transpired by using elements hewn from real material. The design process initially mirrored my previous long-form non-fiction cinematic process. The first step was to gather material that describes an incident while it unfolds – the same type of *verité* moment that marks the best in documentary filmmaking. I commissioned a team to collect audio and video while we also began a review of archives in search of a commanding depiction or event that reflected the larger issues we were trying to convey.[2]

The first version of *Project Syria* had two scenes. The first part recreated video footage of a young girl singing on the street in the Old City area of Aleppo. Behind her, the street shows a busy afternoon, with vendors selling wares from carts

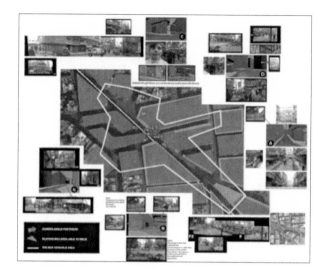

Fig. 3: One page from the art bible used to create *Project Syria*.

and stalls, a boy rests on a bicycle, a photographer and friends cluster together and cars and trucks drive past in the nearby street. Suddenly, a mortar shell hits and the ensuing explosion causes chaos, with debris and smoke filling the air. Screams are heard and the camera shakes as the filmmaker runs.

Although the original video was compelling, the footage ends abruptly after the explosion. In order to meet design goals that allowed the audience to remain on the scene, extensive research was done to find other video and audio material that could supplement the aftermath and extend the piece.[3] Additionally, the streets needed to be fully documented in order to make an accurate reconstruction. Photographic archives and Google Earth images helped to provide the images necessary to guide the modelling of the street before and after the mortal shell hits.

For the sections that follow the bombing, a film crew was specifically sent to a refugee camp to capture material that would help convey the anxiety over food deprivation and the breath-taking growth of refugee camps. Led by filmmaker Namak Khoshaw, a two-person camera and audio crew were directed to focus on the plight of children, as human rights organisations were reporting that children were being specifically targeted in the violence and making up disproportionate populations in camps.[4] As Khoshaw and his crew were Kurdish in origin, they chose Kawergosk, a refugee camp in the Kurdish area of Iraq bordering Syria.

Once the material was in hand, scenes were translated into three-dimensional imagery that could be viewed in real time using the game engine Unity and linked to goggles so that the imagery responded without any noticeable lag to viewpoint changes when the audience looked or moved around. The goal was to give the important sensation of being able to walk along the street scene before, during and after the blast. Viewers were also placed at key vantage points in the following scenes so that they would bear witness to the terrible circumstances of the refugees trying to survive.

However, with this project there was a chasm between the desire for realism and the budget for the digital reconstruction. For example, we began the piece hoping to reproduce the facial expressions of the singing Syrian girl. Unfortunately, we had neither the skillset, funding or time to make the kind of work that could achieve the quality we desired. Instead, the virtual young girl held her eyes wide-open and moved her lips unnaturally – perhaps even laughably. Her shape, size and movements could be considered acceptable as 'real enough' but a close examination of her face would have been off-putting. No doubt allowing the audience to watch her sing would destroy any illusion that a real event was occurring around them.

We dealt with the problem by keeping her turned to the side, so that the audience could hear her sing, but not readily witness the inexpert modeling and animation. (Viewers could have walked around to the front of her, but few did.) Similar problems were hidden, such as when it became clear that coding navigational paths created strange movements when a car or person tried to make adjustments for an object in front of them. We found that it was better to just drive a car straight even if it meant colliding into a building 'down the street' where it was out of sight for the audience because they could not walk to a place where they could see that far.

Fig. 4: Singing Girl in *Project Syria*.

The final results were extremely successful, first at the World Economic Forum premiere, where world leaders left dozens of notecards describing their reactions on a bulletin board. Then, as noted at the start of this chapter, it travelled to the Victoria and Albert Museum, where an audience comprised of museum-goers from around the world, from children to senior citizens, described a visceral experience that connected them to the real world events in Syria in a way that previous exposure from newspaper articles or news broadcasts had not been able to achieve. One museum-goer said that the piece gave her – 'a real feeling as if you are in the middle of something you normally see on TV news'.

While focusing on the virtual girl character's facial animations may have caused viewers to be distracted from the story, she was never so 'real looking' as to have entered the supposedly defined space of the 'uncanny valley' which requires the character to look just shy of real. While her facial expressions could be considered bad art, more relevant was how she acted within the context of the piece. Audiences accepted *Project Syria* as journalism because her behaviour was appropriate in relation to other characters, to the scene and to audio. Moreover, by carefully ensuring that she and other characters or objects did not defy physics such as penetrating the street, walls or their own 'bodies', or acting robotic in movement, *Project Syria* made viewers comfortable with the truth of what they were witnessing. How the scene felt rather than how the scene looked was the crucial dynamic for how the piece was experienced.

USE OF FORCE

Use of Force (2014b) tells the story of the night 35-year-old Anastacio Hernandez Rojas was beaten and tasered to death by the US border patrol, one of more than a dozen migrants who have been killed by the border patrol under questionable circumstances in the past few years. Hernandez Rojas had been brought to the US as a young teenager and had been living for over 27 years under the radar as an undocumented construction worker. In the late spring of 2010, he stole a bottle of tequila and a steak on Mother's Day, presumably for his wife, at a time when the soured economy in the United States had made it extremely difficult to find labour for undocumented workers in particular. He had never been in trouble with the law before but, when he was arrested, he was quickly deported. Just a few days later, on 28 May, he tried unsuccessfully to sneak back into the country, and the border patrol officer who caught him treated him roughly. Hernandez Rojas complained to a supervisor but, rather than take action, the supervisor allowed the same offending officer to take him into the dark pen on his own. Later the officer would claim Hernandez Rojas was trying to 'resist', although evidence would emerge indicating that Hernandez Rojas remained handcuffed throughout his ordeal. As the events escalated, at least fourteen officers became involved in his death. Two witnesses recorded the events with their cell phones from separate vantage points, although the footage would remain out of public view for over two years. While the San Diego coroner's office ultimately ruled Anastacio's death to be a homicide and testified that his death was caused by the injuries he sustained, no action was taken against the officers involved.

The decision to make the piece was made directly after seeing the powerful images and the tragic audio captured in grainy video by witnesses Humberto Navarette and Ashley Young. The border patrol had seized cell phones and cameras from multiple witnesses, yet Navarette and Young had managed to surreptitiously leave the scene with their videos in hand. Investigative reporter John Carlos Frey had tracked the two witnesses down and convinced them to make their recordings publicly available. His report aired on PBS nearly two years after Hernandez Rojas's death but it was picked up by only a handful of news organisations and there was little public outcry.[5]

Documentation photography of the original scene on which to base the digital models was not possible, as the border patrol had demolished the bridge that overlooked the scene. Construction around the site also prevented access to the iron fence outside of which witnesses had filmed the beating of Hernandez Rojas. However, photographs were taken of streets, sidewalks and buildings in the directly adjacent areas. Utilising these photographs and a collection of archive material obtained from news organisations and Google maps, models were built primarily in 3D Studio Max in order to reconstruct the environment to correspond with the original physical world setting as much as possible.

At the same time body-scanning procedures of characters were begun. Key witness Ashley Young, who had captured footage from above the bridge, agreed to be facial scanned, body scanned, facial motion-captured and body motion-captured. The concept here was that she would retell her recollection of the events of the evening through her body as much as through her words. This would help to ensure that the recreation would be personal and come directly from her. Navarette could not be located, with associates reporting that he feared for his wellbeing and was keeping his whereabouts hidden.

Young's face was scanned at the Institute for Creative Technologies using their patented light-stage system, providing the data for building a model with a true likeness. Her body scan was produced by Icon Imaging, which provides similar scans for big-budget Hollywood special effects needs. The same Phasespace motion-capture system that allows for tracking when users wear the virtual reality goggles was used to record Young's body motion and facial movements. Her voice was also recorded as she tried to speak and yell the same words as she had on the night of event. In fact, she was specifically instructed to only say and do the things that she remembered doing that night and to re-enact them in the order that she remembered them occurring. The videos she captured that night were used as guides.

Three other 'look-alikes' were scanned as 'stand-ins' for characters that we could not access. These included using a look-alike for witness Navarette, the key officer who committed the final and probably fatal tasing, and the victim himself. Models of all of the characters, as well as skin and clothing textures, were created in Maya and the models were then given body and facial rigs, i.e. a digital bone structure that could be animated. Other 'bystander' characters came from a pre-built library provided by AXYZ Design.

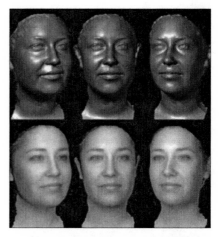

Elaborate motion capture was utilised to recreate the drama and action of the events. Actors wearing body suits had to re-enact events as portrayed in both the videos and as described in court documents. (Young also donned

Fig. 5: Facial captures used to create a CG model of Ashley Young, a real witness to the events depicted in *Use of Force*.

a motion-capture suit, to re-enact her own recollections and her interviews provided additional detail used to direct the motion capture done by actors.) All assets were assembled and programmed in Unity 3D and C# was used for coding requirements. Audio from the real event was augmented with clips to support the surrounding environments – cars passing, crickets, an occasional siren.

Participants experienced the piece wearing bespoke virtual reality goggles, designed with 130-degree field-of-view lenses and tracked through the Phasespace camera system. An HDMI wireless transmitter was used so that participants could walk freely within the footprint of the camera system without being tied to a computer. Later a virtual camera was added which allowed participants the ability to film their own experience for one minute and retain a video of that 'in world/in game' footage. This served two experimental purposes: the first was to make the participant understand more deeply the experience of the real witnesses who were trying to capture crucial evidence; the second was to offer a takeaway video that the participant could post to their social media sites so that publics who had not actually donned the goggles could learn about the original event.[6]

Audience reaction has been consistently strong, with users reporting feeling the piece in their 'whole body' as opposed to just watching a scene in a film clip.[7] The photographs below show how individuals tried to lean over the 'edge' of the bridge to watch more clearly the action unfolding 'below', even though no such edge actually existed in the physical world.

Reviews of the work were also very positive, including comments from Japan's largest gaming magazine that 'this is what video game technology can of-

Figs. 6–8: Viewers try to see 'over' the virtual bridge while experiencing *Use of Force*.

fer to society, gut-wrenching, the most shocking experience in my career.' The piece also won the 'Impact Award' at Indiecade, the world's largest independent games festival.

The questions raised by *Use of Force* when viewed through the 'uncanny valley' lens are multifold. All attempts were made towards depicting the scene as realistically as possible in terms of the models' presentation and their movement and behaviour. This is key, as it is contrary to what Mori suggested and is often held as an important guiding principal in digital design: to find a way to make the scene more palatable by toning down realism. The original paper suggested that a wooden hand was more acceptable than the pink rubbery flesh of the then state-of-the-art fake limb.

Yet there is a clear distinction between reality and the virtual reconstruction in *Use of Force* and, despite attempts to imbue models with lifelike qualities, in no way did they perfectly resemble their real-world counterparts even though the high-end scanning provided high-quality models. Given the appropriate reactions of the audience, does this imply that these models display just the right amount of lifelike characteristics so as to avoid evoking a sensation of being 'creeped out' for the majority of the audience? I would argue that this not the point and that it is the strong audio, plus the fact that multiple characters are moving with baseline motions captured from actual human movement, that makes the action so dense and 'natural enough' to keep audience engagement. This is because motion-capture helps, but does not create, exact human motion. In addition, the knowledge that *Use of Force* is based on a true story perhaps primes the audience to understand that the piece depicts a real moment.[8]

ACROSS THE LINE

Across the Line (2016) screened at the Sundance Film Festival, SXSW and the Sheffield Film Festival in the first half of 2016. Made in collaboration with Planned Parenthood, an organisation that provides reproductive health centres across America, and 371 Productions, the experience puts the audience on scene with anti-abortion extremists who are trying to intimidate patients. The over-arching goal of the content was to offer insight into the experience of young women seeking sexual and reproductive health care by giving the audience an embodied experience. The success of the piece is underscored not only by the multitude of positive press reviews,[9] but was also given a 'Social Impact Award' by the US organisation Media Impact Funders.

The piece unfolds in two consecutive sections. The first was made with an ar-ray of eight GoPro cameras designed to film in 360 degrees, and footage was cap-tured inside and outside a clinic while a protest against Planned Parenthood was underway. The second half, which will be my focus here, places the audience on a virtual street to face a barrage of vitriolic language – an edit from recordings col-lected from across the United States of verbal abuse towards young women trying to enter clinics. Virtual characters, created from scanned models, were animated with facial capture synced to the authentic sourced audio so that they scream at the user much like at the real event. Characters also turn and track the user as they pass so that the delivery is pointed and direct.

With commercial headsets finally reaching the market, viewers were shown *Across the Line* on three different types of goggles. The first, a Vive, was made in collaboration between mobile phone maker HTC and gaming company Valve. This headset achieved what our previously handmade goggles allowed users to do: walk around the scene in a one-to-one correspondence with their movements in the natural world. The other two headsets, the Samsung Gear VR and Google Cardboard, both use mobile phones and do not allow any movement aside from head rotation in all directions. The user can spin their body in a circle, but their translational movement is fixed so that the user cannot walk around. This means that virtual characters are reduced to screen dimensions and that nothing is ex-perienced in the life-sized manner that the positional tracking of the Vive or our bespoke headsets allow.

More than 170 surveys were collected at the SXSW Interactive Festival where *Across the Line* was shown. While these were not evenly distributed between the GearVR mobile phone version and the walk-around Vive version, the reac-tions further support my thesis that the uncanny valley theory, heavily dependent on appearance, becomes irrelevant in virtual reality. The Vive experience was described repeatedly as 'amazing', with a reviewer from Yahoo writing, 'the characters become CGI, but are rendered relatively well; there is no uncanny valley when you're being screamed at and told you're going to invoke God's wrath.'[10]

However, the GearVR experience was viewed as problematic, in that viewers wrote that the characters, 'feel cartoonish and that takes away from the overall seriousness of subject matter.' What mattered, it seems, was whether the users were able to engage with the material, i.e. able to walk around a scene, or whether they were fixed in one position. This was despite the fact that in both experiences the characters and their animations were exactly the same. In fact, the only crucial distinction was how the audience corresponded to the characters – either being able to move naturally down the line, akin to a real-world experience (using the Vive), or frozen in location while the camera moves from character to character so they can 'yell' in turn at the user (on the GearVR).

This suggests that when the sense of presence is violated, rather than fidelity to realism (or lack thereof), the flow and connection to the narrative is compromised. These results therefore deepen my proposition that user experience, rather than the appearance of characters, is key to audience reaction.

CONCLUSION

Recently, I was offered this comment from a reporter: 'With the VR you're creating, we get to experience a point of view, or, better yet, a situatedness in a situation, which it is otherwise highly unlikely that we would have the opportunity to experience and reflect upon.'

What creates that feeling of 'situatedness' – the 'duality of presence'? Certainly, it shares similarities to the phenomenological immersion of watching a film, while still remaining as distinct an experience as reading an engrossing novel is in comparison to seeing a movie. A more relevant description might be the feelings of a daydream in which we feel both here and there, as described by Gaston Bachelard: 'The daydream transports the dreamer outside the immediate world to a world that bears the mark of infinity. [...] However paradoxical this may seem, it is often this inner immensity that gives real meaning to ... expressions concerning the visible world. [...] We can sense the with intimate depth of being' (1994: 189).

Surely that intimate immensity would be eviscerated by a stumble into the uncanny valley. Yet, even with the clumsy graphics, these virtual reality pieces about real scenarios do not destroy the daydream. Instead, I have found that many different levels of modelling and animation are acceptable if the focus is on behavioural realism. It is not necessary to replace virtual humans, even if they display a mediocre rendering, for lower fidelity but 'friendlier,' non-human characters.

Rather, the audience can be disconnected from the feeling of situatedness when the user feels the automation is unacceptable. This can be a virtual human visibly intersecting with physical objects, including their own body; or a virtual human walking or moving in a robotic way. Believable and appropriate audio also seems to be equally crucial in keeping a deep connection alive, a standard also expected in traditional cinema, or television broadcasting. Most importantly, allowing the viewer to engage with natural body movements, not just head movements, helps to eliminate disconnections with the narrative.

Also crucial to the sensation of the daydream, of being both here and there at the same time, is a careful use of 'embodied edits' to the narrative (Weil and de la Peña 2008). The audience needs to be moved carefully along the narrative in a way that doesn't disrupt the physiology of their connected mind and body. Indeed, if there is an uncanny valley in virtual reality, perhaps this might be the definition: the place one feels oneself to be when the camera is moving but the body is still. When the audience feels present on scene, it means that their entire bodies are along for the ride. That means that if the camera is moving, the participant's eyes are telling the brain that the body is moving. Yet the inner ear is saying something completely different, claiming, correctly, that the body is still and with that disconnect creating what is known in the field as 'sim sickness'.

Surprisingly, an article called 'Feeling Woozy? It May Be Cyber Sickness' was published in the *New York Times* in the fall of 2015: 'The more realistic something is, the more likely you are going to get sick', said Thomas Stoffregen, professor of kinesiology at the University of Minnesota, who has done extant research on digital motion sickness. 'No one got sick playing Pac-Man' (Murphy 2015).

However, I would argue that it is camera movement, not realism, which is at the root of the problem. By allowing a one-to-one match of a person's physical movement to the virtual imagery seen through allowing the audience member to walk around, the signals are unified, thereby significantly reducing this type of discomfort. Until we can (or if we can) overcome the conflicting signals sent to the brain by the eyes and the inner ear, the nausea caused by a camera movement out of our personal control, means that the daydream is subject to a horrible disruption.

It seems, therefore, that utilising the arguments in Masahiro Mori's thesis on the uncanny valley to frame virtual reality experiences is an error. Given the desire to offer audiences the greatest sensation of presence, of situatedness, in the non-fiction narrative, I have found behavioural realism to offer an alternative and successful focus. Indeed, this chapter has offered varied examples, which suggest that the valley never needs to be crossed.

NOTES

1. I have found this to be true even though the audience typically has no digital manifestation of a body in the virtual space. In many ways, they travel through the events like 'a ghost', something I have frequently heard commented about. This is interesting in that we are always ghosts in the cinema – in the sense that we are witnessing events unseen – but because VR has evoked a sense of presence, the lack of a body suddenly becomes noticeable.

2. In one tragic occurrence during the research process, a Spanish photographer was announced as kidnapped twenty minutes after we had reached out to ask whether he might have appropriate supporting material we could use.

3. Evangelos Lympouridis did critical research in finding and translating footage to supplement the experience, along with his other creative roles.

4. See http://www.oxfordresearchgroup.org.uk/publications/briefing_papers_and_reports/stolen_futures. Accessed 31 October 2016.

5. I was made of aware of the material through a Twitter posting by the Latino news organisation News Taco.

6. This turned out to be extremely successful when BuzzFeed News had its employees try the experience and their posting received nearly a million views on YouTube as of this writing, with pages of commentary about race issues in America; https://www.buzzfeed.com/chris-lam/being-a-witness-in-virtual-reality

7. This was told to me by the reporter Chelsea Stark during the interview for a piece later published on Mashable; http://mashable.com/2014/06/26/virtual-reality-memory/#8Mt1Sd8VmkqT. Accessed 31 October 2016.

8. There is another crucial distinction between Mori's original thesis and a virtual reality experience. Mori's arguments were framed for the robotics community and more specifically around reactions to being situated in the same physical location as the robot or robotic prosthesis.

9. A few examples: *New York Magazine* and MTV, 22 January 2016: 'A powerful depiction of the often toxic environment that many patients must walk through.'

10. Yahoo, post by Jordan Zakarin Writer, posted 22 January 2016.

REFERENCES

Bachelard, Gaston (1994) *The Poetics of Space*. Boston: Beacon Press.

Brenton, Harry, Marco Gillies, Daniel Ballin and David Chatting (2005) 'The Uncanny Valley: Does It Exist?', Proceedings of Conference of Human Computer Interaction, Las Vegas, Nevada USA, 22–27 July. Published on CD-ROM by Mira Digital Publishing: ISBN 0-8058-5807-5.

De la Peña, Nonny (2012) *Hunger in Los Angeles*. Immersive journalism experience putting people on the street in Los Angeles at a food bank when a man waiting in the long line for food collapses into a diabetic. Premiered at Sundance in January 2012.

_____ (2014a) *Project Syria*. Immersive journalism experience putting people on the street of Aleppo and in a refugee camp. Commissioned by the World Economic Forum and premiered there in January 2014.

____ (2014b) *Use of Force*. Immersive journalism experience about deaths of an immigrant Anastacio Hernandez Rojas at the hands of border patrol. Funded by Tribeca and an Online News Association Google/AP grant.

____ (2014c) 'Embodied Digital Rhetoric: Soft Selves, Plastic Presence, and the Non-fiction Narrative', in Gustav Verhulsdonck and Marohang Limbu (eds) *Digital Rhetoric and Global Literacies: Communication Modes and Digital Practices in the Networked World*. Hershey: IGI Global, 312–27.

____ (2016) *Across the Line*. Immersive journalism experience that put the audience on scene to face protesters at health clinics. Executive produced by Planned Parenthood and created in collaboration with 371 Productions.

Mori, Masahiro (2012 [1970]) 'The Uncanny Valley [From the Field]'. Trans. Karl Macdorman and Norri Kageki, *IEEE Robotics & Automation Magazine,* 19, 2, 98–100; https://www. scribd.com/doc/203887410/The-Uncanny-Valley-Masahiro-Mori. Accessed 31 October 2016.

Murphy, Kate (2015) 'Feeling Woozy: It May be Cybersickness', *New York Times*, 14 November; http://well.blogs.nytimes.com/2015/11/14/feeling-woozy-it-may-be-cyber-sickness/?_ r=0. Accessed 31 October 2016.

Pollick, Frank E. (2010) 'In Search of the Uncanny Valley', in Petros Daras and Oscar Mayora Ibarra (eds) *User Centric Media*. Berlin: Springer, 69–78.

Slater, Mel (2009) 'Place illusion and plausibility can lead to realistic behaviour in immersive virtual environments', *Philos Trans R Soc Lond B Biol Sci,* 364: 1535, 3549–57.

Weil, Peggy and Nonny de la Peña (2008) 'Avatar Mediated Cinema', *ACM International Conference Proceeding Series*, 352, 209–12.

INTERACTIVE DOCUMENTARY AND LIVE PERFORMANCE
FROM EMBODIED TO EMPLACED INTERACTION

Judith Aston

INTRODUCTION

In 2015, I gave a keynote lecture on 'Interactive Documentary and Live Performance' (Aston 2015), a subject which has received little attention to date within the field of interactive documentary practice. My argument was that the sense of time, place and occasion that surrounds live performance has a role to play within interactive documentary, and that there is much to be learnt about this from the world of interactive theatre. I showed a number of examples, suggesting that performative approaches could inform mediated as well as live work, and that there was much scope for creating interesting synergies between these two processes. This chapter builds on this keynote, by tightening up my argument and bringing in some new examples. It also situates my work alongside Julie Fischer's MSc dissertation (2014) on 'the emerging field of live documentary practice', the work of Paul Dourish (2001) on 'embodied interaction', and the work of David Howes (2004) and Sarah Pink (2009) on the emerging paradigm of 'emplacement'. In bringing together these different strands, I suggest a new term through which to interrogate i-docs: 'emplaced interaction'.

My intention is to offer a fresh perspective on how audience has a central role to play within i-docs – one which goes beyond 'clictivism' in order to incorporate broader thinking around 'collectivism'. In so doing, I am re-visiting Jay Rosen's 2006 post on 'the people formally known as the audience' in which he states that the Internet is democratising politics and enabling us to become active and engaged citizens as opposed to passive consumers. In a warning about the dangers of over-claiming, Holmes suggested in 2007 that cyberspace may in

fact be turning us into disembodied consumers controlled by global corpora-
tions and ultimately devoid of political identity and agency. Without wishing to
labour these conflicting positions, my aim here is to argue that live performance
should be considered as being a key part of the palette of possibilities for interactive documentary and its claims for active audience engagement. As a means of
expression, which has the potential to bring people together and to engage all the
senses, my argument is that it is a powerful way to help keep us connected both
to each other and to the physicality of the world in which we live. This seems
pressing at a time in which simulated realities, automation and data tracking are
becoming ever more a part of our everyday lives.

TIME, PLACE AND OCCASION

In my keynote, I situated live performance as being something that happens in
the 'here and now', as having an ephemerality and fleetingness which means that
every performance has the potential to be different from the next. This relates to
the dynamics between performers and their audience, which can be configured in
different ways across different settings and which is what makes live performance
different from the experience of engaging with pre-recorded material in a cinema
or through broadcast media. In a world swamped by screens and pre-recorded
media, I argued, we are witnessing a resurgence of interest in live performance, as
a way of creating an antidote to the sterility of having everything always on tap. I
cited Bill Drummond, the rebel-rouser extraordinaire from the 1980s pop group
KLF, as an inspiration. In particular, I referenced his comments in the film *Press
Pause Play* (Dworsky and Köhler, 2011), where he confirms his frustration with
the iPod and with music playlists and states his belief that the generation to come
are not going to want to make music that anyone can download anywhere and
listen to at any point. Instead, he claims, they are going to want to do something
special, something that is about place, about time and about a sense of occasion.
Drummond's project, *The 17* (2009), is the ultimate expression of this approach
– an ever-changing choir, which writes and performs improvised music scores and
does not make recordings of its performances.

In my own work, I too have felt Drummond's frustration, as screen-based culture is becoming ever more prevalent – through mobile phones, consoles and now
virtual reality. When I first started working with interactive media, it was a little
known phenomenon, but now it is everywhere – even if interactive documentary
by name still remains a more niche activity. Also, having an interdisciplinary background in anthropology, film and interaction design brought together through my
work in multimedia, I have a long-standing interest in Wagner's concept of the

Gesamtskunstwerk, or total artwork, which strives to make use of all or many art forms to create a universal artwork. For Wagner, this could be best achieved through using theatre as the unifying medium, as he argues in 'Art and Revolution' ('Die Kunst und die Revolution', 1849) and 'The Artwork of the Future' ('Das Kunstwerk der Zukunft', 1849), coming closest to the full expression of this vision in his Ring Cycle (*Der Ring des Nibelungen*, 1848–74). Following on from Wagner, the Intermedia movement in the 1960s focused on the interdisciplinary art activities that were occurring between genres and across art and media (Higgins 2001). Gene Youngblood also described intermedia as a part of a global network of multiple media that was 'expanding consciousness' – the intermedia network – that would turn all people into artists by proxy. He gathered his ideas together in his 1970 book *Expanded Cinema*, which had an introduction written by global thinking pioneer, Buckminster Fuller.

Having studied Interaction Design at the Royal College of Art and been working as an art school lecturer for almost twenty years, these influences have stayed with me and have very much been informing the way in which I think about interactive documentary. In the initial stages, it was the multimedia aspect that drew me in – the potential for 'the seamless integration of data, text, sound and images of all kinds within a single digital information environment' (Feldman, quoted in England and Finney 1996: 4), alongside the potential for juxtaposing multiple points of view through spatial montage (Aston 2010). Initially exploring this potential through videodisc, then CD-ROM and then online media, it was only later on that I came to extend my practice into working with musicians and theatre practitioners, partly inspired by Ken Jordon and Randall Packer's work on *Multimedia: From Wagner to Virtual Reality* (2001). This was when I became interested in concepts of immersion and breaking the fourth wall, to create forms of audience engagement and participation that went beyond the 'point-and-click' interactivity of much screen-based work. As a parallel interest, I also became interested in the more 'one-to-one' or readerly aspects of the iPad, as another way of moving beyond point-and-click to create more immersive forms of cognitive engagement. Ultimately, I see the use of these different forms as offering a range of ways to combine the material with the digital, and to create both experiential and readerly ways into documentary content.

PERFORMANCE THEORY

When we think of the *Gesamstkunstwerk* in a twentieth- and twenty-first-century context, we cannot ignore the ways in which live and mediated forms of media are becoming ever more intermeshed. Performance scholar Philip Auslander has written about this in his text on 'Liveness: Performance in a Mediatized Culture' (1999). He points out that prior to the advent of recording technologies such as photography, motion pictures and sound, there was no such thing as a 'live' performance, as that category has meaning only in contrast to an opposing possibility. So, whilst 'the default definition of live performance is that it is the kind of performance in which the performers and the audience are both physically and temporally co-present ... over time, we have come to use "live" to describe performance situations that do not meet those basic conditions. In a live broadcast, for example, performers and audience are temporally but not physically co-present' (1999: 60).

Additionally, Live Aid, one of the largest-scale satellite link-ups and television broadcasts of all time, set up a precedent where audience members could be physically and temporally co-present with some performers but only temporally co-present with others. And online role-playing games can be said to incorporate elements of liveness as they bring players together co-temporally and create the illusion of co-presence within their virtual worlds. Virtual liveness, which does not connect at all to physical co-presence, is not my core interest. However, there has been scholarship which shows that live role-play in virtual worlds feeds directly into face-to-face physical play (Giddings 2014), thus creating synergies between online and face-to-face experience. As such, I have been careful to include examples of interactive projects, which knowingly blend real and virtual exchanges, as part of the scope of this chapter.

A physical live performance can be a play performed in a theatre, a concert performed in a music venue or a live narration or musical performance to accompany the screening of a film. In these instances, the fourth wall between audience and performers is often clearly defined through the demarcation of stage and auditorium. However, live performances can also take place in unconventional settings, involving site-specific venues around which the audience may be free to roam. For example, National Theatre Wales has no permanent building and puts on plays in unusual venues – from beaches, to train stations and mountainsides. Likewise the Punchdrunk theatre company creates 'site-sympathetic work' in which audience members, often wearing masks, are free to choose what to watch and where to go.

Punchdrunk's founder and artistic director, Felix Barrett, has said that he sees the Internet as having skewed the way we read the world, making us more passive and making life too easy. His aim is to work with interactive theatre to make things feel a little more difficult, to make the hairs stand up on the back of peoples' necks, and to make them feel 'alive'. For him, the future of storytelling is absolutely about placing the audience at the heart of the experience (Barrett 2013). Having experienced Punchdrunk's *The Drowned Man: A Hollywood Fable* (2013) and subsequently participated in a professional enrichment masterclass with Barrett, I have some insight into their devising process. It is deeply intuitive and very responsive to the specifics of site, and it has most definitely had a deep influence on the development of my own thinking around time, place and occasion and the role of live performance in 'emplaced interaction'.

RELATED STUDIES

Fischer's MSc dissertation was the first of its kind to provide a 'structured analysis of the emerging form of Live Documentary', with a view to providing 'some support for the foundation of a Live Documentary practice' (2014: 141). It provides some very helpful mapping of the territory, focusing in on three emergent forms which she calls 'Live Performance Documentary', 'Live Subject Documentary' and 'Live Data Documentary'. Fischer also calls for a re-examination of the role of audience as well as subjects within interactive documentary (2014: 137) and hopes that we are moving into a period where documentary-making will be theorised as being as much about process as it is about product. In so doing, she hopes that this will allow for interesting new configurations to emerge around the dynamic between subjects, makers and audiences within interactive work (2014: 88).

Fischer's work accords with my own view that documentary has a rich tradition which is not just about filmmaking and that, although technology is key to the debates, 'it is ultimately people and not machines that should be at the centre of the (interactive) design process' (Aston 2016). Fischer posits her three forms as being a starting point for further discussion and so, in the spirit within which her dissertation is written, I want here to expand the discussion by adding in some other trajectories and influences. In order to do this, I will first summarise her three forms and then go on to consider how they might be used as inspiration for further thinking around the role of live performance in helping to create a dynamic relationship between audience, subjects and makers within interactive work.

Fischer describes the first of these forms, 'Live Performance Documentary', as involving the spatial and temporal co-presence of an audience in a theatrical setting. Whilst she is clear in stating that she is referring to theatre in its broadest sense, she underlines that 'today's representative works in this form engage with performance practices that date back to early days of cinema' (2014: 114). Though this is true in relation to the projects which she describes, my own keynote showed that other possibilities for live presentation have also begun to emerge, as will be illustrated below. Also, Dale Hudson and Patricia Zimmermann's analysis in *Thinking Through Digital Media* (2015) de-centres i-docs thinking by exploring digital media modes which are emerging around the world away from the main centres of interactive documentary production. These modes are often in response to localised creativity and needs, in support of my point that awareness of context and sense of place is central to our developing understanding of interactive documentary.

The second of Fischer's forms is 'Live Subject Documentary' as a form of live performance which 'relies on the Internet for its form of televisual interactivity' (2014: 114). Again I wish to expand the scope of the discussion as, although there is much interesting work emerging which is built around live streaming on the Internet, there are other ways too in which audiences can be brought into contact with documentary subjects, as I will illustrate below. I do, however, concur with Fischer that 'Live Subject Documentary' can absolutely take 'an important step in pushing viewers to engage with people outside their own spheres – and not just to see them, but to interact with them' (2014: 138).

Fischer's third category – 'Live Data Documentary' – involves bringing real time data into a live process of documentary construction which she describes as being more about human/computer interaction than human/human interaction. In analysing this form, she states that whilst it has much potential as a set of possibilities, it would be a shame if interactive documentary were to become limited to a consideration of interaction between viewer and computer. In so doing, she calls for the field to remain as open as it can be 'to the full sense of interaction, including interactions with people out there in the reality we are trying to capture in our work' (2014: 142). This is a statement with which I completely agree.

In response to these three categories and to the ever-evolving nature of interactive documentary practices, what follows below is an extension of Fischer's work, to broaden out the debates and incorporate a wider range of influences from beyond the world of broadcasting. I offer three categories for consideration, based on varying degrees of audience participation, and then I work my way through various theories of emplacement and embodied interaction to arrive at my own concept of 'emplaced interaction'.

PERFORMANCE AS LIVE PRESENTATION

Here I reference pre-recorded interactive work performed live in front of an audience. IDFA DocLab has been a champion of such work, having commissioned interactive performances as part of the annual festival in Amsterdam since 2008. For example in 2012, Caspar Sonnen commissioned a live performance of the interactive documentary *Bear 71* (Allison and Mendes 2012) with Jeremy Mendes orchestrating the event on-stage to live music. Even earlier in 2010, the offline premiere of the 360-degree documentary *Out My Window* (2010) was screened at a live cinema event by director Kat Cizek (whose work features in an extensive interview with her elsewhere in this volume). These are examples similar to screenings of films where the director is on hand to present the work and/ or additional components are added to the screening itself. As with my 'Future Documentary' work with artist and filmmaker Jeanie Finlay (Aston 2014), in which we combined live performance with documentary screening, DocLab takes pre-recorded media back into live settings and create one-off experiences for the audience which can significantly add to viewers' engagement with the work.

There are also projects within this category which can only be experienced live, these being the ones that I wish to focus on here. The first of these examples is filmmaker Adam Curtis and artist/musician Robert del Naja's collaborative project *Adam Curtis v Massive Attack,* which premiered at the 2013 Manchester International Festival. It is a film-work specifically intended for live performance with the band performing behind a bank of immersive film screens to Adam Curtis' pre-recorded film materials and accompanying narration. Though more immersive than interactive in terms of offering the audience navigational choices or setting up a virtual conversation, the audience is bombarded with an intense sensory experience, intended to actively engage the viewer. There is a call to arms at the end when Curtis says 'the future is not predictable, anything is possible, don't be afraid'. Describing the performance as a 'Gilm', Curtis sees it as a new way of integrating a gig with a film that has a powerful overall narrative and emotional individual stories. For him, it is a move towards creating a 'total experience' in which you are 'surrounded by all kinds of images and sounds' but which is 'also about ideas' (2013).

Having not experienced the work for myself, others have relayed to me in personal conversations that experiencing this work was indeed a very active process. Though generally well received, one comment on Curtis' blog about the work (posted on 14 July 2013) was that 'the event missed just one thing – a camera turned on the camera, or perhaps on the audience'. His comment was that 'we were all consumers in that depot – simply gazing at the screens, fixated on the narrative – so it felt like subversion was being subverted. I made the trip to Manchester for a political experience, but ended up with entertainment.'

Without wishing to claim that this would have necessarily made the work 'better', it would have been a way to build on Vertov's early experimentation in *The Man With a Movie Camera* (*Cheloveks Kino-apparatom*, 1929) in which he filmed an audience watching his film and then incorporated it into his final edit. In so doing, it can be said that he created a more 'interactive' relationship between audience and performance.

Another piece involving live presentation is *Hearts and Minds: The Interrogations Project* (Coover *et al* 2014), described on the project's website as being an 'interactive, immersive, and cinematic gaming environment that draws users into the haunting memories of ordinary American soldiers who became torturers in the course of serving their country'. The project presents the audience or individual user with a narrative environment that begins in a reflective temple space with four doors opening into four ordinary American domestic spaces – a boy's bedroom, a family room, a suburban back yard and a kitchen. In the rooms are 3D objects, which when triggered, take users into a strange landscape – an interior abstracted world of memory. Once the performer or individual user has entered a room, he/she cannot leave until all the objects in the room have been triggered. The project was developed in the immersive 3D CAVE2 at the University of Illinois-Chicago (UIC). Though not just designed to be experienced in this environment, it is the version performed in situ as a series of special screenings in June and July 2014 that is of interest here, as documented in an interview with one of the project's directors Rod Coover (Badani 2014).

For these screenings, a performance artist took on the role of the user, carrying an audience of up to thirty people at a time through the experience. This enabled it to become a communal one, as the CAVE2 is a 320-degree immersive space which can only be operated by one person at a time. The audience, having been informed that the experience would last around fifty minutes, sat together at one end of the CAVE2 with the performer sitting in front of them. The performer carried with him a chair and wherever he placed it, would help trigger a visual change. Using a hand-held wand, he took them through several virtual rooms, triggering objects in each, which acted as a portal to audio recordings of the soldiers' experiences. Although the audience were not able to participate in the actual performance, there was an integral discussion at the end, facilitated by members of the project team. In a follow-up interview with me, Coover explained how sitting with others helped viewers to engage with the distressing nature of the material, with the discussion at the end allowing them to share their responses to the work. For him, subsequent 2D versions work really well as 'individual reading and learning tools, but nothing can match the group immersion and experience-sharing of the CAVE2 event' (personal communication, August 2016).

PERFORMANCE AS LIVE PARTICIPATION

Moving on to the next set of possibilities, I described these in my keynote as projects where the authorship explicitly intends the audience to interact with the presenter of the work or with the documentary subjects through temporal and/or spatial co-presence in order to affect the manner in which the content is delivered. Here, there is a strong cross-over with Fischer's 'Live Performance' form, with us both referencing Nathan Penlington's *Choose Your Own Documentary* (2014) project. However, after discussing this work below, I take a more expansive view of the possibilities by moving on to an example which builds more on interactive theatre conventions than on traditions which come out of early cinema.

In *Choose Your Own Documentary,* Penlington performs live on stage, acting as the narrator and bringing the audience in and out of the pre-recorded film clips which he presents. His interaction with the audience is crucial to the work, as he asks them to vote on which way to progress the filmed part of the narrative. This style of interactive performance relies heavily on the performer's skills as a storyteller, and is explicitly designed to encourage as much audience participation as possible. That said, the performance still has a set duration with a beginning, a middle and an end, very much predicated on the idea of a seated cinema-going audience with an onstage performer. Whenever the audience is required to make a choice, Penlington pauses his narration and the house lights are raised slightly to encourage audience members to discuss their decisions with each other. This creates an active dynamic between audience and performer, thus breaking the fourth wall of more traditional forms of theatrical performance.[1]

Bordergame (Norton and Wright 2014) is an example of live participation which moves beyond Fischer's examples to configure a different dynamic between fact and fiction, and between physical and virtual co-presence. Produced by National Theatre Wales and funded by The Space, it involved three sets of 'players' on three separate evenings signing up to meet at Temple Meads station in Bristol, where they were required to catch a train into Wales. On arriving in Wales, they had to convince a fictional group of border guards that they were eligible to enter the world of the 'autonomous republic'. Whilst this scenario was being acted, other 'players' were connected to the performance via webcams, observing their every move with a view to voting towards the end on who they thought should be let in and who should be turned away. Once the vote was cast and the decision was announced, players were bundled off in a mini bus to a safe house where they were invited to share a meal with a group of genuine asylum seekers.

The performances used refugees as both players and informers, with the show being based on and including some of their real experiences. Integral to this experience was a genuine desire on behalf of its creators to create a sense of integrity and authenticity, reflecting real peoples' stories of migration and allowing the audience to share those experiences. The live performance put the audience in the shoes of the migrants, whilst the online experience was based on the Milgram Experiment, asking participants to obey an authority figure instructing them to perform acts likely to conflict with their conscience. In order to 'play' *Border-game* online, participants had to first become an 'active citizen' by signing up and working through a series of preparatory multiple choice questions. They were designed to implicate online players as spies and to ultimately encourage them to consider the impact of their choices on others. Though the reviews were mixed,[2] audience feedback suggests that the performance did succeed in putting players inside the storyline and in melding live with mediated experience to create a new form of part fictional and part factual interactive experience (personal communication with creators, April 2015).

PERFORMANCE AS LIVE CREATION

This approach to live performance involves a range of collaborative possibilities between audience, subjects and makers in which live participation actually leads to at least some of the documentary content being constructed through the performance itself. Often this will involve interesting combinations of live and mediated experience, sometimes involving virtual co-presence through the Internet and sometimes not, with the examples I provide here giving a sense of the range of approaches that might be taken. Again, there is crossover here with Fischer's work – this time with her 'Live Subject' and 'Live Data' categories, the former which she sees as involving live streaming and the latter as involving the incorporation of real-time data feeds into documentary content. Though I can see that the Live Data documentary is dependent on the Internet for its real-time feeds, live televisual streaming is only one of many ways in which subjects, makers and audiences can engage with each other through interactive work. As such, I will start with an example that fits with Fischer's 'Live Subject' category and then move onto two examples which expand the notion into other areas.

My Neck of the Woods (Blast Theory 2013) was a collaboration between Blast Theory and the Manchester Royal Exchange Theatre, described on its website as being part documentary, part performance, part live-stream video experience online. It played out over two consecutive nights and used live video feeds to enable a conversation between six teenagers on the streets of Manchester, UK, and a wider online audience. Audience members signed up on the website where they could watch introductory videos for each teenager and decide who to follow. They would then be dropped into their video stream as they told the audience about their lives and asked the audience questions about theirs. No two conversations were the same, as each teenager had their own approach and interests, with their own unique set of questions and places to explore. In addition to this, it was a two-way experience with the conversation evolving according to the dynamic between the online audience and the teenagers on the ground. Audience members could sit back and listen to other people's conversations or they could play a more active role by responding to questions and/or asking them. Fischer refers to this project as an example of how 'Live Subject Documentary' can take 'an important step in pushing viewers to engage with people outside their own spheres – and not just to see them, but to interact with them' (2014: 138).

Another example of a live-creation event, which did use live video streaming but which very much had a spatially located intervention at its core is David Dufresne's *Dada-Data* project, produced in conjunction with Anita Hugi and the Akufen design agency in Montreal. As documented on the project's website, in March 2016 more than eighty 'brave souls' converged on the Cabaret Voltaire in Zurich for thirty hours to imagine a Digital Dada manifesto one hundred years on from the original launch of the Dada movement. The aim was to use the event to stimulate a series of 'hacktions' as a 'subversive means of combating advertising and the constant surveillance of our online activities'. Using 'bad wi-fi and historic walls, a disco ball and ceiling projections', the participants created a 'doc-by-doing' which was retransmitted live to some seven thousand people connected remotely via their computer screens.

This project has subsequently gone on the road and also continues as an 'online anti-museum' with its very own ad blocker free to download which replaces adverts with art (Zucker 2016). Dufresne has spoken of his interest in using live performance within a wider transmedia strategy to create 'temporary autonomous zones' (for example at Inter-DocsBarcelona, June 2016) – a term originally coined in 1991 by Hakim Bey (2011) for spaces which use their ephemerality to focus on the present and elude formal structures of control. For Dufresne, a key aim of the Cabaret Voltaire was to 'remake the world through laughter, through the absurd, through the fact of being in that space, together' (personal communication, August 2016) in a way that was absolutely grounded in the here and now of live performance. This is a sentiment which very much accords with my own motivation for bringing elements of live performance into interactive documentary practice, and is a key part of the experiences that I am trying to create through my own projects.

EMPLACED INTERACTION

To finish, I would like to explain my desire to situate interactive documentary and live performance within a wider theoretical context of 'emplaced interaction'. This is a term that I have come up with as a step on from Paul Dourish's work on 'embodied interaction' and David Howes' and Sarah Pink's work on 'emplacement'. I define it as being the creation, manipulation and sharing of meaning through engaged interaction, bringing our bodies and minds into direct interplay with the wider environment. It brings the senses to centre stage as a way of thinking about how we might work with interactive documentary, to create experiences which, as Felix Barrett (2013) has said, might help to make us feel 'alive' through maintaining some direct physical contact with our fellow humans and with the world at large. I offer it at a time when the Internet and now virtual reality is becoming ever more a part of the way in which we relate to the world and to each other, in the hope that as humans we will be intelligent enough never to allow ourselves to lose touch with the physical directness of the tactile world that surrounds us. Its provenance is as follows.

Dourish describes embodied interaction as being a way of thinking about human computer interaction which privileges engaged action over disembodied cognition (2001: 189). Starting from the premise that 'the social and the physical are intertwined and inescapable aspects of our everyday experiences' (2001: 99), embodied interaction is not a technology or a set of rules, more 'a perspective on the relationship between people and systems' (2001: 192). With this in mind, Dourish argues that new directions in tangible and social computing should be seen as one and the same activity, brought together through the unity of mind and body that lies at the heart of embodied interaction. In terms of human computer interface design, he sees this as leading to a definition of the term which involves 'the creation, manipulation and sharing of meaning through engaged interaction with artifacts' (2001: 126). His work has been very influential in bringing computer science into dialogue with the field of interaction design, and in moving it away from a mechanistic focus on plans, procedures, tasks and goals towards more of a focus on how things are done in a wider physical and social context.

However, whilst Dourish offers a powerful argument for taking a people- as opposed to systems-led approach to the design and implementation of human/computer interfaces, the work of anthropologists David Howes and Sarah Pink can be drawn upon to take this argument a step further into what I have called 'emplaced interaction'. Through his work on the senses, Howes has become critical of embodiment's focus on the body/mind relationship and has suggested that a new paradigm is emerging – one which adds environment into the equation. He calls this paradigm 'emplacement' in recognition of the fact that it suggests the sensuous interrelationship of body/mind/environment (2005: 7). Pink has picked up on this idea to foreground the idea of the 'emplaced ethnographer' as one who 'attends to the question of experience by accounting for the relationship between bodies, minds and the materiality and sensoriality of the environment'. As such, she states that it is now frequently recognised that ethnographers need to investigate 'both the emplacement of the people who participate in our ethnographic research and ethnographers' own emplacement as individuals in and as part of specific research contexts' (2015: 28).

In applying these ideas to interactive documentary, I have focused on Bill Drummond's ideas about time, sense and occasion. In so doing, I have argued that incorporating elements of live performance into i-docs, whether as process or as end-product, can be a way to engage our full complement of senses by bringing us together through physical co-presence. We can learn here from current approaches to interactive theatre which breaks down the fourth wall, to play with the dynamics between audience and performer, as well as from earlier movements such as Fluxus and the 'happenings' of the 1950s and 1960s. My argument is that this can open up possibilities to create interventions which might help to inspire audiences to become active citizens as opposed to passive consumers. In no way am I suggesting that this is the sole purpose of interactive documentary, or that other forms cannot achieve the same. I am simply offering it up as another way of thinking about interactive documentary's role in facilitating what the on-going process of creative improvisation that is everyday life (Hallam and Ingold 2007). In so doing, it might help us to keep technology in its place, thus ensuring that the Internet, virtual reality and ultimately robots do not take us over. My hope is that in considering these ways of thinking, this chapter will help to open up interactive documentary to these possibilities.[3]

NOTES

1. We invited Penlington to perform at i-Docs 2014, an event which was well received as a highly engaging example of live interactive documentary performance.
2. See, for example, https://www.theguardian.com/stage/2014/nov/11/border-game-review-national-theatre-wales and http://www.walesonline.co.uk/whats-on/arts-culture-news/bordergame-thought-provoking-piece-national-theatre-8090121. Accessed 31 October 2016.
3. I am very grateful to RMIT Melbourne, in particular to Adrian Miles at the non/fictionLab, for offering me a writing residency in June 2016. It led to much fruitful exchange and gave me invaluable headspace to consolidate my thoughts, as preparation for writing this chapter.

REFERENCES

Allison, Leanne and Jeremy Mendes (2012) *Bear 71*. Web documentary. Produced by NFB; http://bear71.nfb.ca/#/bear71. Accessed 31 October 2016.

Aston, Judith (2010) 'Spatial Montage and Multimedia Ethnography: Using Computers to Visualise Aspects of Migration and Social Division Among a Displaced Community', *Forum:*

Qualitative Social Research, 11, 2; http://www.qualitative-research.net/index.php/fqs/article/view/1479/2982. Accessed 31 October 2016.

_____ (2014) '*I Am Orion* as a wraparound approach to documentary filmmaking'. Project report; http://www.react-hub.org.uk/articles/future-documentary/i-am-orion-and-wrap-around-filmmaking. Accessed 31 October 2016.

_____ (2015) 'Interactive Documentary and Live Performance'. Keynote delivered at InterDocs Barcelona; http://www.inter-doc.org/interdocs-2013/interdocsbarcelona-2015/videos-de-la-conferencia/. Accessed 31 October 2016.

_____ (2016) 'Interactive Documentary – What Does It Mean And Why Does It Matter?' Blog post on i-docs.org, posted 27 March 2016; http://i-docs.org/2016/03/27/interactive-documentary-what-does-it-mean-and-why-does-it-matter/. Accessed 31 October 2016.

Auslander, Phillip (1999) *Liveness: Performance in a Mediatized Culture.* New York: Routledge.

Badani, Pat (2014) 'Roderick Coover in conversation with Pat Badani on *Hearts and Minds: The Interrogations Project*'. Screened at the Electronic Visualization Laboratory, University of Illinois at Chicago. *Journal of the New Media Caucus,* 2, 3; http://crchange.net/cr-change/documents/MEDIANreview_coover.pdf. Accessed 31 October 2016.

Barrett, Felix (2013) 'Burn the Seats: Audience Immersion in Interactive Theatre. Future of Storytelling Film'; https://futureofstorytelling.org/video/felix-barrett-burn-the-seats-audience-immersion-in-interactive-theater. Accessed 31 October 2016.

Bey, Hakim (2011 [1991]) *TAZ: The Temporary Autonomous Zone, Ontological Anarchy, Poetic Terrorism.* New York: Pacific Publishing Studio.

Blast Theory (2013) *My Neck of the Woods.* Live documentary from the streets of Manchester. In cooperation with Royal Exchange Theatre's Truth about Youth programme. https://www.blasttheory.co.uk/projects/my-neck-of-the-woods/. Accessed 31 October 2016.

Cizek, Kat (2010) *Out My Window.* 360-degree documentary. Part of the multi award winning *Highrise* Project, directed by Kat Cizek, produced by Gerry Flahive, co-produced by NFB; http://interactive.nfb.ca/#/outmywindow. Accessed 31 October 2016.

Coover, Roderick, Scott Rettberg, Daria Tsoupikova, Arthur Nishimoto, Arthur Partridge, Mark Baratta, Jeffrey Murer and John Tsukayama (2014) *Hearts and Minds: The Interrogations Project.* Interactive immersive and cinematic environment. Produced by Electronic Visual-ization Lab (EVL) at the University of Illinois Chicago; http://theinterrogationsproject.com/. Accessed 31 October 2016.

Curtis, Adam (2013) 'The Medium and the Message'. Blog; http://www.bbc.co.uk/blogs/adamcurtis/entries/f431c7d1-3da0-3c56-bc67-fbc3bca2debc. Accessed 31 October 2016.

Curtis, Adam and Robert del Naja (2013) *Adam Curtis v Massive Attack.* Live Interactive documentary performance with multiple screens and live music. Premiered at Manchester International Festival 2013.

Dufresne, David and Anita Hugi (2016) *Dada Data. A doc by doing.* Live events, hacktions, web and app. Co-produced by ARTE, ARTE Creative, SSR/SRG, BR, Upian and Akufen design agency; http://dada-data.net/en/. Accessed 31 October 2016.

Dourish, Paul (2001) *Where the Action Is. The Foundations of Embodied Interaction.* Cambridge, MA: MIT Press.

Drummond, Bill (2009) *The 17.* Project homepage; http://www.the17.org/about.php. Acces-sed 31 October 2016.

Dworsky, David and Victor Köhler (2011) *Press Pause Play*. Film. Co-produced by Einar Bodström, Philip Marthinsen and Adam Svanell.

England, Elaine and Andy Finney (1996) *Managing Multimedia*. Guildford: Addison-Wesley.

Fischer, Julie (2014) *To Create Live Treatments of Actuality: An Investigation of the Emerging Field of Live Documentary Practice*. Unpublished MSc Thesis, Department of Comparative Media Studies, Massachusetts Institute of Technology.

Giddings, Seth (2014) *Gameworlds: Virtual Media and Children's Everyday Play*. New York: Bloomsbury.

Green, Sam and Yo La Tengo (2012) *The Love Song of R. Buckminster Fuller*. Live Documentary. Premiered at the San Francisco Film Festival, San Francisco Museum of Art, 2 May 2012.

Hallam, Elizabeth and Tim Ingold (2007) *Creativity and Cultural Improvisation*. London: Berg.

Higgins, Dick (2001 [1965]) 'Synesthesia and Intersenses: Intermedia', *Leonardo*, 34, 1, 49–54; https://muse.jhu.edu/article/19618. Accessed 31 October 2016.

Holmes, David (2007) *Virtual Politics: Identity and Community in Cyberspace*. London: Sage.

Howes, David (ed.) (2004) *Empire of the Senses: The Sensual Culture Reader*. Oxford: Berg.

Hudson, Dale and Patricia Zimmermann (2015) *Thinking Through Digital Media: Transnational Environments and Locative Places*. New York: Palgrave Macmillan.

Jordan, Ken and Randall Packer (eds) (2001) *Multimedia: From Wagner to Virtual Reality*. New York: W.W. Norton.

Norton, John and Matthew Wright (2014) *Bordergame*. Immersive interactive theatre experience inspired partly by the UK Citizenship test, developed in consultation with refugees and asylum seekers now living in south Wales. National Theatre, Wales and The Space. https://www.nationaltheatrewales.org/bordergame. Accessed 31 October 2016.

Penlington, Nathan (2014) *Choose Your Own Documentary*. Live experience. Created by writer and performer Nathan Penlington and filmmakers Fernando Gutierrez De Jesus, Sam Smaïl and Nick Watson. Previewed in 2013, toured in 2014; http://www.cyod.co.uk/about/. Accessed 31 October 2016.

Pink, Sarah (2009) *Doing Sensory Ethnography*. London: Sage.

Punchdrunk (2013) *The Drowned Man: A Hollywood Fable*. Immersive theatre production, Presented by Punchdrunk and the National Theatre. Creative Director Felix Barrett; http://www.punchdrunk.org.uk/the-drowned-man/. Accessed 31 October 2016.

Rosen, Jay (2006) 'The People Formerly Known as the Audience'; http://www.archive.pressthink.org/2006/06/27/ppl_frmr.html. Accessed 31 October 2016.

Uricchio, William (2004) 'Storage, Simultaneity, and the Media Technologies of Modernity', in John Fullerton and Jan Olsson (eds) *Allegories of Communication: Intermedial Concerns from Cinema to the Digital*. Bloomington: Indiana University Press.

Vertov, Dziga (1929) *The Man With a Movie Camera (Chelovek's kino-apparatom)*. Film.

Wagner, Richard (1993 [1849]) *The Artwork of the Future and Other Works [Das Kunstwerk der Zukunft und andere Schriften]*. Trans. William Ashton Ellis. Lincoln, NE: University of Nebraska Press.

Youngblood, Gene (1970) *Expanded Cinema*. New York: Dutton.

Zucker, Stefan (2016) '*Dada Data* replaces ads with art'. Reporting for Deutsche Welle; http://www.dw.com/en/dada-data-replace-ads-with-art/av-19036729. Accessed 31 October 2016.

THE TRAVELLING I-DOC
REFLECTIONS ON THE MEANING OF INTERACTIVE DOCUMENTARY-BASED IMAGE-MAKING PRACTICES IN CONTEMPORARY INDIA

Paolo Favero

One of the key qualities of i-docs that has been stressed by many scholars and that is today almost becoming taken for granted is their capacity to translate the engagement with a screen into a kind of direct and perhaps also material engagement with the world that surrounds us (Aston and Gaudenzi 2012, Favero 2013a, Aston 2016). Addressing the hybrid space between life 'off-line' and 'online' (de Sousa e Silva 2006, Kabisch 2008), i-docs have the potentiality to function as generators of new social relations and new forms of participation in the material, physical and social exigencies of everyday life. I-docs seem to show us the extent to which the digital is a terrain in and through which we can better grasp (and potentially intervene in) the lived world that surrounds us. A part of the set of possibilities for 'the construction and representation of "reality" brought about by the human/computer interface' (Aston 2016), i-docs are also a tool, I suggest elsewhere, for 'getting our hands dirty again' (Favero 2013a; see also Gaudenzi 2013).

New image-making practices seem to offer us a precious window onto the social and political transformations that are affecting contemporary capitalist societies at large (Favero 2014b). They offer 'clues' (Ginzburg 2000) for understanding local contexts and the times in which we live. In this chapter, I would like – inspired by this range of reading – to take this issue a step further and look at the capacity of this visual form to adapt to new contexts. Looking at i-docs as a travelling practice, I enquire into their adaptation in a territory beyond the West, i.e. India. To do this, I rely on my on-going research on image-making practices in contemporary India and attempt to create a map of interactive documentary practices in the subcontinent. As the reader may have already understood by my usage of the terms 'interactive documentary practices' rather than i-docs, this exploration leads me to question the meaning of i-docs at large. In line with the work of other scholars in the field (Gifreu-Castells 2011, Aston and Gaudenzi 2012), I suggest the need to move beyond a definition of the field of interactive documentary as a 'genre' acknowledging instead the need to look at it as a 'field of practice' (Aston 2016). What will emerge from my mapping of the Indian space is, in other words, an enlargement of the notion of interactive image-making. The relative absence of i-docs in India, but the simultaneous abundance of projects containing the same logic, will spur these reflections while inviting us simultaneously to reflect critically upon questions of infrastructure, technology and geopolitics but also of culture and ideology. In other words, this chapter offers a fairly conventional, culturally situated, cultural relativist, anthropological approach to what we conventionally refer to as i-docs.

It starts with a brief introduction to the context of digital technologies and documentary film in India. After that, I describe in four sections different aspects of interactive documentary practices in India. In the conclusions, I will sum up my argument by inviting readers and future scholars to devote more attention to the emergence of such practices beyond the West.

IN A DIGITAL INDIA

When, about seven or eight years ago, I started interrogating documentary filmmakers and artists in India about whether they had worked with interactive documentaries, the conventional replies were often along the lines of: 'I would love to do one, but where shall I begin?' Most of the artists and filmmakers I encountered seemed to have an idea of what this language was but did not have a direct relation to it. Today, a few years down the line, the awareness and popularity of i-docs has not changed much, even though the number of projects working with formats, notions and technologies that we could label as belonging to the realm of i-docs has boomed. Such a growth is indeed part of a much wider scenario that today seems to be giving the digital/visual nexus an unprecedented centrality in India. Advertisements and articles on new image-making technologies fill the pages of newspapers and magazines. Mainstream media are increasingly adopting footage or photographs taken by viewers with their mobile phones as journalistic evidence. Also, the speed of landlines and the accessibility of 3G and 4G have improved immensely. Despite being characterised by a low percentage of penetration, the relative growth of numbers of users is pretty impressive: 20 per cent for year 2014, 52 for 2015 and 30.5 per cent for 2016.[1] And the booming sector is that of the mobile platform which, according to 2016 statistics, accounted for approximately 75 per cent of the total of access to the net.[2]

Indeed, the digital has also become the symbol of a new India capable of moving towards the future while strengthening, as contemporary slogans would put it, its firm roots in its past, culture and traditions. Launched on 21 August 2014, by the government led by Narendra Modi, 'Digital India' promotes digital technologies as key tools in the scaffolding of a future 'Tiger India'. Aiming to transform India into an electronically empowered economy, the 'Digital India' agenda runs alongside the campaign 'Make in India' which tries to give incentives for companies to manufacture in India and to attract foreign investors to the country. The nationalist undertones of this combined agenda are evident. However, the terrain of digital technologies in India is a very contested and lively one. Many intellectuals, activists and artists are today looking critically at the government's digital agenda, questioning the extent to which such technologies can become tools for an enhanced control of citizens and the cause of new social divisions. At the same time, many of these actors are also actively exploiting the very same terrain, in order to find new tools of cultural resistance. Many filmmakers, photographers, designers, etc, look upon the digital as an 'apparatus' with potential for helping citizens defeat injustice and bring visibility to marginalised social categories. They explore the extent to which digital technologies can allow them to intervene in everyday life and its politics; to function, that is, as tools for making and re-making India. Anandana Kapur's chapter in this volume is one such example and this is the context in which I too have been conducting research over the past ten years.

It may be important to point out that in an Indian context, the impact of digital practices gathers further momentum through its merging with visual practices. A topic addressed by several scholars in a variety of different arenas ranging from photography (Pinney 1997, MacDougall 2006), to popular culture (Jain 2007), cinema (Nandy 1998, Dwyer and Patel 2002), religion (Babb 1981, Eck 1998) and documentary film (Monteiro and Jayasankar 2015), the visual is a fundamental trait of Indian culture. Images in particular are incredibly powerful in this context. Connected to notions of reciprocity, tactility and efficacy, they are powerful tools requiring a rethinking of conventional Western assumptions regarding the visual field. In the next section, I stay a little longer with this issue and introduce the reader to the history of documentaries in India. This passage is fundamental in order to understand the way in which image-makers engage with this visual form and to understand the cultural, political and historical conditions from which the practices that I will describe later on have emerged.

BACKGROUND

Cinema came to India right from its very birth. In 1896, only months after their first presentation in France, the Lumière brothers came to Mumbai to screen their films. The Indians were very quick in identifying and exploiting the power of this new technology, and films were fundamental in generating a sense of nationhood among Indians. Spurring anti-colonial resistance (Chowdhry 2001), they became quickly an important part of modern popular culture. During the colonial period, documentary film occupied a secondary role to fiction. Non-fiction film was primarily the language of the British Raj. The Information Films of India (IFI), that is, the organisation coordinating documentary activities in the subcontinent, was in fact a propaganda organ subjugated to the political agenda of the empire. With independence, the Indian intelligentsia, however, decided not to get rid of the IFI but to found it anew under a different name. The Films Division (FD), founded in 1948, right at the time of India's independence, aimed at producing films for public information, education, motivation and for institutional and cultural purposes. The FD quickly became the single largest producer of documentary films in the world. A natural prolongation of the British model of audio-visual documentation, the FD set the standard for what documentary was perceived to be in independent India.

Most of the filmmakers I have interviewed during the last few years in India have told me that documentary has long been associated with FD clips and hence with notions of propaganda, boredom and educational weight. In the 1970s, however, things started changing. The historical phase known as the 'Emergency', when Indira Gandhi suspended democratic civil rights, ignited instances of resistance among young activists and artists who took to the camera in order to portray the tragic destiny of their country. The launch in 1978 of Anand Pathwardhan's *Prisoners of Conscience* is conventionally considered to mark the birth of Indian independent documentary film. With the arrival of VHS, the popularity of documentary film gained further momentum, allowing filmmakers not only to produce films at a lower cost but also to bypass India's centralised censorship mechanisms. These mechanisms were such that, until recently, the purchase of raw film had to be declared and accompanied by an explanation of the purpose.

The 1980s bore witness also to the emergence of NGOs as key sponsors of documentary films, hence making developmental issues a key trait of the Indian documentary. And today, in the age following the opening of the Indian economy to the global market, young filmmakers have also started finding new opportunities outside the conventional world of NGOs or of government sponsorship. Corporate filming and advertisement have become increasingly important domains of documentary production today. Many young documentarians are in fact able to sustain themselves economically by producing ads, info videos, etc. Combined with cheaper and lightweight digital technologies, this change has paradoxically meant liberation from the need to rent studio space, from production and distribution barons, etc. The new 'DIY documentary-maker' is emerging as a new profession developing a dialectic between new technologies and culturally situated image-making practices.

The contemporary documentary scene, therefore, stands out as a decentralised, heterogeneous space in which the introduction of new technologies is in dialogue with larger contextual issues – with the indigenous notions of visual culture and documentary practice, and with politics and societal issues (Battaglia 2012, Monteiro and Jayasankar 2015). In this scenario, a variety of different approaches to emerging practices and to interaction and participation can be found, which I delineate below. For the sake of coherence, I have divided my investigation of interactive image-making practices in India into four main areas: distribution/production, engaging the local, archiving the local and experimenting. Whilst perhaps seeming rather random, these categories have helped to structure this material and make it more intelligible.

DISTRIBUTION AND PRODUCTION

One of the first observations I was able to make among documentary filmmakers in India is that the digital is instinctively associated first and foremost with questions of distribution as opposed to production. This is a common association that most of the image-makers that I have interviewed have made. They immediately connected my questions regarding digital-visual practices to Facebook and email-based networks such as Vikalp or Docuwhallas[3] explaining how this is the arena of digital culture which has mostly generated benefit for documentary filmmakers in the country. Such networks have made possible the creation of larger and more functional circuits of information regarding screenings, courses, workshops and so forth. They have also helped filmmakers to circumvent the restrictions of the documentary film market and in particular the strict Indian censorship, as any film in India needs to get an approval from the board of censors in order to be officially distributed. Social media and other digital circuits have allowed filmmakers to bypass such mechanisms and get their films into circulation.

Some filmmakers have, however, also addressed this question from a different angle. Sanjay Joshi, a New Delhi-based activist and filmmaker, revealed to me that, for him, the digital has been fundamental for developing his nomadic festival called Cinema of Resistance.[4] Animated by the intent to oppose the contemporary Hindu-nationalist wave, Joshi, along with a group of formerly Marxist-inspired filmmakers, has seen in digital technologies the opportunity to create a mobile festival. After its start in Gorakhpur, Uttar Pradesh, it has now spread to several towns and villages in northern India, as Joshi explained in an interview with me in April 2013 (Favero 2013b). Bringing the notion of the digital to a more down-to-earth terrain and flirting with the practices of mobile film screenings that have characterised the history of Indian cinema in rural areas (see below), Joshi suggests that new technologies allow primarily for the reproduction of film-copies and mobile projections in a cheaper and more moveable manner. Digital technologies (in the shape of cheap projectors, DVD copies, etc.) have been fundamental to allowing films and their constituent critical resistance to travel across the country. Jokingly, Joshi told me also, with respect to a question that I asked him during an interview regarding digital crowdsourcing, that this is what they have always done, 'with the help of a hat, my friend!' (Hudson and Zimmermann 2015).

Cinema of Resistance's approach to technology, like that of many social actors in the field of digital practices in India, opens up the space for several types of reflection. In the first place, underlying its mission, there seems to be, as mentioned, the lively tradition of wandering cinemas, the 'bioscope whallas' that, as Prem Chowdhry (2001) suggested, were also fundamental to creating momentum for the anti-colonial struggle. However, this organisation is also in dialogue with practices relating to the circulation of videos (Battaglia 2012, 2014) that have been a key characteristic of the Indian consumption of images. They also speak of the present significance of piracy, which, as Ravi Sundaram (2009) has argued, could be looked upon as a form of modernity. We could, however, also view the solutions promoted by Cinema of Resistance as an example of '*jugaad*'.[5] Emerging as an established practice within innovation (Radjou *et al* 2012) *jugaad* entails that technologies can be creatively morphed so as to fit specific needs. Finally, organisations and events such as the Cinema of Resistance speak also of the fluctuating media boundaries that characterise digital practices at large today (see Gifreu-Castells 2011 and Favero 2014a for reflections on this in the context of i-docs).

Indeed, the leap from distribution to production is a small one. And in fact, while putting the accent on distribution, the documentary filmmakers that I have interviewed over the years have also acknowledged the importance of digital technologies as a tool for enhancing the production of documentary films. Digital technologies can allow, in particular, the liberation of production from the conventional circuits of institutional funding. Governmental agencies such as Films Division and non-governmental organisations such as the Public Service Broadcasting Trust (PSBT) have, together with NGOs, constituted the major share of funding available to filmmakers. The new forms of distribution allow filmmakers to break free from these commissioners. Thanks to new distribution formats, money can, with due limitation, be raised for producing new films without having to fall back on government funds or NGOs. Through a mixture of high technology, *jugaad* and self-piracy, a lot of filmmakers use screening opportunities as occasions to raise funding by either pitching new ideas or by selling 'self-pirated' copies of their films.

ENGAGING THE LOCAL

The Cinema of Resistance also uses its festivals as opportunities for supporting the production of new films. They customarily organise workshops whose aim is to attract the young to engage with image-making. Having taught them the basics of filmmaking, they send these young men and women out to narrate their life-worlds. These materials then constitute the body of future screenings and act as an incitement to new filmmakers to keep the process of self-documentation alive. This kind of format is quite established in India. I suggest that it constitutes a significant aspect of documentary production inspired by nonlinear, web-based and participatory techniques in the subcontinent. Let me give a few examples.

The project *Bell Bajao (Ring the Bell* 2008) by the organisation Break Through is a campaign targeting men to intervene against domestic violence. Made up of a series of online video clips (uploaded by amateur filmmakers but also by some well-known filmmakers), this project aims at telling true stories of men stopping violence with one ring of a bell. *Bell Bajao* has now reached more than 130 million people in India alone and won 25 awards, and its clips can be explored online or seen on television. In order to reach smaller places *Bell Bajao* has also organised 'video vans', which have travelled across the country. It has also been referenced in soap operas and television quizzes. Another similar example is *Project Kalki*. Born from the initiative of activist actress Kalki Subramaniam, *Project Kalki* aims at training underprivileged transgender women of Tamilnadu as community journalists and documentary film-makers. Addressing mainly the transgender community of southern India, the project aims to create a space for third-gender subjects to produce and share their stories.

I could give more examples of this sort. However, what is already evident is that in all these projects the image has found in the web the space for connecting back to everyday life (Gaudenzi 2013, Favero 2013a). These two platforms, albeit in different ways, speak of the capacity of the digital image to help social actors to attempt to enact changes. Once again, this approach, which dominates the panorama of digital-imaging practices, constitutes a link with the various forms of activism and of engagement with local critical issues that have been at the core of the tradition of documentary filmmaking in India. The collaborative spirit contained in this project can also be found in some other platforms that

Fig. 1: Screenshot of *Remembering 1992*. School of Media and Cultural Studies, Tata Institute of Social Sciences; http://mumbairiots.tiss.edu/#/

utilise formats and aesthetics that connect more evidently to what we conventionally refer to as i-docs.

Remembering 1992 (figure 1) is a platform developed in 2012 by students from the Tata Institute of Social Sciences in Mumbai. Based on official justice documents and reports, this site catalogues and maps all the events that happened during the 1992/93 Mumbai riots. Part of a larger project devoted to exploring questions of marginality in the city, the database, which has been created by the students of the school, allows viewers to explore the materials by date and place. The structure of the website is provided by the different types of memories connected to these events. Organised around a set of themes such as dislocation, divided city, struggles for justice, peace initiative and media representations, such memories offer multiple possibilities activating the viewer in their searches.

The ideal precursor of this type of collaborative, participatory image-based practice is probably *Cybermohalla*, a project created in 2001 by SARAI, an experimental arts group born in New Delhi, India out of the collaboration between academics and RAQS Media Collective.[6] SARAI explored the possibility of shaping material localities and communities through the creation and use of virtual environments. A web-based project, *Cybermohalla* saw the creation of self-administered media labs and studios in various neighbourhoods of New Delhi. Connecting them through the web, it aimed at drawing resources from the intellectual life of these various localities.

ARCHIVING THE LOCAL

All the projects mentioned above seem indeed to contain what we could call an 'archival spirit'. The form of the archive is in fact the root around which the rest grows. It is instructive to look beyond documentary examples and mention another set of experiences, which have recently become very popular in India. In an altogether different field of digital culture, mention could be made for instance of the *Traditional Knowledge Digital Library* (2001), an online archive of traditional systems of medicine, or *Sahopedia* (2016), the online encyclopaedia of Indian culture. Another project would be *TasveerGhar* (literally 'the house of pictures'), a deposit, as the site declares, for posters, calendar art, pilgrimage maps, cinema hoardings, advertisements and other forms of street and bazaar art. The common goal of all these projects is to strengthen awareness of India's history and cultural heritage. There are also many projects that, while using an archival spirit, have a different goal. More innovative in terms of both content and form is, for instance, the Public Access Digital Media Archive, better known as *Pad.ma*.

Launched in February 2008, *Pad.ma* is a collection of hard-to-access footage (such as unfinished, found, digitised or out-date films) that can be explored through a varied set of possibilities. Building on the idea that today video-making needs to be in dialogue with open online platforms, *Pad.ma* aims at stimulating an interactive connection with moving images among

Fig. 2: Screenshot of *Pad.ma*, online archive initiated by CAMP (Mumbai), 0x2620 (Berlin), the Alternative Law Forum (Bangalore) and also Majlis and Point of View (Mumbai).

film practitioners in India and also between filmmakers and academia. *Pad. ma* is basically a nonlinear archive with a participatory element. Footage is presented here along with annotations that can be produced by users. Users can also, through the site, make contact with the filmmaker (who created or uploaded the audio-visual material) and request to make use of the images for other projects, etc. The software on which the interface builds has also been adapted to other projects. Of particular value is here *IndianCine.Ma* (2013–), a database of Indian film intended to serve as a shared resource for film scholars and enthusiasts in India and beyond.

The concept of shared footage and/or an interactive archive, however, does not belong to *Pad.ma* alone. In recent years I have followed the fortunes of the materials produced by a group of activists from all over India who collected images of the aftermath of the Gujarat genocide of 2002. Mainly, but not exclusively, filmmakers, this group of activists wanted to prevent the evidence of the carnage from disappearing. Their goal was, however, not to make a film but to produce raw footage that could be used by journalists, activists, lawyers and filmmakers. The project did officially fail in the sense that the materials were never used for the making of a film, and today, parts of this material has been deposited with *Pad.ma*. This archive can be regarded as a forerunner of today's shared documentary practices in India.[7] Let me, however, now direct my attention to a last set of examples that take us into a more experimental terrain and one that we can more easily connect to conventional visions of what is an i-doc.

EXPERIMENTING

During a 2016 conference (Diginaka) at the Tata Institute of Social Sciences in Mumbai, after I had given my lecture on the politics of i-docs, I was approached by a young scholar/artist who told me that she had only just realised that in 2006 she had created something that probably was an interactive documentary. Namita Aavriti, a collaborator to the above mentioned *Pad.ma*, showed me, later that day, the work that she'd created together with her colleague Lawrence Liang. Entitled *Now Showing,* this is a research-driven project on the connection between cinema and law. Presented through a series of graphically appealing interfaces, the project consisted of a variety of video clips, links, photographs, scans and texts distributed according to a set of conceptual themes. Not convinced about how to distribute it further, Namita and Lawrence sadly abandoned the project.[8]

Now Showing is, however, not the only example of a work that looks like an i-doc (as per Aston and Gaudenzi's 2012 definition) that I have come across in India. A similar product was also produced in 2011 by Bharat Haridas, a

Fig. 3: Screenshot from *Traverse*, i-doc by Bharat Haridas, Bangalore. Available at: http://bh.mrinal. net/#/?snu=56

graduate student in visual communication from Bangalore. Entitled *Traverse*, this project was generated with the help of the Korsakow open-source software for interactive audio-visual storytelling. According to Haridas this software allowed him to produce a form capable of sharing his understanding of a changing India. Reflections on the ongoing exchanges between India and the outer world needed, he felt, a nonlinear format allowing for the creation of a set of disparate narratives to be created by viewers. Conceptually maximising the use of the software adopted, this film uses multiple screens (hosting videos, photos and sounds) in order to generate a series of overlaps and disjunctures between space and time.

The apparently simple structure of the documentary (always presenting a main media in the centre and three parallel media to choose among below it) perfectly fits the experience that is being shared with the viewer. According to Haridas, nonlinearity is the expression of a particular worldview, a (more immersive) way of portraying reality that is closer to the experiences of everyday life of many individuals today, particularly to those young men and women who have been raised in the age of digital technologies and of diasporas.

Both *Traverse* and *Now Showing* were hence born by necessity, rather than through adherence to new trends in image-making or as a direct response to the engagement with new technologies. Their authors were looking for a way to communicate a particular experience and were faced by the need to host a variety of different materials (sounds, photographs, video-clips, documents, texts) in the same space. Constituting a clear example of how multiple-media platforms can be seen as translations of image-making practices in a digital habitat, such examples generate also, as a surplus, a particular activation of the viewer (or better the 'interactor', as Arnau Gifreu-Castells (2011) puts it). They trigger in fact a dynamic relationship with the viewer that can also be found in other experiences bringing documentary film into other artistic territories. This is the case of Amar Kanwar who in his recent installation *The Sovereign Forest* (2016) explores a world, to paraphrase him, on the brink of extinction. Dealing with the multiple threats that are surrounding Orissa's rural and tribal areas, this installation is made up of a variety of documents in different media: videos screened in cinema format, clips projected on the pages of a book that can be flipped; newspaper clips hanging on the walls, photographs and posters; maps and a variety of identity documents. One room also hosts different varieties of rice corns and booklets containing images of murdered or suicidal farmers. This space, rather than offering a ready-made narrative, instigates in the viewers the production of new stories through their own 'knowledge-seeking strategies' (Färber 2007). What can be found in this exhibition is therefore a conceptual blueprint for the multimodal structure that characterises i-docs (with the exception perhaps of the tactility that Kanwar seems to be very eager to highlight).

Indeed, this kind of trend is not really something new in the subcontinent. Looking back into my material from the late 1990s, 'audio-visionary' artist Ashim Ghosh was working on a set of multiple media performances aiming at making dialogue across cultural and technological boundaries possible. Among these works was, for instance, a multiple location play that would happen through a set of phone calls. This performance never took place but the multiple media approach gave birth later to a series of works such as his *New Delhi Belly* (2009), a live multiple-media performance in which live music, narration and acting alternate with projections of documentary material and photographs. Pushing this scenario further, it could also be said that a lot of artists and activists engaging with digital practices have today chosen to move towards the creation of apps devoted to address specific social issues. Overall, the market for apps in India has become a booming one. In recent years a wide variety of apps have been created responding to the local needs of the growing middle classes and beyond. To mention but one example, in the aftermath of the gang rape on a bus in New Delhi in December 2012 that outraged India and the world, there has been a plethora of apps designed to help women to protect themselves from possible aggressions.[9] The above-mentioned Sahodari Foundation has also gone the 'mobile way'. Instead of creating an app they have simply adapted their requirements to available platforms. They have therefore created a WhatsApp group that offers 24 hours counselling.[10]

The *Priya Shakti* project (Devineni *et al* 2014–) is probably the most avant-garde of multiple media and cross-platform projects that I have come across. Also born in the aftermath of the New Delhi December 2012 rape, the project gathers inspiration from the mythological figure of Priya, a devotee of Goddess Parvati, who survived a brutal rape. Ideated by Indian-American filmmaker Ram Devineni, this project plays with Hindu mythology for the construction of a narrative in which Priya and Parvati join hands in struggling against gender-based violence. Aiming at reinserting in public consciousness 'ancient matriarchal traditions that have been displaced in modern representations of Hindu culture', the project results in a mixture of comic books, augmented reality and exhibitions. The main characteristic of Priya Shakti is that it engages with the world off-line. One of the strands of the project is in fact the use of the augmented reality app Blippar which allows viewers to get extra content while exploring images in physical space. Exploring/scanning these images with the help of the app, viewers get access to special animation and movies that pop out of the walls.

All the projects mentioned in this section do seem to highlight another important trait of images and image-making in India. As conventionally indicated with the help of the notion of Darshan, which encompasses the simultaneous act of seeing and being seen and which lies at the core of Hindu practices of devotion,

Fig. 4: Screenshot of promotional trailer *Priya Shakti*. Source: https://www.youtube.com/watch?v=tLSsdl_FJKc

the act of seeing in the Indian context entails a physical contact containing also a strong reciprocal and dialogic connotation. As Lawrence Babb (1981) suggested, in seeing each other, deity and devotee engage in a reciprocal act of emanation of substance. Christopher Pinney (2001) pushes this notion even further. Through his analysis of popular religious chromolithographs in village India, he indicates how visual practices are in the context of Indian popular culture, a matter of 'corpothetics' rather than aesthetics (2001: 157). Prioritising questions of efficacy and effect, images are hence, in this context, just as much a matter of performing and acting as a matter of representation.

CONCLUSIONS

The experiences described above indicate that the spirit of i-docs is very much present in India today even though the form is not, or at least is not easily recognizable. This gap does indeed open up the space for a set of interesting reflections regarding the meaning and future of i-docs at large.

Indian interactive image-making practices do, in the first place, immediately ask us to pay careful attention to the role of infrastructure. Questions of speed of information, of availability of networks and so forth do matter (Hudson and Zimmermann 2015, Kapur 2016). Below these hide 'simple' questions of electricity, transport, etc, which are fundamental for the construction of communication networks. Infrastructure is a necessary platform on which networks, interfaces, software and eventually form and aesthetics can develop. As my examples may have shown, Indian image-makers today respond to such limitations by generating solutions and practices that are adapted to the local context. The popularity of app-driven experiments responds, for instance, to the growing accessibility of 3G and 4G networks. The limitations imposed by infrastructure have in the context of India also generated creative adaptations to local needs – instances of *jugaad* – that lead us to rethink the relationship between technology and practice, forcing us to rethink our conventional understanding of i-docs – and of the digital, too. This transcultural space of creative practices is perhaps the one we need to monitor in the future, in order to discover leading trends in the field of interactive documentary practices.

We have also seen, however, how interactive image-making practices seem to respond to the broader traditions of image-making (and image-viewing) that characterise Indian culture. The dominance of projects aiming, somehow, at intervening upon the social world surrounding the image-makers constitutes a direct dialogue with the Indian history of documentary films which, as discussed above, has been characterised by this activist ethos. This is also true for the performative spirit which characterises many of these projects and which is again in dialogue with indigenous notions of visual culture.

Finally, I would like to suggest that attention to interactive image-making practices can offer precious clues about specific societies. In the case of India, I have shown for instance how the destiny of such practices is tightly connected to ideologically informed investments and celebrations of the digital/visual. Some of the projects addressed in this chapter offer insights into the ongoing struggles for producing instances of Indian-ness in a globalising India, a topic which, as I have discussed elsewhere (Favero 2005), is central for understanding contemporary Indian culture.

Altogether, such reflections seem to ask us to briefly stop and rethink our conventional understandings of i-docs. As I have shown with my examples, in the adaptation to a different context (with specific infrastructural, cultural and political challenges) the conceptual notions that inform i-docs give birth to materials and practices that can at times be significantly different from what is elsewhere defined as an i-doc. In the Indian context, the dialogue with indigenous traditions of documentary film and with situated notions of images and image-making give birth to a set of practices putting social intervention, performance and archival urgency at the centre. So, how much can we stretch the definition of an interactive documentary? This is indeed an open question and one that needs to be constantly reconsidered. As Judith Aston suggests, with digital technologies becoming 'ever more embedded into everyday life, the possibilities of interactive documentary continue to evolve, along with our understanding of these possibilities' (2016). The Indian experience shows that i-docs are a privileged window onto the potentialities of image-making in a digital habitat. Rather than approaching i-docs as a set of specific formats and technologies, we should therefore perhaps look upon them as a direction, an inspiration for creating more inclusive participatory and multi-modal experiences capable of responding to the changing world that surrounds us.

NOTES

1. http://www.internetlivestats.com/internet-users/india/
2. https://www.statista.com/statistics/309866/india-digital-population/; http://www.internetlivestats.com/internet-users/india/
3. Vikalp and Docuwhallas are entirely contained by their email newsletters and produce at times cross-communication with social media.
4. Cinema of Resistance is an organisation functioning entirely via their activities and via Facebook. For more information see https://www.facebook.com/Cinema-of-Resistance-152483288189680/. Accessed 31 October 2016.

5. A colloquial Hindi term indicating the fix and work-around solutions that are used for cir-cumscribing rules and difficulties, '*jugaad*' is emerging today as key term in defining the subcontinent's varied responses to technological change.

6. '*Cybermohalla*' means cyber neighbourhood, and was realised in collaboration with Ankur: Society for Alternatives in Education.

7. Other projects with a similar inclination that followed in the years are *Godaam* by Majlis (2007), *Images from Conflict Zones* (2008), *City Images* (2008) and *Cinema City* (2009). For a brief discussion of these see Battaglia and Favero 2014).

8. It was my impression, however, that our conversation may have triggered in her the desire to do something with it in the future.

9. Among them, probably the most popular is the *Circle of 6*, an iPhone and Android app that lets the user pre-program six friends and a set of SMS messages such as 'Call me, I need an interruption' or 'Come pick me up, I'm in trouble'. With two easy taps the user can hence alert their 'circle' of their whereabouts through GPS location.

10. The same has also been done by WhatsApp group Baliraja which provides a space in which more than a hundred farmers from different villages in Maharastra can seek and share advice on agricultural practises, connecting with experts in various fields and learning new practices.

REFERENCES

Aston, Judith (2016) 'Interactive Documentary – What Does It Mean And Why Does It Matter?' Blog post on i-docs.org, posted 27 March; http://i-docs.org/2016/03/27/interac:ve-documentary-what-does-it-mean-and-why-does-itma?er/. Accessed 20 October 2016.

Aston, Judith and Sandra Gaudenzi (2012) 'Interactive documentary: setting the field', *Studies in Documentary Film*, 6, 2, 125–39.

Aavriti, Namita and Lawrence Liang (n.d) *Now Showing*. Research-driven project on the connection between cinema and law.

Babb, Lawrence A. (1981) 'Glancing: Visual Interaction in Hinduism', *Journal of Anthropological Research*, 37, 4, 387–401.

Battaglia, Giulia (2012) *Documentary Film Practices in India: History of the Present*. PhD thesis. SOAS, University of London.

____ (2014) 'The Video Turn: Documentary Film Practices in 1980s India', *Visual Anthropology*, 27, 1/2, 72–90.

Battaglia, Giulia and Paolo Favero (2014) 'Reflections upon the Meaning of Contemporary Digital Image-Making Practices in India', in Raminder Kaur and Dave-Mukherj Parul (eds) *Arts and Aesthetics in a Globalizing World*. Oxford: Berg.

Break Through (2008) *Bell Bajao*. Web project and online platform; http://www.bellbajao.org/. Accessed 31 October 2016.

Cabus, Thomas and Nancy Schwartzman (2015) *Circle of 6*. App. Co-produced by circle of 6 and Tech4Good; http://www.circleof6app.com/. Accessed 31 October 2016.

Chowdhry, Prem (2001) *Colonial India and the Making of Empire Cinema: Image, Ideology, and Identity*. New Delhi: Vistaar Publications.

de Souza e Silva, Adriana (2006) 'From Cyber to Hybrid Mobile Technologies as Interfaces of Hybrid Spaces', *Space and Culture*, 9, 3, 261–78.

Devineni, Ram, Lina Srivastava and Dan Goldman (2014-) *Priya Shakti*. Cross platform project; http://www.priyashakti.com/. Accessed 31 October 2016.

Dwyer, Rachel and Divia Patel (2002) *Cinema India: The Visual Culture of Hindi Film*. London: Reaktion Books.

Eck, Diana (1998) *Darsan: Seeing the Divine Image in India*. New York: Columbia University Press.

Färber, Alexa (2007) 'Exposing Expo: Exhibition Entrepreneurship and Experimental Reflexivity in Late Modernity', in Paul Basu and Sharon MacDonald (eds) *Exhibition Experiments*. London: Blackwells.

Favero, Paolo (2005) *India Dreams: Cultural Identity Among Young Middle Class Men in New Delhi*. Stockholm: Almkvist & Wiksell.

_____ (2013a) 'Getting our hands dirty (again): Interactive documentaries and the meaning of images in the digital age', *Journal of Material Culture*, 18, 3, 259–77.

_____ (2013b) Interview with Sanjay Joshi on Cinema of Resistance. April 2013.

_____ (2014a) 'Learning to Look Beyond the Frame: Reflections on the Changing Meaning of Images in the Age of Digital Media Practices', *Visual Studies*, 26, 2, 166–79.

_____ (2014b) *'Look Away from Me!' – what images mean and want in the age of digital practices*. Exposition. *The Transparent Performer/Surface Tension*. Performance. Hosted by Art Heritage, Triveni Kala Sangam, Dehli, February 2014.

Gifreu-Castells, Arnau (2011) 'Basic characteristics of the interactive documentary', posted 25 November; http://i-docs.org/2011/12/25/basic-characteristics-of-the-interactive-documentary-featuring-the-interactive-documentary-ii/. Accessed 31 October 2016.

Ginzburg, Carlo (2000) *Miti, emblemi e spie. Morfologia e storia*. Torino: Einaudi.

Gaudenzi, Sandra (2013) *The Living Documentary: From Representing Reality to Co-creating Reality in Digital Interactive Documentary*. PhD Thesis. Goldsmiths, University of London; http://research.gold.ac.uk/7997/1/Cultural_thesis_Gaudenzi.pdf. Accessed 31 October 2016.

Ghosh, Ashim (2009) *New Delhi Belly*. Multiple media performance; http://www.audiovisionary.net/Country_n_Eastern_Music.html. Accessed 31 October 2016.

Haridas, Barath (2011) *Traverse*. Interactive video database; http://thetraverseproject.tk/. Accessed 31 October 2016.

Hudson, Dale and Patricia Zimmermann (2015) *Thinking Through Digital Media: Transnational Environments and Locative Places*. New York: Palgrave Macmillan.

Indiancine.ma (2013-) An annotated online archive of Indian film, initiated by Pad.ma, and operated in collaboration with a number of organisations and film studies institutions. https://indiancine.ma/. Accessed 31 October 2016.

Kabisch, Eric (2008) 'Datascape: A Synthesis of Digital and Embodied Worlds', *Space and Culture*, 11, 3, 222–38.

Kanwar, Amar (2016) *The Sovereign Forest*. Installation. 30 July -9 October 2016, NTU CCA Singapore.

Kapur, Anandana (2016) 'Digital diversity and its implications for i-docs'. Abstract submitted for i-Docs 2016, University of the West of England, Bristol, 2–4 March 2016; http://idocs 2016.dcrc.org.uk/abstracts/digital-diversity-and-its-implications-for-i-docs/. Accessed 31 October 2016.

Jain, Jyotindra (ed.) 2007. *India's popular culture : iconic spaces and fluid images*. Mumbai: Marg Publications.

Majlis (2007) *Godaam*. Online archive; http://majlisbombay.org/godamm/. Accessed 31 October 2016.

_____ (2008a) *Images from Conflict Zones*. Online archive; http://majlisbombay.org/images-from-conflict-zones/. Accessed 31 October 2016.

_____ (2008b) *City Images*. Online archive; http://majlisbombay.org/city-images/. Accessed 31 October 2016.

_____ (2009) *Cinema City*. Online archive and research art and documentary practices project; http://projectcinemacity.com/. Accessed 31 October 2016.

MacDougall, David (2006) *The Corporeal Image*. Princeton: Princeton University Press.

Monteiro, Anjali and K.P. Jayasankar (2015) *A Fly in the Curry: Independent Documentary Film in India*. New Delhi: Sage.

Nandy, Ashid (ed.) (1998) *The Secret Politics of our Desires: Innocence, Culpability and Indian Popular Cinema*. New Delhi: Oxford University Press.

Pad.ma. (2008-). Public Access Digital Archive. An online archive of densely text-annotated video material. https://pad.ma/. Accessed 20 October 2016.

Pathwardhan, Anand (1978) *Prisoners of conscience*. Film.

Pinney, Christopher (1997) *Camera Indica: The Social Life of Indian Photographs*. London: Reaktion Books.

_____ (2001) 'Piercing the Skin of the Idol', in Christopher Pinney and Nicholas Thomas (eds) *Beyond Aesthetics*. London: Bloomsbury, 157–179.

Radjou, Navi, Jaideep Prabhu and Simone Ahuja (2012) *Jugaad Innovation*. Jossey-Bass: Wiley.

Sahapedia (2016). Encyclopedia project of India's cultural heritage launched by Sudha Gopalakrishnan; http://www.sahapedia.org/. Accessed 31 October 2016.

SARAI (n.d.) *Cybermohalla*. Web project and online platform; http://sarai.net/category/projects/cybermohalla/. Accessed 20 October 2016.

Subramaniam, Kalki (n.d.) *ProjectKalki.com*. Web project and online platform; http://www.projectkalki.com. Accessed 20 October 2016.

Sundaram, Ravi (2009) *Pirate Modernity: Media Urbanism in Delhi*. London: Routledge.

TasveerGhar (2006–) Digital archive of South Asian popular visual culture; http://tasveerghar.net/. Accessed 31 October 2016.

Tata Institute of Social Sciences of Mumbai (2012-) *Remembering 1992*. Web project and online platform; http://mumbairiots.tiss.edu/about-remembering-1992. Accessed 31 October 2016.

Traditional Knowledge Digital Library (2005) Online archive. Co-initiated by Council of Scientific & Industrial Research (CSIR) and Department of Ayurveda, Yoga & Naturopathy, Unani, Siddha and Homeopathy (AYUSH); http://www.tkdl.res.in/tkdl/langdefault/common/Home.asp?GL=Eng. Accessed 31 October 2016.

INTERACTIVE DOCUMENTARY AQUÍ Y AHORA - HERE & NOW
THEMES AND DIRECTIONS IN SOUTH AMERICA

Arnau Gifreu-Castells

INTRODUCTION

Although the majority of interactive documentary production has been concentrated mainly in northern hemisphere countries, such as Canada, France and the United States, and to a lesser degree in the Netherlands, the United Kingdom and Germany, in recent years there has been some movement in Latin American countries around this form of narrative expression. Documentaries have historically played an important role in South America, a region with a strong narrative tradition – with non-fiction storytelling at times seeming like a collective catharsis in response to the problems and conflicts that people in the region have faced (Gifreu-Castells 2014).

This work looks to new geographical horizons for i-docs in South America. Through a dialogue with producers, I chart the emergence of interactive documentary production and its state of development in several South American countries. I compare the contexts of commissioning and consider audience demand, as well as the forms and approaches that are coming to the fore within these cultural, political and linguistic contexts. To do this, I analyse three representative projects: *Ressaca* (Vianna 2008), *Malvinas 30* (Liuzzi 2013) and *The Quipu Project* (Court *et al* 2015). These examples show how different cultures other than the Anglophone and Francophone cultures imagine and develop interactive and transmedia documentaries and by extension create new ways of storytelling with unique traits and points of view.

STATE OF DEVELOPMENT IN LATIN AMERICAN COUNTRIES

The late development of interactive narratives is, at least in part, a consequence of the limited resources in these countries which do not have the help of public institutions that finance films and other storytelling forms in many other parts of the world (Gifreu-Castells 2013b). Without money and business models, Latin American storytellers have looked to non-conventional formulas to produce their works at the lowest possible cost, turning to the Internet in order to reach and engage with audiences. However, over the last few years, specific funds for Latin countries – such as the Tribeca Latin America Fund – have appeared on the scene, as well as i-docs from outside Latin America, which deal with specific topics in the region. One example is Guatemalan gang culture in the case of *Alma: A Tale of Violence* (Dewever-Plana and Fougere 2012). Latin America is experiencing a growth in online users in all of the countries that form the region. EMarketer estimates that in 2017 there will be more than 310 million users throughout the region – more than a third being from Brazil, almost double the number of the next country on the list, which is Mexico. In terms of internet penetration, Chile leads the list, at 66.7 per cent in late 2015, predicted to reach 73.5 per cent by 2018.

Interest in interactive documentaries is often linked to social and activist topics such as migration routes, drug trafficking, youth violence, problems in education and political conflicts, etc. Many of these interactive documentaries use different media such as audio, photos, video and text. These, are placed, or structured, within the confines of one platform – most commonly the Internet. Often in these early works, the interactive narrative structure is very simple or just doesn't exist at all, with the user facing a mosaic of choices or a menu with videos. This is because a new medium has to forge a new language – so Latin American countries need time to experiment and play with the form itself across different contexts.

The Argentine newspaper *Clarín* was a pioneer medium in using the Internet to produce multimedia stories in a series that was halfway between reports and documentary. The newspaper created more than forty multimedia works using Flash software in a small format. One of the most outstanding multimedia features was *En la tierra del Diego* (*In the land of Diego*, Sierra 2009). This seminal multimedia documentary used a combination of videos, photos and interactive infographics to portray the barrios of Villa Fiorita where the famous Argentine footballer Diego Maradona grew up. Other Latin American creators from Argentina, such as Alvaro Liuzzi or Fernando Irigaray, are also exploring transmedia storytelling applied to interactive documentary (see Giannoti 2014a). This differs from multimedia works in that different media platforms are used to tell separate narrative elements of the story.

Colombia and Brazil are also important countries entering the field. Colombia has different funding mechanisms such as Crea Digital, Ministry of Culture, Colombia 3.0, Bogota Audiovisual Market and, moreover, Brazil is considered a BRICS country experiencing advanced economic development, so there is room to deal with associated issues. In addition, Brazil has recognised researchers and producers such as Denis Porto and André Paz, with Nina Simoes also being originally from Brazil. Denis Porto is a postdoctoral researcher on interactive and transmedia journalism and documentary; André Paz is a professor, producer and researcher doing a postdoctorate on interactive narratives; and Nina Simoes received a scholarship in 2002 from the University of the Arts, London to explore the use of new media to address and illustrate her work. *Rehearsing Reality* (2007), the practical work of her PhD, which addresses social justice in Latin American countries, has been presented at many festivals in Europe, Brazil and the USA. I have studied some of the most representative projects, in terms of budget and impact, from the larger Latin American countries – Argentina, Brazil, Colombia, Mexico, Chile and Peru. The following table summarises the major contributions to the field from those and from some smaller countries:

Countries	Representative projects
Argentina	Gustavo Sierra and Multimedia Team from *Clarin* newspaper, e.g. *El viaje en que Ernesto se convirtió en el Che* (1996–2009); Fernando Irigaray and the Multimedia Communication Department of the National University of Rosario, e.g. *Vibrato* (2008); Alvaro Liuzzi *et al*, e.g. *Proyecto Walsh* (2011)
Brazil	Bruno Vianna *et al*, e.g. *Ressaca* (2008); Marcelo Bauer *et al*, e.g. *Rio de Janeiro – Autorretrato* (2011). Cross Content Production Company / Webdocumentario; Maryse Williquet and Switch Asbl, e.g. *Copa para quem?* (2014)
Colombia	El País Colombia *Reportaje 360*. Interactive report. Marcelo Dematei *et al* and Hierro Animación, Piaggiodematei and Señal Colombia, e.g. *Cuentos de viejos* (2012) Elder Manuel Tobar, Orgánica Digital, e.g. *4 ríos* (2014) Angela Carabali, Thibault Durand and Grupo Carabalí, e.g. *Pregoneros de Medellín* (2015)
Mexico	Ecnológico de Monterey, UNC-Chapel Hill, e.g. *Repensando México* (2011); Mónica González and Sacbé Producciones, e.g. *Frío en el alma* (2014a); Mónica González and Sacbé Producciones, e.g. *Geografía del dolor* (2014b)

Chile	Pablo Ocqueteau, e.g. *Aysén profundo* (2012); Christopher Murray *et al*, e.g. *Mafi TV. Mapa fílmico de un país* (2013) Andrea Chamorro, e.g. *Vida humana en el desierto* (2015)
Peru	Cesar Torres, El Comercio, e.g. *Cerro de Pasco: el Éxodo (de una ciudad improvisada* (2009); Jimmy Carrillo, Sociedad Peruana de derecho Ambiental, e.g. *Las rutas del oro* (2015)
Other countries	Guatemala: *Guatemala nuestro siglo* (interactive CD) Jamaica: Kwame Dawes and Pulitzer Center on Crisis Reporting, e.g. *Hope: living and loving with HIV in Jamaica* (2008) Paraguay:Andrea Ruffini, e.g. *Chaco-py* (2015)[o]

Fig. 1: Representative projects produced in the Latin American region.

CASE STUDIES

To characterize some interactive documentary practices in South America, I have focused my analysis on three representative countries in this area: Brazil, Peru and Argentina. I have selected one work from each of these three countries: I have chosen the work from Brazil because it is an early example, which proposes a very innovative way to representing reality. The work from Peru entered this corpus of case studies, as it is offers an innovative and novel way of alleviating the pain of many women and families; and the work from Argentina explores the transmedia documentary form as a historical re-enactment of facts for the first time in South America. These three case studies are outstanding projects from Latin America: they are experimental and creative, they push new boundaries, and reflect issues and concerns that are specific to the countries and regions from which they come.

RESSACA

Ressaca (Vianna et al 2008) is an audiovisual work, which is edited and run in real time by the author, with an interface allowing each sequence of the film to be manipulated. The story is told differently in each presentation through the selection and arrangement of the elements. *Ressaca* is the story of a Brazilian family in Rio de Janeiro in the 1980s, living through a period of economic and social chaos.

The interactive feature film tells how the family lives through the Latin American debt crisis. The story focuses on how a young teenager is growing up in a troubled country facing currency changes, corruption, hyperinflation and political

	Ressaca	*The Quipu Project*	*Malvinas 30*
Team	Bruno Vianna (director) Daniel Scatena (producer) Maira Salas (interaction designer)	Rosemarie Lerner, Maria Court and Sebastian Melo (directors) Ewan Cass-Kavanagh (creative technologist) Chaka Studio (production Company) Credits: http://www.quipu-project.com/team/	Álvaro Luizzi (coordination) Guadalupe López, Ezequiel Apesteguía and Tomás Berguero Trpin (production) Romina Vásquez (design) The Project received the support of the Facultad de Periodismo y Comunicación Social de la Universidad Nacional de la Plata. Credits: http://www.malvinastreinta.com.ar/autores/
Origin	Brazil	Peru	Argentina
Year of Production	2008	2013–present	2013
Subject	art-artists/diffusion, cultural dissemination, economic crisis, historical memory	health, politics, remembrance	war/conflict, remembrance
Support	interactive installation, web	multiplatform (web, viral campaign, telephone line with VOIP)	multiplatform (web, TV, computer graphics, social networks)
User Experience	game, Performative	Branched, participatory	Branched, participatory
URL	http://ressaca.net/	http://www.quipu-project.com	http://www.malvinastreinta.com.ar/

Fig. 2: Features and details of the selected case studies.

259

instability and has to become an adult in a very short period of time. Although the project was directed by Bruno Vianna, the interactive project was part of Maira Salas's final project for her Digital Arts degree at the University Pompeu Fabra in Barcelona, and was produced by Daniel Scatena.

When speaking about the interface of the film, which was developed specifically for the project with support from the Arts Center Hangar in Barcelona, Vianna and his team refer to it as '*engranaje*' (gear). The platform allows for manipulation of moving videos and complete sequences during the screening of the film. The user can also choose a mix of his or her own. The project was not designed for continuous projection and requires live music composition and a director who 'plays' with it to compose dozens of versions of the film. This is why it was proposed to project it in a theatre during five sessions across a week. Reactable, a music synthesis programme used by artists like Bjork live on stage was used for the music composition for the film, making it possible to incorporate and mix the pieces of the soundtrack.

Vianna came up with the idea to create a piece on the border between film and live performance, starting at the time that VJs began to make live presentations accompanied by electronic music. The project consists of a story composed by a network of more than 120 short sequences. The selection and ordering of these sequences is not predetermined: in each section, the director has to choose a series of scenes and the order in which they are presented.

In a personal conversation with Vianna in 2015, he explained to me that the interface consists of a touch fabric that allows the player to move elements of the film with his or her fingers. As the fabric measures a metre in diameter and is positioned to one side of the main movie screen, the audience can follow the whole editing process. The interface allows the player to view all the material of the film and its organisation through links that define the order of the sequences.

Fig. 3: The director Bruno Vianna manipulating the interface during an exhibition.

Fig. 4. Bruno Vianna selecting sequences from a thematic block in an exhibition in Barcelona.

Ressaca tells the story of a boy who goes through puberty in the 1980s during the political and economic adolescence of his country, Brazil. His family suffers the consequences of the economic boom and the monetary crisis. Here is what the film's director has to say about it: '*Ressaca* is a project that was planned long ago. I wanted to explain the confusion that reigned in Brazil from the 1980s to the 1990s but from the point of view of the middle class: the death of the president, a half-dozen different currencies, lack of an economic system, hyperinflation. [...] It was like the country was growing up, so it was appropriate to talk about a teenager who also goes through a maturation process' (personal communication, 2010).

Bruno Vianna is a filmmaker born in Rio de Janeiro, Brazil, in 1971. His first short film was *Geraldo Voador* in 1994, which received several awards at festivals in Brazil and beyond. His first feature, *Cafuné* (2006), was the first Brazilian feature film that used a Creative Commons license. *Cafuné* was created as an unfinished story as a way of showing the public that the film could be interpreted in different ways. The users could construct it themselves and then download it from the Internet. The *Cafuné* experience made him realise that *Ressaca* would make much more sense with a nonlinear structure where things could happen twice, not happen at all or have other endings.

MALVINAS 30

Alvaro Liuzzi, director of *Malvinas 30*, is a journalist, consultant and researcher in Digital Media and Design, and Project Management and Digital Communication Strategies Specialist, based in La Plata, Argentina. Since 2008, Liuzzi has been creating multimedia documentaries closely linked to journalism: blog documental, documental multimedia, sobre blogs y periodismo (2008) and documental multimedia (e.g. *Redacciones On Line* 2009). Since 2011, he has created the first Latin American transmedia documentaries: *Proyecto Walsh* (*Walsh Project*) (2011), *Malvinas 30* (2012), *#Voto83* (2013) and *70 Octubres* (2015).

While his early work was focused on the analysis of journalism from blogs and essays, in his later works, Liuzzi experiments with multiplatform production to explore historical memory: *Malvinas 30* responds to the thirtieth anniversary of the war between Argentina and Britain, the *Walsh Project* recreates the identity of Rodolfo Walsh in a digital key, and *#Voto83* is a special production for the newspaper La Nación on the occasion of the celebration of thirty years of democracy in Argentina in real time through social networks, focusing on the relationship with the audience. His last production, *70 Octubres*, focuses on the political and social mobilisation of 17 October 1945, a date that changed forever the history of Argentina.

Before *Malvinas 30*, in 2010, Liuzzi launched *Proyecto Walsh*, a documentary about Rodolfo Walsh, an Argentine journalist famous for his book, *Operación Masacre* (*Operation Massacre*, 1957). The aim was to use various platforms and tools to give more historical depth and context to Walsh's book. Liuzzi created a Rodolfo Walsh Twitter account and tweeted as though he was him, talking about his life and the progress of his investigations during 1956 and 1957. He also held a Twitcam live session in which Rodolfo 'talked' about his investigation. He used Prezi, a cloud-based presentation programme, to create interactive infographics about executions that took place, and Google Maps to geotag places of illegal executions. Alvaro Liuzzi and Vanina Verghella produced this journalistic experiment aiming to 'remix' a remarkable work of classic Argentine journalism, *Operación Masacre*, combining it with a modern vision and supported by various digital publishing tools.

In 1957, with *Operación Masacre*, Walsh started a new trend by writing newspaper articles, which later received several names – literary journalism, non-fiction, new journalism. Walsh's work redefined the borders that separated the practices of journalism and literary narrative, reporting shootings that occurred in June 1956 in Jose Leon Suarez under the government of General Aramburu. This was a milestone in the commitment to journalistic research and protest in times of persecution and political assassinations. Five decades later, two journalists and academics projected a tribute experience and re-construction of the Walsh investigation using digital tools.

In 2012, Liuzzi launched his second transmedia documentary, *Malvinas 30*, as a digital commemoration of the thirtieth anniversary of the Malvinas (Falklands) war. Liuzzi and his team produced this experimental transmedia documentary as a proposal to relive the past in order to think about the present. The project played out over a period of four months to propose a new way of telling the story of the war 'in real time'. It re-lived the events on the same dates on which they occurred, but thirty years later, facilitating the collaboration of the public from different platforms. Luizzi produced the project with a team of four members – Guadalupe López, Ezequiel

Apesteguía, Tomás Berguero Trpin and Romina Vásquez – and with the support of the Facultad de Periodismo y Comunicación Social de la Universidad Nacional de la Plata. The project also allowed history to be reconstructed so that new generations could reflect on the effects through readings, chats, contributions, and so forth.

Each platform focused on a different aspect of the conflict: Luizzi used Twitter to narrate the conflict in real time, interactive computer graphics to explain the sinking of the Argentine cruiser *General Belgrano*, Ustream to broadcast a daily TV show that pretended to be broadcasting actual live events, and Facebook as a general space to post about these diverse narrative strands. As these examples show, and according to the director himself, 'transmedia storytelling can offer more narrative possibilities than multimedia stories, because it isn't confined to a single platform. Instead, transmedia stories can travel through social networks and mobile devices, augmenting the narrative and creating a more complete experience for users' (Liuzzi 2015a).

In a personal interview with Liuzzi in 2015, he told me that, while production of interactive documentary is at an initial stage in Argentina, mainly driven from separate projects, there is a vast potential to lay the groundwork for future developments. He believes that both interactive and transmedia documentaries have managed to incorporate disruptive narratives into classic analogue documentary. These new ways of producing and publishing different types of content can become more profound and can be used to analyse different time periods and many topics without relying on the frenzied forms of consumption of traditional media. His personal interests have allowed him to go deeper into historical topics, extending the story through various digital platforms and giving a central role to users in the construction of the narrative universe.

Fig. 5: Website of *Malvinas 30*, one of the main platforms of the multiplatform project.

Fig. 6: Interactive infographic in *Malvinas 30*, explaining the sinking of General Belgrano.

THE QUIPU PROJECT

The Quipu Project (Proyecto Quipu) is a transmedia documentary project that provides the tools to help make the voices heard of the 300,000 women and 20,000 men who were forcibly sterilised through a government campaign in Peru in the mid-1990s. Using a specially developed phone line, an interactive web documentary, a radio campaign and a forthcoming feature documentary, it creates a context to facilitate audience listening experiences which reach well beyond the Peruvian borders. *The Quipu Project*, directed and produced by Maria Court and Rosemarie Lerner with further production from Sebastian Melo, is a collaboration between a core team with strong connections to Peru and a wider community of designers, programmers, researchers and academics. The project was developed in the UK by Chaka Studio in collaboration with Matthew Brown and Karen Tucker, researchers at the University of Bristol, and creative technologist Ewan Cass-Kavanagh.

In 1995 in Peru, the government of President Alberto Fujimori introduced a new National Program for Family Planning and Reproductive Health. It was promoted as a way to provide access to a wide range of birth control methods, including voluntary sterilisation. At the time, the policy was welcomed by women's groups and the international community, as it was seen as a positive step for women and as a potential approach to reducing poverty. In reality, however, sterilisation was promoted aggressively in indigenous, rural and impoverished communities. In many cases, consent was tampered with or was absent. There are testimonies of people who were forced by the medical profession or sterilised without their knowledge while they were in the hospital for another reason.

Almost twenty years later, the legacy of this policy still affects lives: many of the women are still suffering from emotional trauma and in pain. Many are unable to work. This translates to entire generations because the people who did not have children do not have anyone to support them in their old age. Since 2000, organised groups of women and men have campaigned for their experience of sterilisation to be recognised and compensated. Still, they are facing many challenges: most of them live in remote areas without access to the Internet, many have not completed primary education, and their first language is not Spanish, the language spoken by the majority of legislators, but Quechua.

The latest legal investigation was filed in January 2014. In the documentation of the process, the prosecutor claimed to have found no evidence of systematic sterilisation. Nonetheless, lawyers representing women's organisations are preparing a new appeal to prove that there were human rights violations in this case. Beyond the campaigns of those affected, sterilisations have not had much media coverage in Peru, and therefore many Peruvians still do not recognise what has happened.

From the beginning, the authors developed the project in collaboration with the people who were sterilised in Peru. A combination of a low-tech phone line and high-tech digital interface has made it possible for this initiative to reach politically, geographically and digitally marginalised communities and allow them to tell their stories around the world using the Internet. Contributors can also use the telephone line to be heard – and they can answer each other, as *The Quipu Project* provides a platform that also operates with dispersed communities. As such, the project can be regarded as a 'living documentary' (Gaudenzi 2013) – a story that continues to grow and transform after being released online. This open-ended structure also reflects on justice, as an open case will not be closed until the scars that it caused are healed.

The telephone line uses VOIP technology (voice-over internet protocol), which needs an Internet connection. Once recorded, the evidence is checked, transcribed

Fig. 7: One of the affected women protagonists of *The Quipu Project.*

and translated into Quechua, Spanish and English. The testimonies which were given are uploaded to the online archive where they can be heard by anyone in the world via the Internet. In addition, the audience can record a reply to the statements and upload the file. These messages are translated, rewritten and sent to the contributors of the phone line, letting them know that there are people who have listened to them, who are supporting them and who are engaging in a dialogue. For many contributors, it will be the first time that their stories will be heard outside their communities.

A *quipu* is an ancient Inca accounting system made from ropes and knots. It was used to store information in a predominantly oral culture. The strings were made of cotton, alpaca wool or llama wool. *Quipu* were used for everything from tax accounting to crop records and censuses, in which knotted cords served as a mnemonic tool for remembering events that happened. In short, a *quipu* is a physical memory, a file. It is articulated as a symbol and metaphor that allows the oral information to enter our collective memory and help prevent forced sterilisations from being forgotten. The structure of the *quipu* is also the inspiration for the way in which the collected information is presented: each record is a string, each answer a knot.

The pilot version of *The Quipu Project* was supported by the React-Hub Future Documentary Sandbox and was presented at the third i-Docs Conference in Bristol, UK, in 2014. It contained a version of the digital prototype and a video filmed in Huancabamba, in the Peruvian Andes. The pilot project was conducted in Piura when directors contacted Iamamc, an organisation representing more than two hundred women sterilised in the area. More than forty women went to the workshop from remote and inaccessible places.

On the strength of the pilot, *The Quipu Project* was awarded the Tribeca New Media Fund and CrossCurrents Doc Fund 'Hot Docs'. During November and December 2014, the team behind this project launched a successful crowdfunding campaign to develop the technology to expand the *The Quipu Project* to a new region – Anta-Cusco – where a group of women activists representing more than 1,300 women has been organised for over fifteen years. They raised more than £22,000.

Currently, the team is developing a documentary film which focuses on some of the women who have contributed to *The Quipu Project* in different communities in Peru and who are using this new tool in their struggle for justice. This will cover the story of Esperanza, for instance, who is fighting for justice after having been sterilised against her will eighteen years ago. She is just one of those affected by the Peruvian government's health campaign that was promoted aggressively in rural and indigenous communities.

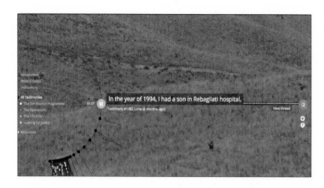

Fig. 8: The digital interface of *The Quipu Project.*

In a personal conversation in 2015. Maria Court explained how she saw the intersection between new digital technologies and documentaries as opening up an interesting space to explore non-fiction storytelling. On the one hand, she stated, it involves thinking of projects with a focus on the audience: how they can interact with the content, generate parts of the story, choose addresses where to take the story – or interactive projects enable them to live an immersive experience. On the other, these projects have the potential to renew what documentary has always been able to do: to enter into social situations and to build relationships between authors, subjects and audiences in order to challenge us to understand our reality in new ways.

To conclude – here is what Court said during our 2015 interview: 'The Latin interactive documentary has great potential and will clearly be an important form of expression for future generations. Because there are many communities that are digitally excluded, the challenge is to continue to explore new ways of telling stories across the digital gap. This could help these communities whose main priorities today are to obtain basic needs such as food, water or electricity. Mobile telephones and radio, in this sense, are means that can be reinterpreted with new features. The topics to be addressed in issues of identity in Latin America are endless in terms of their social, environmental, political and cultural impact and new and interesting ways to narrate in collaboration with different audiences will certainly appear.' As Maria Court pointed out, *The Quipu Project* showcases how technology and design approaches were designed to be sensitive to the Latin American context because a lot of of families do not have access to electricity, let alone the Internet.

CONCLUSION

Evolving audience/user expectations present a challenge for storytellers in both the production stage and in the editing and distribution of documentary content.

In the Latin American context, many projects are still searching for suitable ways to represent reality and to improve the user experience. Narratives are needed that allow users to become immersed in the story, regardless of which screen they are using. Creators also need to devote more time to finding new languages for presenting content on different screens, as well as new ways of merging and mixing media across platforms.

So far, Canada and France have been the pioneering leaders in the production of interactive documentaries. However, Latin American cultures do not only have different stories, codes and motivations, they also require their own specific approaches. These factors will affect how interactive documentary is made in Latin America and how narratives are constructed. One key factor, in my view, is that Latin countries are led by emotional perspectives and approaches – they live 'from the heart'. This means that their documentaries are often made from an emotional point of view – a key ingredient for this kind of narrative. Community-based projects are another type of production that is likely to increase in the forthcoming years in these countries, with new technologies providing a sense of connection between different remote people, services and areas. While there was some growth in this field in other regions of the world by the end of the first decade of the present century, we are now witnessing that web and transmedia documentaries are being made in the Latin area, and that they are here to stay.

In addition, Latin America has a great advantage in comparison with other areas if we take into account the different regions and various digital embodiments that can be made. Being such a large area that shares the same language (or a few languages), the potential to interconnect local projects and historical representations opens up a huge market for documentary production and consumption. It is undeniable that there is an emerging scene – a scene in gestation. This scene may currently be somewhat under-developed but it has some foundational projects, with more to come. And it has a firm intention to develop further in the future.

REFERENCES

Bauer, Marcelo (2011) *Rio de Janeiro – Autorretrato*. Web documentary. Produced by Cross Content Production Company; http://riodejaneiroautorretrato.com.br/dev2011/Content/Swf/index_portugues.html. Accessed 31 October 2016.

Carabali, Angela and Thibault Durand (2015) *Pregoneros de Medellín*. Web documentary. Produced by Grupo Carabalí; http://www.pregonerosdemedellin.com/#es. Accessed 31 October 2016.

Carrillo, Jimmy (2015) *Las rutas del oro*. Web documentary. Produced by Sociedad Peruana de Derecho Ambiental; http://www.lasrutasdeloro.com/. Accessed 31 October 2016.

Chamorro, Andrea (2015) *Vida humana en el desierto*. Web documentary; http://www.

vidahumanaeneldesierto.cl/. Accessed 31 October 2016

Court, Maria, Ros Lerner and Sebastian Melo (2014) *The Quipu Project*. Web documentary. Co-produced by Chaka Studio and Helios Design Labs. First presented at i-Docs in 2014. https://interactive.quipu-project.com/#/en/quipu/intro. Accessed 31 October 2016.

Dawes, Kwame (2008) *Hope: living and loving with HIV in Jamaica*. Web documentary. Produced by Pulitzer Center on Crisis Reporting; http://www.livehopelove.com/. Accessed 31 October 2016.

Dematei, Marcelo, Ana Ferrer, Carlos Smith and Laura Piaggio (2012) *Cuentos de viejos*. Web documentary. Produced by Hierro Animación, Piaggiodematei and Señal Colombia; http://cuentosdeviejos.com/. Accessed 31 October 2016.

Dewever-Plana, Miquel and Isabelle Fougere (2012) *Alma: A Tale of Violence*. Web documentary and app. Directed by Miquel Dewever-Plana and Isabelle Fougere. Co-produced by Arte, Upian and L'Agence Vu; http://alma.arte.tv/en/. Accessed 31 October 2106.

Gaudenzi, Sandra (2013) *The Living Documentary: From Representing Reality to Co-creating Reality in Digital Interactive Documentary*. PhD Thesis. Goldsmiths, University of London; http://research.gold.ac.uk/7997/1/Cultural_thesis_Gaudenzi.pdf. Accessed 31 October 2016.

Giannoti, Federico (2014a) 'Panorama de las producciones interactivas en argentina (1)'. Blog post on *El Blog Nuevos Medios*; http://elblognuevosmedios.wordpress.com/2014/06/24/159/. Accessed 31 October 2016.

____ (2014b) 'Panorama de las producciones interactivas en argentina (2)'. Blog post on *El Blog Nuevos Medios*. https://elblognuevosmedios.wordpress.com/2014/07/21/panorama-de-las-producciones-interactivas-en-argentina-2da-parte/. Accessed 2 October 2016.

Gifreu-Castells, Arnau (2013a) *El documental interactivo. Evolución, caracterización y perspectivas de desarrollo*. Barcelona: Editorial UOC.

____ (2013b) 'Production of interactive documentary in the Latin area'. Blog post on *i-docs.org*; http://i-docs.org/2013/09/30/production-of-interactive-documentary-in-the-latin-area-v/. Accessed 31 October 2016.

____ (2014) 'The interactive documentary: My favourite Latin projects'. *MIT Docubase*; http://docubase.mit.edu/playlist/arnau-gifreu-playlist/. Accessed 2 October 2016.

González, Mónica (2014a) *Frío en el alma*. Web documentary. Produced by Sacbé Producciones; http://frioenelalma.com/. Accessed 2 October 2016.

____ (2014b) *Geografía del dolor*. Web documentary. Produced by Sacbé Producciones; http://www.geografiadeldolor.com/. Accessed 31 October 2016.

GSM Association (2015) 'The Mobile Economy'. www.gsmamobileeconomy.com. Accessed 31 October 2016.

Irigaray, Fernando (2008) *Vibrato*. Web documentary. Produced by Departamento de Comunicación Multimedia. Universidad de Rosario; http://www.unr.edu.ar/resources/documedia/vibrato/vibrato.htm. Accessed 2 October 2016.

USMC (2015) '4 Key Changes in Latin America's Mobile Market'. *Latin Link;* http://latinlink.usmediaconsulting.com/2014/10/4-key-changes-in-latin-americas-mobile-market/. Accessed 31 October 2016.

Liuzzi, Álvaro (2008) *Documental Multimedia sobre blogs y periodismo*. Web documentary. Produced by Observatorio Platense de Internet (OPLADI) and Segundo Plano; http://

documentalblog.blogspot.com.es/. Accessed 31 October 2016.

____ (2013) # *Voto83*. Multiplatform documentary. Produced by Diario La Nación. https://www.flickr.com/people/voto83/. https://twitter.com/search?q=%23voto83. Accessed 31 October 2016

____ (2015a) 'Latin America's growing appetite for digital storytelling', *DW Akademie*; http://www.dw.com/en/latin-americas-growing-appetite-for-digital-storytelling/a-18411613. Accessed 31 October 2016.

____ (2015b) *70 Octubres*. Web documentary. Produced by Facultad de Periodismo y Comunicación Social, Universidad de la Plata; http://perio.unlp.edu.ar/70octubres/. Accessed 31 October 2016.

Liuzzi, Álvaro and Máximo Ponz (2009) *Documental Multimedia Redacciones On Line*. Blog; http://redaccionesonline.blogspot.com.es/. Accessed 31 October 2016.

Liuzzi, Alvaro and Berghella, Vanina (2011) *Proyecto Walsh*. Multiplatform documentary; http://proyectowalsh.com.ar/. Accessed 2 October 2016.

Liuzzi, Álvaro, Lopez Guadalupe, Ezequiel Apesteguía, Tomas Trpin Bergero and Romina Vázquez (2012) *Malvinas 30*; http://www.malvinastreinta.com.ar/. Accessed 31 October 2016.

Lloreda, Felipe, Mauricio González, Marco J. Guerrero, Sandra Cano, Katherine Arredondo and Jonathan Herrera (2009) *Cali, la ciudad que nunca duerme*. Web documentary. Produced by Nuevos Medios El País; http://www.elpais.com.co/reportaje360/web/home.html. Accessed 31 October 2016.

Murray, Christopher, Luco, Antonio, Rojas, Ignacio and Carrera, Pablo (2013) M*afi TV. Mapa fílmico de un país*. Web documentary; http://mafi.tv/. Accessed 31 October 2016.

Ocqueteau, Pablo (2012) *Aysén profundo*. Web documentary.; http://www.aysenprofundo.cl/. Accessed 31 October 2016.

Ruffini, Andrea (2015) *Chaco-py*. Web documentary.; http://chaco-py.com/. Accessed 31 October 2016.

Sierra, Gustavo (2007) *El viaje en que Ernesto se convirtió en el Che*. Web documentary. Produced by Clarin newspaper; http://edant.clarin.com/diario/2007/10/08/conexiones/home.html. Accessed 31 October 2016.

____ (2009) *En la tierra del Diego*. Web documentary. Produced by Clarin newspaper; http://edant.clarin.com/diario/2009/11/23/conexiones/home.html. Accessed 31 October 2016.

Simoes, Nina (2007) *Rehearsing Reality*. A docufragmentary audiovisual experiment.

Tecnológico de Monterey and UNC-Chapel Hill (2011) *Repensando* México. International multimedia project by the students of UNC-Chapel Hill with students from Tecnológico de Monterre Mexico City; http://reframingmexico.org/. Accessed 31 October 2016.

Tobar, Elder Manuel (2014) *4 ríos*. Web documentary. Produced by Orgánica Digital; http://4rios.co/. Accessed 31 October 2016.

Torres, Cesar (2009) Cerro de Pasco: el Éxodo *(de una ciudad improvisada)*. Web documentary. Produced by El Comercio; http://elcomercio.pe/ediciononline/especiales/cerrodepasco/. Accessed 31 October 2016.

Vianna, Bruno (2015a) Personal website; http://brunovianna.net/. Accessed Accessed 31 October 2016.

Vianna, Bruno, Daniel Scatena and Maira Salas (2008) *Ressaca*. Web documentary; http://ressaca.net/. Accessed 31 October 2016.

Vianna, Bruno (2006). *Cafuné*. Feature film; http://cafuneofilme.com.br/. Accessed 31 October 2016.

Williquet, Maryse (2014) *Copa para quem?* Web documentary. Produced by Switch Asbl; http://www.copaparaquem.com/. Accessed 31 October 2016.

WHO WANTS TO BECOME BANAL?
THE I-DOC FROM EXPERIMENT TO INDUSTRY

Jon Dovey

In this chapter I want to mark a moment in the evolving story of the interactive documentary and to look at its developmental trajectory to date. I want to think about how we would establish a timeline for the development of the i-doc and further, how we might plot its progress against such a timeline. I want to also look at the development of the i-doc as cultural form and explore its chances of becoming banal, an everyday part of our media experience rather than a niche tech experiment. I will address the wider questions of what kinds of factual mediation we might expect networked societies to produce. This bigger question is set against the turbid discursive frameworks of 'upgrade culture' (Dovey and Kennedy 2006: 52–3) that shape the way that media development is currently understood. This chapter is part of a continuing investigation in trying to understand media in perpetual transition. My argument therefore finds its way to media historiography, and asks what kinds of media histories can we mobilise that might offer us some perspective beyond enthusiasm for novelty. What historical resources do we have that get us beyond 'awesome' as a response to media innovation?

In my previous writing in documentary, television studies, games studies and 'New Media Studies', I have sought to identify the genuine margin of novelty produced by digital innovation, to distinguish between utopian hype, remediation and material affordance. On reflection, I think I imagined that we were witnessing and constituting, as critics and practitioners, the emergence of new cultural forms and new genres; participating in the long transitional period between analogue and digital, mass media and micro, lean-back and lean-in media experiences. Underpinning this was a default attachment to a teleological account of media histories that assumes that stability will emerge from transition, that the rate of innovation will slow down and forms of publics that I can recognise will emerge around common mediated conversations. Within this paradigm, forms of experimental practice can be understood not only as critique of a decaying mainstream but as the seedbed for future innovation. I think I began this piece of writing imagining that the interactive documentary filled this space, a steadily developing set of institutional and audience practices emerging round technological affordance building a cultural form that would establish itself as an identifiable genre of the documentary and factual media offer. I think I was wrong.

IS THIS A CULTURAL FORM?

What indicators would we turn to assess the state of development of the interactive documentary? How can we understand where we have got to? What resources are available to understand the present moment in such a way that we might reasonably hope to understand the future? We can first of all think about the rate of development of practice and culture by looking at what has changed since the idea of the i-doc was first posited. (For reasons of space I avoid the question of defining the i-doc in this chapter, but work with an emergent corpus of titles that are in the main forms of webdoc.)

The editors of this volume and I convened the first UK-based interactive documentary event as a one-day symposium for 120 people in 2011, by 2014 we had 200 people for two days. Since then, the i-doc has become a key part of the international documentary festival and conference circuit. Sheffield Documentary Festival for instance is the premiere industry documentary event in the UK and now runs its 'Crossover Market' for online-first projects alongside its 'Meet Market' for linear projects seeking funding. Tribeca in New York and IDFA in Amsterdam now both run regular digital-first and interactive festival and market strands with screenings, awards and debates. An international festival circuit has started to develop, suggesting that there is a substantial infrastructure of production in development. The i-doc is now also on the awards circuit, *The Guardian's NSA Files* (Macaskill and Dance 2013) won a Pulitzer Prize in 2014 and ARTE's *Alma: A Tale of Violence* (Dewever-Plana and Fougere 2012) won the World Press Photo Multimedia Award in 2013. *Highrise* (Cizek *et al* 2010–15) won an Emmy in the New Approaches News & Documentary category in 2014.

Apparently, starting from an experimental position a little over five years ago, the i-doc has begun the process of developing an *industrial* base, which is particularly apparent within the field of journalism. Significantly, journalism has been powerfully threatened by digital disruption; some organisations have responded with innovation, particularly *The Guardian*, *The New York Times* and *Die Zeit*. *The Guardian* in particular has a strong reputation as a news organisation who understood the potential of digital networks early on. As the MIT Open Documentary Lab report (Uricchio *et al* 2015: 49–50) shows, from 2011 when Francesca Panetta was appointed as Special Projects editor, a small team of in-house staff and freelancers have been building up a body of industrial expertise around the production of a series of ground-breaking webdocs.

In the television and documentary markets, however, there is still what Jess Linington (2015) described as 'a broad disconnect with industry when discussing interactive non-fiction and transmedia productions', reporting from the Sunny Side of the Doc festival in the summer of 2015. Panels from Nordic and German producers and broadcasters pointed out how the budgets for transmedia projects were understood as add-ons to be funded from marketing, wrung out of existing budgets for the linear project component. Whilst international partnerships are a way forward they are immensely complex to set up for players with low levels of starting resource. The overall picture from the TV and film sector was that the case for interactive and transmedia production is not yet made – with the notable exceptions of NFB and ARTE, projects struggle to find champions or budgets; expertise is patchy, unreliable and inconsistent.

This developing but uncertain picture is related to what I argue is the key problematic in our long transition from mass mediation to networked mediation, that is the problem of the attention economy in the early twenty-first century (Arvidsson and Colleoni 2012). Essentially, this problem revolves around the conflict between an eyeballs-for-advertisers business model (Smythe 1981) and the development of the new valuing practices associated with social media, search optimisation, community management and targeted advertising. Paradoxically, this conflict produces a lack of good public data on audiences or engagement. Although analytics are available for every web documentary project, unlike ratings or overnight figures, they are rarely made public but instead circulate as part of an advertising-led discursive framework that does not always produce transparency. This is not an issue confined to the i-doc: the whole spectrum of networked media is confused by the disconnect between mass media ratings systems and the much smaller numbers attracted by digital-first productions. For instance, the producers of *Fort McMoney* (Dufresne 2013) shared their Google analytics, showing that the project had half a million visits, 450,000 players and 25,000 'hard core' players. The problem for legacy media industries is in understanding what the true meaning is of the relationship between the 25,000 hard-core players and the 450,000 other players. Where exactly is the value being created? For whom? These questions are conventionally addressed by recourse to the idea of engagement; small numbers will be compensated by higher value engagement, which may produce long-term benefit for the brand or platform.

However, as William Uricchio *et al* have noted in their report on interactive documentary and digital journalism, this question of engagement is far from settled, indeed it is perhaps the key problematic in the dynamics between legacy cultures and digital-first innovations: '"Engagement" has fast replaced "exposure" and "unit sales" as the desideratum of the digital information economy. But its meanings are many, as are strategies for achieving and measuring it. Engagement is a metric of value that correlates to interest and influence, both of which are significant concerns to the advertisers and non-profit foundations that support most commercial and non-commercial news organizations' (2015: 25). Engagement is an inevitably ambiguous term: ambiguous in that it may apply to audiences and users or to the 'interest and influence' of a number of different agents in the webdoc system. In this argument, 'engagement' might be understood as a circuit, where platform, plus brand, plus interface, plus user produce a deeper sense of identification than legacy media.

On the supply side, the brand of the producers themselves may also be part of the engagement circuit. In that sense, a studio like Paris-based Upian has a very high 'engagement index'; the small number of people building the i-doc as a form will all know Upian. Since 2005, they have produced 39 web-documentary projects of exemplary quality and style, developing a strong reputation in the nascent field. They are the Universal Studios (founded 1912) of the proto industry. However, the attention that the i-docs and design fields devote to them is disproportionate to the audience and user numbers for their work. The critically acclaimed *Alma* (Dewever-Plana and Fougere 2012) for instance was, at its height, ranked 127th most popular app in France, for one month (AppAnnie 2015).

If 'engagement' is uncertain, we might also look at the development of the i-doc in terms of its global reach, so as part of this research we made an analysis of the projects listed on the MIT Docubase (2013), which is by no means comprehensive and is US-based, but nevertheless is a good resource for assessing the scope and reach of the form. As of June 2016, the site had listings for 251 projects that it has defined in scope; all of these titles were produced in sixteen countries with 61 per cent from North America:

Country of Production	Count
United States	108
Canada	46
France	28

Multinational	16
United Kingdom	13
Netherlands	8
Spain	8
Australia	6
Germany	4
Argentina	3
Italy	3
Colombia	2
Ireland	2
Chile	1
Denmark	1
Greece	1
Japan	1

Fig. 1: Country of origin for projects featured on the MIT Docubase.

This concentration of country of origin is also reflected in the geography of topic areas. However, here we also see the i-doc emerging as a genuinely global form where 'other countries' (the subject of two or less projects) are actually the third largest group after Global, i.e. projects that are equally addressed to everywhere.

Location of topic	Count
United States	69
Global	62
Canada	28
France	9
United Kingdom	8
Spain	7
Russia and Former Soviet Union	5
Syria	5
Australia	4
Argentina	3

China	3
Germany	3
India	3
Other countries	43

Fig. 2: Topic locations for projects featured on MIT Docubase.

These 251 projects have all been made since 2004 (with four outlier exceptions from 1980s and 1990s of interest to future media archaeologists). A little under 247 projects are listed as having been produced in twelve years. In global media market terms, this is still very much an experimental niche; clearly it is growing, and its 'influence and attention', as evidenced by its entry onto the festival and prize-giving circuit, is already established as 'interesting innovations' to 'look out for'. Whilst not being comprehensive, I think that this evidence is sufficient to suggest that its reach is not yet matching its ambition or potential.

I turn next to some evidence from producers that helps to explain how these conditions are experienced at the industrial level.

THE REAR-VIEW MIRROR

How does this big picture look from the point of view of producers coming into the field? In 2013, the UK REACT Creative Economy research network (which I directed) invested in six innovative projects as part of a 'Future Documentary' theme inspired by developments in digital documentary. The aim of REACT was for project teams to create original prototypes that would have commercial or cultural impact in the world beyond our research and development phase; investment was aimed at producing long-term commercial, social or cultural impact in the dynamic spaces of emerging markets. I have revisited two of the producers in the light of this research, interested to understand how they now understand themselves in the market place as it is shaping up. Rosemary Lerner is a producer at Chaka Studio who was funded to work with a Bristol University research team to develop *The Quipu Project* (Court *et al* 2014), a participatory project aimed at telling the stories of some of the thousands of women and men sterilised against their will by Peru's Fujimori government in the 1990s.

Working in Peru, the Chaka team developed a platform for collecting and listening to the women's stories based on appropriate technology: the *campesinas* commonly used mobile phones and relied on local radio communications systems, no TV, no internet. The platform was used to collect testimony that took the eventual form of an interactive audio documentary available through a website, but which is also available to the women themselves through a server connected to the phone system in Peru. Eventually, the team also hope to produce a linear documentary version of the story. Rosemary thinks she first became aware of the idea of interactive documentary at the IDFA Academy in 2011, having just graduated from Goldsmiths London with an MA in Documentary: 'I was very critical and very reluctant at the beginning. I found it interesting, but even today, I cannot say that an interactive has ever had the same impact on me as really, really good documentary – but I do think there's amazing potential' (Lerner, personal communication with the author, November 2015).

However, this scepticism was overcome by the demands of the sterilisation story – especially the need as the team expressed it to collaborate with the women – supporting them in finding their voices and connecting with one another in a way that a linear project, on its own, would not. Four years on from encountering the idea of the i-doc and having produced a major, prize-winning participatory piece, Rosemary Lerner is still not sure where the field is going: 'In terms of the market I still don't know where it can go to make money – it's still very niche. We did user-testing a couple of weeks ago and 90 per cent of people had never heard of interactive documentary, so it's hard to think about a market. On the other hand, it's easier to target your market online' (ibid.).

The participatory platform developed by Chaka for the *The Quipu Project* clearly has developmental potential for other projects with NGOs or third-sector bodies interested in citizen engagement. However, the company is committed to telling great factual stories – not to platform development: 'From the first time I went to IDFA to Power to the Pixel a couple of weeks ago, people in the industry keep saying "Someone will find suddenly the business model for this and it will be a big thing." And I think "Yeah, eventually people do consume more and more content online." … I don't think necessarily that [documentary] is going to be the one that sets the ground for people to start using it – maybe that's going to be VR or fiction in an interactive way. Documentary audiences are always smaller, anyway' (ibid.).

Matt Golding is a producer with a different background working as a writer and director for Team Rubber, the commercial company he co-founded that deals in viral communications. Like Rosemary, he learnt about documentary at film school, but Matt has been following the interactive storytelling movement for ten years, arriving at the i-doc around 2011, following the National Film Board of Canada, Upian and Honkytonk Films with a view to learning how to incorporate the powerful potential in the field into his creative business. Matt worked with a film academic at Exeter University to produce *The Risktakers Guide to Survival*

(Golding 2014), an interactive inside a linear film format about the nature of risk and the user's personal approach to it. The film uses quiz formats, sliders and questions to build a risk profile for each user as they watch the film. Matt's approach to the i-doc has been conditioned by the commercial imperative to make anything new a comfortable user experience for his audience. He had previously been involved in Alternate Reality Games (ARGs) for movie marketing and knew that it was necessary to spend a lot of time on UX to create a welcoming intuitive experience that would lower the barriers to participation as he explains in a conversation on the production process: 'When I saw some of these interactive documentaries, I was like "you haven't done that bit at all, you haven't told people how long they're going to be sitting here at the start, you haven't told people what the hell this is". They use this mystique and peoples' desire for the new more than they used user experience. And I found that frustrating and infuriating because it's like you've got this amazing stuff, but you're not really holding anyone's hand through it. You are not drawing them in' (Golding, personal communication with the author, December 2015).

Software platforms come and go – Klynt, Zeega, Popcorn Maker, Korsakow and now VideoPath, Engajer and HTML5 – as an authoring environment. Every product made in these environments is a bit different. That means that every user experience is a bit different: there are no rules for interaction, in contrast, for instance, to the computer game, which has developed a cultural grammar of navigation and UX design over the past thirty years. So for Golding, the prospect for the field depends entirely on shedding its experimental elitism and supporting users. 'If you are going to invent a medium, simplistically as creators you can do it in a nice or nasty way. You can either be like "I've invented a new medium and they don't understand, so I've got to invite them in I've got to explain to them what's going on make them comfortable and take them on that journey". Or you do what I'd call the nasty way which is to go "There's a dark door in this wall and brave people can come through, but anyone who's not very brave can't 'cos I'm not going to tell you what's through it and I'm not even going to tell you why it's there." That's interesting as an artistic practice but it's not interesting if you want to engage people because it's threatening' (ibid.).

Even then the main problem for the development of the i-doc remains, in Golding's view, to do with the economic models of attention that are designed into video players. 'The problem is the distribution. The distribution dictates the flow of money, but the reality is that so much money has been spent on building video servers that are tied hand-in-glove to ad servers, and those things don't really support interactivity. So to put interactive documentary into the current market in a big way is very hard' (ibid.). Thus, he predicts that this issue will only be solved when i-docs move into the VR platform, in a move that parallels the development of the games market in the early 1980s from choose-your-own-adventure-formats to 3D graphics on PCs and later consoles. Golding argues that subscription platforms like Steam will make it possible for us to download VR products that interest a wide range of users. Especially, if the value is centred on the user's investment in the work: 'Because it's a user-guided experience, the film-maker is giving the user the space to explore something about themselves, so the core value will be in things that help the user reflect on things or learn about themselves or explore the world through the lens of themselves' (ibid.).

These views from the frontline of the experimental and emerging field offer us a sense of the challenging, uneven and circuitous path followed by media innovation. These views from *inside* the emergent field illustrate how the lack of a financial model, and the lack of a sense of UX standards make the i-doc a confusing creative space to occupy.

ADOPTIONS AND ADAPTATIONS

Because the i-doc is produced at the overlap of tech innovation and legacy media, it finds itself subject to the developmental dynamics of the tech sector as much as traditional content businesses (as the current hype around the VR i-doc demonstrates). Understanding the adoption of technological innovation has become a major site of business school training, speculation and systematised guesswork on which fortunes are made and lost. The complexity of the innovation landscape is such that there is no formula for predicting exactly which technological innovations find a foothold in the market place and which don't. However, matching audience need with appropriately presented technological innovation are key features of business plans designed to persuade imagined investors that there is a market for their product or service. Such business plans frequently begin with the wide frame of the market as a whole, in this case a consideration of what the conditions in the landscape for the interactive documentary are. Recent research from the UK industry regulator Ofcom would suggest that the market place for interactive services is very healthy. They report for instance that the *average* UK household now 'is most likely to own a laptop, smartphone, games console and VoD set-top box' (2015: 345). Moreover the lean-back experience of TV viewing is increasingly sharing its platform with the lean-in experience of interactive content as 56 per cent of homes now own TVs that are connected to the internet – mostly through set top boxes – but sales of 'smart' internet-connected TVs were 54 per cent of all TV sales in Q1 of 2015 (2015: 151).

Moreover the changing demographics of media consumption might be interpreted as suggesting a positive future for different kinds of content, with Ofcom's 'Digital Day' research showing that 16-to-24 year olds were averaging 21 minutes a day of 'short form' video content, watching news, entertainment and music clips (2015: 58).

Market forecasting in the field of innovation frequently has recourse to the trend data collected by Gartner, the international technology research consultancy. In particular the Gartner hype cycle has become a way for businesses and analysts to understand where to place their products in the rapidly changing field of technology innovation. In 2014, for instance, Gartner predicted that augmented reality and TV app platforms were on the rising curve of the cycle, that automatic content recognition, social network analysis and data-driven marketing were at the top of the curve and those sliding toward disillusion included social TV, connected televisions, enhanced e-books and online video publishing platforms. Games consoles as Media Hubs, rich media, live streaming and consumer-generated media were marked as entering the happy uplands of productivity.

In July 2015, Michel Reilhac addressed the situation of interactive storytelling at the Power to the Pixel event in London. He also adapted the Gartner Cycle to argue that in his view interactive storytelling was about two-thirds down the slope of disillusion where negative critique surrounds the form, companies fail, and those that remain need further rounds of investment to survive. This, he argued, was due to disappointment in the performance of interactive products from the media commissioners, poor impacts on broadcasters' web traffic, and cultural resistance to change from both producers and audiences, before suggesting that the field is comparable to early cinema, looking for a form and a market (Reilhac 2015). This is a familiar and significant trope in commentary on New Media developments. It mobilises the idea that interactive storytelling could stabilise into a recognisable form on the 'plateau' of stable business performance. Reilhac argues that the way forward for interactive storytelling will take the route of VR as the next inevitable wonder to storm the gates of media monopoly. Reilhac's account begins with the idea of transmedia springing into public consciousness in 2010. As we will see, its upbeat sense of inevitability radically oversimplifies the ways that technologies and cultures interact historically.

ARCHAEOLOGIES OF ANTICIPATION

'The use of concepts of discontinuity, rupture, threshold, limit, series, and transformation present all historical analysis not only with questions of procedure, but with theoretical problems.' (Foucault 1974: 24)

One of the roles of scholarship in these debates might be to mobilise cultural history against a technologically determined embrace of short-term prediction. In this case Reilhac's history needs some revision. First of all, 'interactive storytelling' did not spring into the world fully-formed through the idea of transmedia. Michael Joyce published his *afternoon, a story* in 1987. It is considered the first 'hypertext' novel that allowed the reader to navigate through a database of different story fragments. It was followed by ten more years of theoretical enquiry and industry speculation around interactive literary platforms (for example, Landow 1992, Aarseth 1997, Murray 1997, Moulthrop 2004) which traced a field as it developed from hypertextual to more fluid, game-oriented forms of interaction. In this reading, we can understand that 'interactive storytelling' may have been on the 'slope of enlightenment' already for the better part of thirty years. To really understand where the i-docs field has got to, perhaps we need a better theoretical perspective on technology and cultural form – a mode of analysis that can understand long-term change over time.

There is no shortage of approaches to media history. Whilst Raymond Williams' socially constructivist historical work (1974) was foundational to media studies, his centrality has been long displaced by various kinds of materialist history deriving from Marshall McLuhan (1964) via either a route influenced by Gilles Deleuze (1986, 1987, 1989) or Friedrich Kittler (1999) and on in into the currently fashionable historical approaches of media archaeology of, for example, Jussi Parrika (2012). These approaches to media histories have been influenced by the post-representational theory of – among others – Nigel Thrift (2008) and the so-called 'new materialism' derived from a feminist tradition of Science and Technology Studies with its roots in Donna Harraway (1985) and Bruno Latour's (2005) Actor Network Theory (see, for example, Coole and Frost 2010, Dolphijn and van der Tuin 2012). Much of this work concerns itself with the nature of media, their ontologies, how they work within us, through us and with us to determine 'the pace and scale of human affairs' (McLuhan 1964: 8). The influence of Deleuze's writing on cinema has been particularly significant in this regard, arguing for the ways in which the body, apparatus and affective responses create new kinds of mental automata 'consisting in nerves, flesh and light' (Lister *et al* 2009: 384). As we shall see below, Adrian Miles (2014) has used a Deleuzian approach to elaborate the nature of interactive documentary. However, this strain of media historical research tends toward the phenomenology of mediation – not without its relevance when we want to think about audiences, users and markets – but not the best approach for understanding change.

A genealogical focus on processes of (dis)continuity, threshold, series and transformation (as Foucault has addressed them above) unlocks approaches that reveal the complexities of media histories; the unexpected, surprising and often apparently aleatory narratives through which technologies bloom and die as cultural experience. Following this approach, a materialist media archaeology may excavate, as Errki Huhtamo and Jussi Parikka argue, 'forgotten media-cultural phenomena that have been left outside the canonized narratives about media culture and history' (2011: 203). Angela Piccini asserts in her recently edited special edition that 'media archaeology and archaeology-as-such share concerns with dismantling and reconstructing media technologies in order to reveal secret histories and lost lineages' (2015: 5).

PUTTING THE 'I' IN I-DOCS

If we want to take a longer-term historical analysis, Raymond Williams' approach remains useful in understanding the contemporary situation and future development of the interactive documentary. Williams' virtue here is in his combination of attention to science and technology as well as social formation. (I would also argue that his method actually produces one of the best demonstrations of media historical analysis applied to understanding future potential in the final chapter of *Television Technology and Cultural Form* (1974: 135–52). His method argues for the development of cultural form as the product of very long processes of foresight development that intersect with particular forms of social organisation. Science and technology, he argues, is driven by what he calls 'social investment' – an idea of what a particular scientific development *could* become combined with socially sanctioned resource deployment that sustains progress. However, social investment does not cohere as achieved cultural form without meeting particular historical moments of social need or necessity. By holding on to the subtlety of Williams' approach, whilst attending to the materialist realism of more recent approaches, we may be able to construct a genealogy of the i-doc that understands its potential from a more securely theorised point of view.

First of all, we would extend our timeframe, to escape the five-year cycle of upgrade culture and the immediacy of the hype cycle. Putting aside for now the 'documentary' part of our historical question, I want to focus on its 'interactive' dimension. Long foreseen and multiply instantiated, our history of the i-doc could start with Vannevar Bush's essay 'As We May Think' from 1945 in which he posits a machine, the Memex, that would enable information retrieval by an associative form of indexing rather than alphabetical ordering or according to the Dewey library classification. The idea surfaces again as digital computers begin to become more widespread in 1982 in Ted Nelson's paper 'A New Home for the Mind' in which he argues for 'the jump link facility' which would permit 'fully non-sequential writing' and reading, which could underpin 'a grand library that anybody could store anything in' (1999: 120, 128). So the conception of networked knowledge, usually dated as starting with Tim Berners Lee's coding the first web browser in 1993, can be seen to have at least a fifty-year prehistory. The development of the idea of interaction is entangled with these prefigurations too – originally understood by J.C.R. Licklider (1960) and Douglas C. Englebart (1962) as the process through which computer operators could intervene in batch-processing operations and thus start to 'interact' with the computing in real time. This work can be regarded as setting the foresight conditions for the development of the web in the following decades. However *their* work is part of a genealogy that starts after World War II and is – as Bush and Nelson make clear – one of the constituents of the new modes of production and social organisation predicated on information management and exploitation.

'Post-industrial' societies were foreseen from the 1960s onward (see, for example, Touraine 1969, Smith 1972, Roszak 1986). These visions cannot be separated from technological developments at the microscopic level; they were intimately entangled with Moore's Law. Gordon Moore was the co-founder of Intel in 1965 and predicted, more or less accurately, that the capacity of the silicon chip would double every two years; the increases in the productivity of information technologies is unprecedented. The material reality of new kinds of chips in technology every two years establishes the conditions for a hardware cycle: here machines are designed for future capacity, and thus upgrade culture was instantiated. Manuel Castells (1996) took these developments in micro-electronic-powered communications technologies and analysed their impact in the context of neo-liberal globalisation to define the idea of the 'networked society'. Here, computing technologies and new modes of economic production centred on information and knowledge work together to produce new forms of social organisation based on distributed networks of power: 'In the industrial mode of development, the main source of productivity lies in the introduction of new energy sources, and the ability to decentralise the use of energy throughout the production and circulation process. In the new, informational mode of development, the source of productivity lies in the technology of knowledge generation, information processing, and symbol communication' (1996: 17).

Where Raymond Williams demonstrated that television was created through the need of newly complex but centralised forms of social organisation that produced its own form of 'mobile privatisation' (1974: 26), I argue that the i-doc is produced through the long-term communicative needs of the networked society.

ALWAYS INDETERMINATE

What are the factors in play that may shape the i-doc in this longer-term geneal-ogy? We have witnessed massive 'social investment' in the construction of the internet both at the level of global infrastructure but more especially at the level of 'collective intelligence' (Levy 1997) and participatory cultures (Jenkins *et al* 2009). Our participation – our *engagements* in these circuits of sharing infor-mation and know-how – has become an increasingly important part of how we perform ourselves in networked societies. So our documentary engagements are therefore likely to call upon us to invest some of ourselves, some of our time, at-tention and choice making. The documentary form develops in the context of the network society. In turn, one might reasonably assume that the i-doc would be at once local and global, as the data above from Docubase confirms. It is also likely to mirror the dynamics of network society by being reconfigurable (i.e. 'interac-tive') in at least three modes of interaction: person-to-person, person-to-system and system-to-system. In these conditions, each encounter with a work is unique, a mosaic of fragments that themselves trace their own path through the network. These experiences have the potential to be both social and affective but in new registers and new ways.

This resonates strongly with Adrian Miles' conclusion to his Deleuzian analysis of 'Affective Ecologies', where the sense of potentiality inherent in reconfigurable meanings and encounter is summarised: 'Documentary makers and audiences lie at the intersection of a series of vectors of indeterminacy between the machine's procedural logic, networked affordances, and narrativisation, all literally ren-dered via an interface' (2014: 80). In this reading, the sense of indeterminacy is what we experience as we work out the interface, make our way through the work, experiencing choice-making and noticing through the click, swipe, key-stroke actions of the navigation. Here, then, indeterminacy *is* the dominant user experience for the i-doc: 'This interval needs to be embraced as the centre for indetermination that it is. In other words, online documentary needs to seek rap-prochement with affect and become pluralist, multivocal, multilinear, associative and poetic. This expression of an affective ecology allows documentary to look towards the particular material logic of digital networks as enabling, and allows understanding to reach out of the work to address the world' (2014: 80–1).

TAKING THE LONG VIEW

In these contexts, the Gartner hype cycle can be understood as contingent at-tempts to crystallise the long underpinning historical forces of culture and tech-nology into a snapshot that supports investment decisions. Still, as a way to answer the question of where the i-doc is going as a form, it is less than useful. There are a small number of web documentaries out there in the world (with an even smaller number of experiments in immersion and VR developing, too). There are a very small number of people, as audiences or producers, who understand what an i-doc is or could be. We are at present a very long way from becoming banal, from the i-doc becoming part of everyday life and shedding its experimental nature. However, understanding that media form and social structures are indissoluble means that we can predict the i-doc will continue to grow and expand – not in the next five years but over the next fifty years. Despite the foreshortened timeframes of upgrade culture, we are living through long timescales that I have traced beginning after World War II and which are playing out in the very long afterlife of legacy media in the networked society. In this horizon, the task of the i-doc community is to continue the long patient slow work of building institutional infrastructures, developing audiences and making a culture. The innovation caravanserai will move on soon enough, and when it does, we can continue with the task of understanding exactly what 'engagement' really means and how it can become part of a new economy for critical media practice.

REFERENCES

Arvidsson, Adam and Eleanor Colleoni (2012) 'Value in Informational Capitalism and on the Internet', *The Information Society: An International Journal*, 28, 3, 135–50.

AppAnnie (2015) https://www.appannie.com/. Accessed 31 October 2016.

Aarseth, Espen J. (1997) *Cybertext: Perspectives on Ergodic Literature*. Baltimore: Johns Hopkins University Press.

Bush, Vannevar (1999 [1945]) 'As We May Think', in Paul Mayer (ed.) *Computer Media and Communication: A Reader*. Oxford: Oxford University Press.

Castells, Manuel (1996) *The Rise of the Network Society*. Oxford: Blackwell.

Cizek, Kat *et al* (2010–15) *Highrise*. Web documentary series. Produced by Gerry Flahive, co-produced by NFB; http://highrise.nfb.ca/. Accessed 31 October 2016.

Coole, Diana and Samantha Frost (2010) *New Materialisms: Ontology, Agency and Politics*. Durham, NC: Duke University Press.

Court, Maria, Lerner, Ros, and Melo, Sebastian (2014) *The Quipu Project*. Web documentary. Co-produced by Chaka Studio and Helios Design Labs. First presented at i-Docs in 2014. https://interactive.quipu-project.com/#/en/quipu/intro. Accessed 31 October 2016.

Dewever-Plana, Miquel and Isabelle Fougere (2012) *Alma: A Tale of Violence*. Web documentary and app. Directed by Miquel Dewever-Plana and Isabelle Fougere. Co-produced by Arte, Upian and L'Agence Vu; http://alma.arte.tv/en/. Accessed 31 October 2106.

Deleuze, Gilles (1986) *Cinema 1: The Movement Image*. Trans. Hugh Tomlinson and Barbara Habberjam. Minneapolis: University of Minnesota Press.

____ (1989) *Cinema 2: The Time Image*. Trans. Hugh Tomlinson and Robert Galeta. Minneapolis: University of Minnesota Press.

Deleuze, Gilles and Félix Guattari (1987) *A Thousand Plateaus*. Minneapolis: University of Minnesota Press.

Dolphijn, Rick and Iris van der Tuin (2012) *New Materialism: Interviews and Cartographies*. Ann Arbor: Open Humanities Press.

Dovey, Jon and Helen W. Kennedy (2006) *Game Cultures*. Milton Keynes: Open University Press.

Dufresne, David (2013) *Fort McMoney*. Web Documentary. Co-produced by NFB, ARTE and TOXA; http://fortmcmoney.com/#/fortmcmoney. Accessed 31 October 2016.

Englebart Douglas C. (1999 [1962]) 'Augmenting Human Intellect: A Conceptual Framework', in Peter Mayer (ed.) *Computer Media and Communication: A Reader*. Oxford: Oxford University Press.

Foucault, Michel (1974 [1968]) *The Archaeology of Knowledge*. London: Tavistock.

Gartener, (2014) 'Hype Cycle for Media and Entertainment'. https://www.gartner.com/doc/2797321/hype-cycle-media-entertainment-. Accessed 31 October 2016.

Golding, Matt (2014) *The Risktakers Guide to Survival*. Web documentary. Co-produced by Rubber Republic, REACT and University of Exeter; http://www.risktakersguide.com/. Accessed 31 October 2016.

Harraway, Donna (1985) 'A Cyborg Manifesto: Science, Technology, and Socialist-Feminism in the Late Twentieth Century', *Socialist Review*, 80, 65–108.

Huhtamo, Errki and Jussi Parikka (2011) *Media Archaeology Approaches, Applications, and Implications*. Oakland: University of California Press.

Jenkins, Henry, with Ravi Purushotma, Margaret Weigel, Katie Clinton and Alice J. Robison (2009) *Confronting the Challenges of Participatory Culture: Media Education for the 21st Century*. Cambridge, MA: MIT Press; https://mitpress.mit.edu/sites/default/files/titles/free_download/9780262513623_Confronting_the_Challenges.pdf. Accessed 31 October 2016.

Joyce, Michael (1987) *afternoon, a story*. Hypertext. Published by Eastgate Systems in 1990.

Kittler, Friedrich (1999 [1968]) *Gramophone, Film, Typewriter*. Palo Alto: Stanford University Press.

Landow, George (1992) *The Convergence of Contemporary Literary Theory and Technology*. Baltimore: Johns Hopkins University Press.

Latour, Bruno (2005) *Reassembling the Social: An Introduction to Actor-Network-Theory*. Oxford: Oxford University Press.

Levy, Pierre (1997) *Collective Intelligence: Mankind's Emerging World in Cyberspace*. Cambridge: Perseus Books.

Licklider, J.C.R. (1999 [1960]) 'Man-Computer Symbiosis in Computer Media and Communication', in Peter Mayer (ed.) *Computer Media and Communication: A Reader*. Oxford: Oxford University Press.

Linington, Jess (2015) 'What Happens When Industry Meets Interactive Documentary'; http://i-docs.org/2015/08/07/funding-production-distribution-what-happens-when-industry-meets-interactive-documentary/. Accessed 31 October 2016.

Lister, Martin, Jon Dovey, Seth Giddings, Iain Grant and Kieran Kelly (eds) (2009) *New Media – A Critical Introduction*. New York: Routledge.

Macaskill, Ewan and Gabriel Dance (2013) *NSA Files: Decoded*. Produced by Guardian Interactive. Produced by Feilding Cage and Greg Chen; https://www.theguardian.com/world/interactive/2013/nov/01/snowden-nsa-files-surveillance-revelations-decoded#section/1. Accessed 2 Occtober 2016.

McLuhan, Marshall (1964) *Understanding Media: The Extensions of Man*. Toronto: McGraw Hill.

Miles, Adrian (2014) 'Interactive Documentaries and Affective Ecologies', in Kate Nash, Craig Hight and Catherine Summerhayes (eds) *New Documentary Ecologies: Emerging Platforms, Practices and Discourses*. New York: Palgrave MacMillan, 67–82.

MIT OpenDoc Lab. *Docubase;* http://docubase.mit.edu/. Accessed 31 October 2016. (This author is indebted to Jess Linington for support in compiling the MIT Docubase data).

Moulthrop Stuart (2004) 'From work to Play', in Noah Wardrip-Fruin and Pat Harrigan (eds) *First Person: New Media as Story, Performance and Game*. Cambridge, MA: MIT Press.

Murray, Janet (1997) *Hamlet on the Holodeck: The Future of Narrative in Cyberspace*. Cambridge, MA: MIT Press.

Nelson, Ted (1999 [1982]) 'A New Home for the Mind', in Peter Mayer (ed.) *Computer Media and Communication: A Reader*. Oxford: Oxford University Press.

Ofcom (2015) 'The Communications Market Report'; https://www.ofcom.org.uk/research-and-data/cmr/cmr15. Accessed 31 October 2015.

Parikka, Jussi (2012) *What is Media Archaeology?* Cambridge: Polity Press.

Piccini, Angela (2015) 'Media-Archaeologies: An Invitation', *Journal of Contemporary Archaeology*, 2, 1, 1–8.

Reilhac, Michel (2015) 'What are we learning?' Presentation at Power to the Pixel, London, 30 July; http://www.slideshare.net/tishna/the-pixel-lab-2015-what-are-we-learning-michel-reilhac. Accessed 15 October 2016.

Roszak, Theodore (1986) *The Cult of Information*. Cambridge: Lutterworth Press.

Smith, Ralph Lee (1972) *Wired Nation, Cable Television the Communications Superhighway*. New York: Harper Colophon Books.

Smythe, D.W. (1981) 'On the audience commodity and its work', in Meenakshi Gigi Durham and Douglas M. Kellner (eds) *Media and Cultural Studies*. Malden: Blackwell.

Thrift, Nigel (2008) *Non-Representational Theory*. New York: Routledge.

Touraine, Alain (1969) *La Société Post Industrielle*. Paris: Denoel.

Uricchio, William with Sarah Wolozin, Lily Bui, Sean Flynn and Deniz Tortum (2015) *Mapping the Intersection of Two Cultures: Interactive Documentary and Digital Journalism*. Boston Mass: MIT Press; http://opendoclab.mit.edu/interactivejournalism/Mapping_the_Intersection_of_Two_Cultures_Interactive_Documentary_and_Digital_Journalism.pdf. Accessed 31 October 2016.

Williams, Raymond (1974) *Television Technology and Cultural Form*. London: Fonatana.

INDEX